lonely planet

MOROCCO

Jade Bremner, Narina Exelby, Sarah Gilbert, Paula Hardy, Tharik Hussain, Helen Ranger, Tara Stevens

Meet our writers

Jade Bremner

@jadeob

Born in London, Jade has called many places home across four continents, but without fail she pilgrimages to Southern Morocco's wild coastline every winter to surf perfect waves until her arms can no longer paddle (p216).

Narina Exelby

narinaexelby.substack.com

Narina is a roaming South African writer whose default setting is to seek out quiet places – so hiking in the High Atlas Mountains (p82) and staying in remote Amazigh villages (p98) is her idea of heaven.

Sarah Gilbert

X @SarahGTravels

Sarah loves to explore Morocco's markets, from sheep shopping in the Middle Atlas (p194) to rummaging through the treasure of Essaouira's flea market and sampling olives of every hue at food souqs everywhere.

Paula Hardy

@paulahardy

Paula is a travel journalist who has been working in North Africa for over 20 years. She contributes regularly to Lonely Planet's guides as well as *The Telegraph, FT* and *Condé Nast Traveller Middle East*.

Tharik Hussain

@tharik_hussain X @_tharikhussain

Author of the award-winning *Minarets in the Mountains: a Journey into Muslim Europe*, Tharik has contributed to various Lonely Planet guidebooks and to *National Geographic, The Guardian* and the BBC.

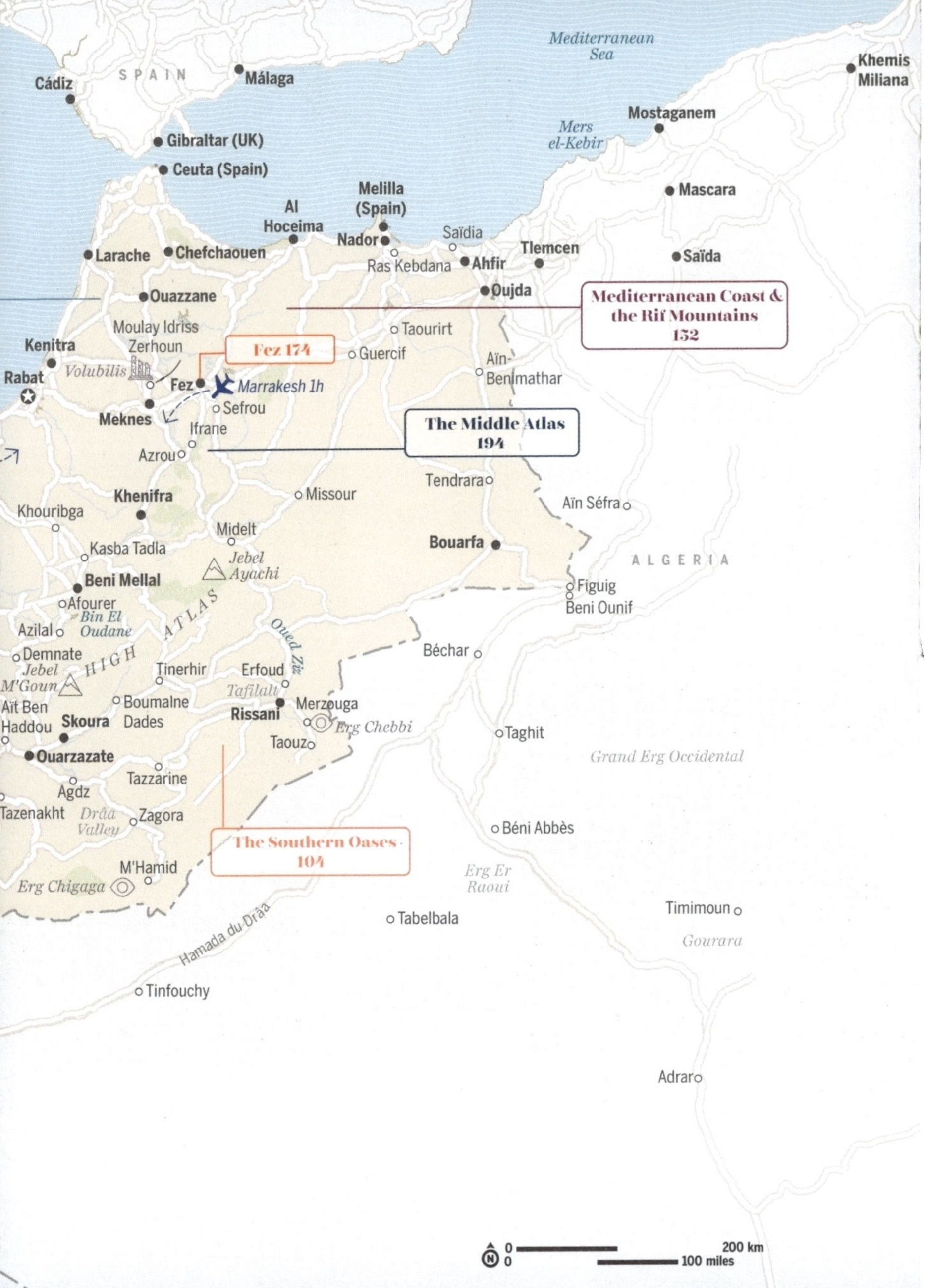

Mediterranean Sea
Khemis Miliana
Cádiz
SPAIN
Málaga
Mostaganem
Mers el-Kebir
Gibraltar (UK)
Ceuta (Spain)
Melilla (Spain)
Mascara
Al Hoceima
Nador
Saïdia
Tlemcen
Saïda
Larache
Chefchaouen
Ras Kebdana
Ahfir
Ouazzane
Oujda
Mediterranean Coast & the Rif Mountains 152
Moulay Idriss Zerhoun
Taourirt
Kenitra
Fez 174
Guercif
Rabat
Volubilis
Aïn-Benimathar
Fez
Marrakesh 1h
Meknes
Sefrou
Ifrane
The Middle Atlas 194
Azrou
Tendrara
Missour
Aïn Séfra
Khenifra
Khouribga
Midelt
Bouarfa
Kasba Tadla
Jebel Ayachi
ALGERIA
Beni Mellal
Figuig
Afourer
Beni Ounif
Bin El Oudane
HIGH ATLAS
Azilal
Oued Ziz
Béchar
Demnate
Jebel M'Goun
Tinerhir
Erfoud
Tafilalt
Aït Ben Haddou
Boumalne Dades
Merzouga
Skoura
Rissani
Erg Chebbi
Taghit
Taouz
Ouarzazate
Grand Erg Occidental
Tazzarine
Agdz
Tazenakht
Drâa Valley
Zagora
Béni Abbès
The Southern Oases 104
M'Hamid
Erg Er Raoui
Erg Chigaga
Timimoun
Tabelbala
Gourara
Hamada du Drâa
Tinfouchy
Adrar
0
200 km
0
100 miles

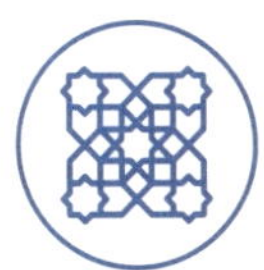

Lose yourself in the narrow alleyways of a medieval medina. Taste the delicious flavours of Moroccan cuisine. Hike majestic mountain ranges or tackle North Africa's highest peak. Pause in Amazigh villages for a glimpse of local life. Ride a camel over Saharan sands and watch the sun set over the dunes. Stay in an impressive kasbah hotel. Catch a music festival and dance to the beat of Gnawa musicians. Surf the perfect wave or learn to kitesurf. Shop for that gorgeous rug.

This is Morocco.

TURN THE PAGE AND START PLANNING YOUR NEXT BEST TRIP →

Western Sahara
CANARY ISLANDS (SPAIN)
Tarfaya
Disputed Border
Tindouf
Erg Iguidi
Laayoune
Al Mahbes
Samara
Bou Craa
ATLANTIC OCEAN
Boujdour
Guelta Zemmur
Bir Mogrein
WESTERN SAHARA
Dakhla
Bir Anzarane
Mijek
Imlil
MAURITANIA
Awsard
Zouérat
Aghoninit
Bir-Gandouz
Tichla
Sahara
Guegarat
Nouâdhibou
Atar
0 200 km
0 100 miles
Northern Atlantic Coast 128
Fez 4h (300km)
Casablanca
Marrakesh 3h (250km)
El Jadida
Settat
Oued Oum er Rbia
Oualidia
Safi
Ben Guérir
Marrakesh 42
Essaouira
or
Tizi n'Tichka
Agafay 80
Agafay
Asni
Ourika Valley
Tizi n'Test
Jebel Toubkal
Taghazout
Agadir
Taroudant
ATLANTIC OCEAN
Southern Morocco 216
Jebel Lekst
ANTI ATLAS
Tata
Mirleft
Tiznit
Tafraoute
Legzira Plage
Sidi Ifni
Akka
Guelmim
Bouizakarne
The High Atlas 82
CANARY ISLANDS (SPAIN)
Taïdalt
Assa
Tan Tan
Tiglite
Oued Drâa
See Western Sahara
Tarfaya
Disputed Border
Tindouf
Erg Iguidi
Al Mahbes
Laayoune

GLEN BERLIN/SHUTTERSTOCK

Above Djemaa El Fna food stall (p49), Marrakesh

Helen Ranger

@helenranger

Helen was born in the UK but has lived in Africa for most of her life, making Fez her home for 16 years. You'll find her wandering medina streets, pausing for people-watching over a pot of mint tea (p174).

Tara Stevens

@tarastevenswrites

Tara is the founder of the Courtyard Kitchen Fez (p180) – a cooking school that explores the next chapter in the country's riveting and delectable cuisine. She is never happier than when on the trail of something delicious to eat.

FIRST SPREAD: VIXIT/SHUTTERSTOCK

Contents

EDOGRAPHY/SHUTTERSTOCK

Souq, Marrakesh (p42)

MEDINA FACT

During the protectorate years (1912–56), the French left medinas to the locals and built shiny, new cities *(villes nouvelles)* for themselves. Result: medinas were preserved and, apart from renovations, ancient buildings have hardly changed for a thousand years.

A MAZE OF MEDINAS

Step through the *bab* (gateway) into a Moroccan medina and be instantly transported to an ancient way of life. Here in the winding, cobbled lanes are artisans plying their trades, boutique *riad* (traditional house built around a garden) hotels, markets bursting with fresh produce, tiny shops full of ceramics or brassware, soaring minarets and stately monuments. Order a pot of mint tea at a pavement cafe and soak up Morocco's famous mystique.

Left Medina, Fez (p174)
Right Metalwork artisan, Fez (p182)
Below Chefchaouen street (p166)

→ ARTISANAL AREAS

Artisans cluster together, so you'll find blacksmiths in one area, and leatherworkers in another. Cedarwood scents the carpenters' neighbourhood, while click-clacking looms denote weavers at work.

RUSLANKPHOTO/SHUTTERSTOCK

NEIGHBOURHOOD NECESSITIES

Spot a minaret? See if you can find other elements nearby: every neighbourhood has a mosque, a *medersa* (theological school), a fountain, a hammam and a community oven.

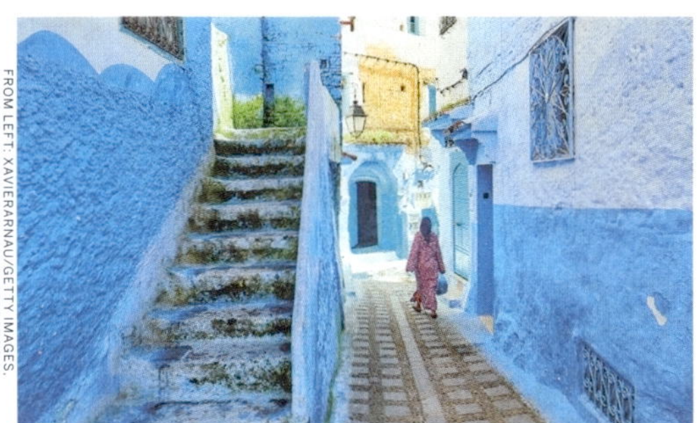

FROM LEFT: XAVIERARNAU/GETTY IMAGES; EKATERINA POKROVSKY/SHUTTERSTOCK

↑ HILLY VS FLAT MEDINAS

Chefchaouen's medina stretches down a mountainside, Tangier's is pretty steep and Fez has punishing hills. Marrakesh and Essaouira are pleasingly flat. All are cobbled, so wear sturdy shoes.

Best Medina Experiences

- **Admire the astounding mosaics, carved plaster and wood at the spectacular Ben Youssef Medersa in Marrakesh.** (p52)
- **Wander the Sultan's garden in Tangier's Kasbah before strolling down to the Petit Socco for coffee.** (p162)
- **Visit the restored *fanadiq* (caravanserais) by Fez's Kairaouine Mosque.** (p192)
- **Capture Chefchaouen's blue walls in the dawn light.** (p166)
- **Breakfast under orange trees in the courtyard of your Marrakesh medina *riad*.** (p58)

BREAD & COUSCOUS

Government initiatives for water management are vital to offset Morocco's severe drought conditions that have reduced wheat harvests. The country was ranked the sixth-largest wheat importer in the world in 2023, satisfying the demand for *khobz* (bread) and *seksu* (couscous).

RELISH MOROCCAN **FLAVOURS**

Take an array of the freshest produce and add a sprinkling of influences from Africa, Andalusia and Arabia to produce savoury and sweet, curiously but deliciously combined: a tajine of beef and prunes, chicken with preserved lemon and pinkish-green olives, lamb with apricots, or *bastilla,* a fine pigeon or chicken pie dusted with cinnamon and powdered sugar. Finish with honey-drenched almond pastries and refreshing mint tea.

ELENA RYKOVA/SHUTTERSTOCK

Left Snails, Djemaa El Fna food stall (p49), Marrakesh
Right Tajine, Djemaa El Fna food stall (p49), Marrakesh
Below Friday couscous lunch

→ TAKE A FOOD TOUR

Arrange a medina food tour to discover local delicacies and try those restaurants you'd never find by yourself (or wouldn't dare to try).

MOROCCAN WINES

Sip a Moroccan wine: vineyards can be found around Meknes and Rabat. Look out for the signature gris: a light wine with a pale pink blush.

FROM LEFT: MURATART/SHUTTERSTOCK, GORDINE N/SHUTTERSTOCK

↑ FRIDAY COUSCOUS

Don't miss the traditional Friday couscous lunch. A pyramid of small pasta-like grains is studded with seven vegetables and topped with sweet onion jam.

Best Foodie Experiences

▸ **Hop between food stalls on Djemaa El Fna, sampling snails, grills, fried fish and *tanjia* (meat stew).** (p49)

▸ **Lunch on sardines fresh from the sea, grilled before your eyes in Taghazout.** (p222)

▸ **Have a feast cooked by *dadas* (cooks) in a traditional *riad* restaurant.** (p178)

▸ **Cook up a storm at Cafe Clock in Chefchaouen.** (p167)

▸ **Munch on *madfouna,* bread stuffed with meat and spices and baked in the Saharan sands of Erg Chebbi.** (p120)

MAJESTIC **MOUNTAINS**

Morocco's mountains offer a range of landscapes and activities for hiking, trekking, mountain biking, climbing and even skiing. The Atlas Mountains offers superb trails, including around Africa's second-highest mountain, Jebel Toubkal in the High Atlas; through the lonely lunar-like reaches of the Jebel Sahro guarding the Sahara; and on the gentler slopes of the Rif and Middle Atlas with their cedar forests. En route, discover Amazigh villages and terraced fields.

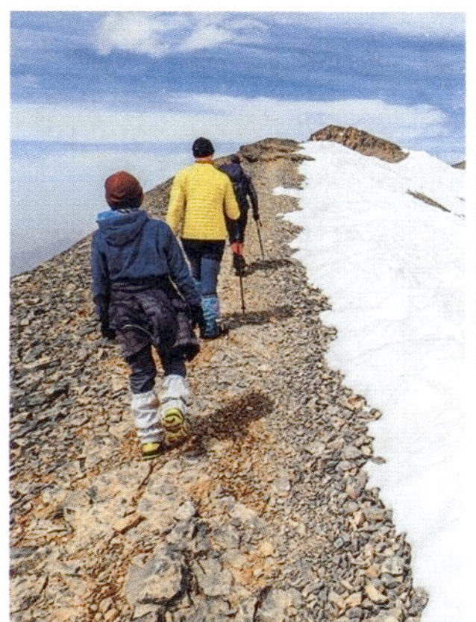

TOLOBALAGUER.COM/SHUTTERSTOCK

→ AVOID THE CROWDS

Head to the lesser known M'Goun Massif for a three-day trek in spectacular mountain landscapes, hiking through river gorges and remote valleys (p84).

Left Hiker faces view of Jebel Toubkal (p88)
Right M'Goun Massif (p99)
Below Hikers near Imlil (p89)

WHERE TO LAY YOUR HEAD

Overnight options when trekking include village *gîtes d'étapes* (homestays), mountain refuges, nomad encampments, luxurious kasbah-style hotels and valley lodges.

FROM LEFT: LUKAS HODON/GETTY IMAGES, ROCKOVER PRODUCTION/SHUTTERSTOCK

↑ HIRE A GUIDE

Imlil is the centre for hiking in the High Atlas, from short rambles to more demanding treks. Hire a guide at the Bureau des Guides d'Imlil (p90).

Best Mountain Experiences

- **Climb Jebel Toubkal (4167m) on a two-day summit hike.** (p88)
- **Hike the Talassemtane National Park around Chefchaouen in the Rif.** (p167)
- **Stroll beneath massive cedar trees in the Ifrane National Park in the Middle Atlas.** (p187)
- **Take an off-road biking tour in the High Atlas.** (p94)
- **Drive the Tizi n'Test, Morocco's most dramatic pass.** (p99)

AMAZIGH POPULATION

The 2024 census put the Moroccan population at 36.82 million, of whom about 40% are Amazigh (formerly known as Berber), though most Moroccans have some Amazigh heritage.

AMAZIGH CULTURE **REVEALED**

The original tribes of North Africa, the Amazigh ('Free People') have a distinct culture, from languages to art, costumes to music. The Ghomara live in the Rif, and speak the Tarafit dialect. The Zaianes are found from Fez to Marrakesh, and, in the High Atlas, are still nomadic. They speak Tamazight. The largest group is the Shilhah from the south, who speak Tashlheit.

Left Amazigh jewellery (p225)
Right Festival National d'Ahidous (p215), Ain Leuh
Below Sign with Tifinagh script, Casablanca (p128)

→ TRADITIONAL FESTIVALS

The Imilchil Marriage Mossem (p103) and Festival National d'Ahidous in Ain Leuh (p215) offer snapshots of Amazigh culture.

ACHLAJI MOHAMED/SHUTTERSTOCK

WHAT TO READ

Delve into Alice Morrison's *Walking with Nomads* about her adventures with Tuareg nomads in the Drâa Valley (p40).

FROM LEFT: SOAD22AVR/SHUTTERSTOCK, FRANTICOO/SHUTTERSTOCK

↑ AMAZIGH MEDIA

Tamazight is taught in some primary schools, there's a dedicated TV channel and you'll see official signs in the Tifinagh script.

Best Cultural Experiences

- **Visit some of the excellent museums that showcase traditional Amazigh lifestyles and cultural artefacts.** (p103)
- **Download Amazigh music: try *ahidous* songs** (p215) **or *reggada*** (p40) **from the north.**
- **Stop off at an artisan cooperative to see Amazigh designs woven into carpets.** (p103)
- **Search out Amazigh silver jewellery in Tiznit.** (p225)

FEEL THE MUSIC

Music permeates every aspect of Moroccan life – from the muezzin's call to *hibhub* (Moroccan pop, rock and hip-hop) and rap. Hear traditional Amazigh music at village *moussems* (festivals), watch Sufi brotherhoods perform at *lilas* (spiritual jam sessions), and catch a classical concert of music from Andalusian Spain and the east in the cities.

VANDERWOLF IMAGES/SHUTTERSTOCK

★ DJEMAA EL FNA

Amazigh musicians singing haunting laments alongside energetic Gnaoua bands in bright satin entertain the crowds every night on Djemaa El Fna in Marrakesh.

EDUCATION IMAGES/GETTY IMAGES

Best Music Experiences

- **Enjoy Amazigh or Gnaoua bands at Cafe Clock's Sunday Sunset Concerts in Fez, Marrakesh and Chefchaouen.** (p61)
- **Dance along to the Gnaoua & World Music Festival held in Essaouira in late June.** (p144)
- **Be entranced at Fez's long-standing Fes Festival of World Sacred Music in May or June.** (p20)
- **Swing to Casablanca's Jazzablanca every June.** (p145)

↙ SUFI NIGHTS

Devotees flock to Sufi brotherhood performances held nightly in the Jnan Sbil Gardens at the Fes Festival of World Sacred Music.

Above Gnaoua musicians, Djemaa El Fna square, Marrakesh (p42)
Right Fes Festival of World Sacred Music

↘ AÏT BEN HADDOU FACTS

This *ksar* (pictured; fortified village) was a strategic trading post on trans-Saharan routes.

Built in the 17th century, it has older origins.

It's one of nine UNESCO World Heritage Sites in Morocco.

Dozens of Hollywood movies have been filmed here.

SCSTOCK/SHUTTERSTOCK

KASBAHS & **KSOUR**

Some of the most spectacular kasbahs and *ksour* lie in the High Atlas from Telouet to Ouarzazate, around Toubkal and the M'Goun Massif, and along the Dadès and Drâa river valleys between the Tafilalet Gorges and Tansikht.

Best Kasbah Experiences

- **Visit Kasbah Amridil at Skoura for a peek at local life.** (p111)
- **Follow in Jacques Majorelle's footsteps and paint (or photograph) a remote High Atlas kasbah.** (p54)
- **Marvel at the interior decor at the Glaoui family kasbah at Telouet.** (p113)
- **Stay in a romantic kasbah hotel in the Drâa Valley.** (p110)

↘ HOW MANY GRAINS OF SAND?

Just over 42%, or 300,000 sq km, of Morocco is in the Sahara, but only 3.3% of the Sahara is in Morocco.

MITZO/SHUTTERSTOCK

INTO THE SAHARA

Soak up the silence of the Sahara (pictured), watch the endless dunes that change colour with the light and, by night, marvel at the intense blue sky thick with stars. Ride a camel, sandboard down a dune, stay in a kasbah hotel or try glamping at a luxurious tented camp.

Best Desert Experiences

- **Watch the dunes turn spectacular shades of orange, pink and purple as the sun sets.** (p120)
- **Travel off-road in a 4WD beyond M'Hamid to Erg Chigaga, the largest sand sea in Morocco.** (p122)
- **Check out the wildlife in the Souss-Massa National Park south of Agadir.** (p231)
- **Wonder at the brilliant night sky above Saharan sands in Merzouga.** (p120)

ADRENALINE ADVENTURES

That long Atlantic coastline and dramatic mountain ranges mean adventure sports have taken off in Morocco. There's exciting off-road cycling in the High Atlas, superb hiking and excellent rock-climbing routes. Try paragliding or windsurfing, or head for the southern beaches for serious surfing opportunities.

Best Sporty Adventures

- **Surf those right points and hollow beach breaks in winter.** (p220)
- **Hike the High Atlas and ascend Jebel Toubkal.** (p88)
- **Try a multi-pitch climb in the Todra Gorge.** (p30)
- **Hire a bike for hair-raising cycling adventures on High Atlas mountain routes.** (p94)

GUENTERGUNI/GETTY IMAGES

★ CYCLING FROM DESERT TO MOUNTAINS

Hop on a gravel bike to ride from Agafay to the Kik Plateau in the High Atlas, discovering valleys, peaks and villages.

CHRISNOE/SHUTTERSTOCK

↙ ALL TOOLED UP FOR CRACK-CLIMBING

Tafraoute in the Anti-Atlas is an exciting place for crack-climbing: the White Dome has five towers to scale.

Above Cyclist, the High Atlas (p94)
Left Climber, Tafraoute (p225)

ARTY CRAFTY

Morocco is famed for its exquisite crafts. Ancient monuments gleam with *zellige* (mosaic tilework) and carved plaster and wood, while ceilings swirl with intricate, painted floral designs called *zouak*. In the medinas, artisans ply centuries-old trades from bone carving to brass etching, embroidery to slipper-making, ceramics, copper beating and carpentry. In the countryside, women weave blankets and rugs with wool from sheep they've raised.

Left *Babouches* (leather slippers), Marrakesh (p42)
Right Threads, Fez workshop (p182)
Below *Tanjia* (crock-pot stew) heated in hammam coals, Marrakesh (p42)

→ BEYOND FAIR TRADE

Check out the artisan store of The Anou (p209) in Fez to meet the artisans. You can also visit their rural cooperatives across Morocco to see them at work.

KUJAWIANKA PODROZUJE/SHUTTERSTOCK

A MODERN TAKE

Marrakesh reigns supreme for contemporary Moroccan design. Search out modern interpretations of ancient crafts such as ceramics, lighting, jewellery and leather.

FROM LEFT: KHRITTHITHAT WEERASIRIRUT/SHUTTERSTOCK, LOIS GOBE/SHUTTERSTOCK

↑ BACHELORS' CONVENIENCE FOOD

Drop off a *tanjia* (crock-pot stew) at the hammam to cook in the coals while you're on your artisan tour, like bachelor craftsmen of old (p56).

Best Arts & Craft Experiences

- **Take an artisans tour to meet craftspeople in medinas and the countryside.** (p103)
- **Visit the Fez tanneries to see how skins are prepared to make fine leather.** (p182)
- **Try your hand at carving plaster or painting *zouak* at a workshop.** (p57)
- **Write your name in Arabic on a calligraphy course.** (p165)
- **Wander the shops and galleries in Marrakesh's Ville Nouvelle for contemporary art and crafts.** (p54)

Heat is fierce in the interior (45°C is not unusual), so make like Moroccans and head for the coast.

Fes Festival of World Sacred Music

This week-long festival in Fez is usually held in late May or early June.

Fez, p174

fesfestival.com

Gnaoua & World Music Festival

Essaouira is the place to be in late June for the Gnaoua & World Music Festival.

Essaouira, p144

festival-gnaoua.net

Demand for seaside accommodation peaks in July and August. View tours and overnight adventures in advance at lonelyplanet.com.

JUNE

Average daytime max: 27°C
Days of rainfall: 0 (Atlantic Coast)

JULY

Morocco in SUMMER

FROM LEFT: MICHELE FALZONE/ALAMY, ABDELMJID RIZKOU/SHUTTERSTOCK, RYZHKOV OLEKSANDR/SHUTTERSTOCK, DAN BACIU/SHUTTERSTOCK, BACKGROUND: RYZHKOV OLEKSANDR/SHUTTERSTOCK

Surf's Up

Surfing for beginners and intermediates is perfect in Essaouira, with waves 0.5m to 1m high.

Essaouira, p140

Casablanca Jazz

Jazzablanca hits the streets of Casablanca in July.

Casablanca, p145

jazzablanca.com

Blown Away

The morning wind in Essaouira and Dakhla is great for kitesurfing, wingfoiling, surfing and windsurfing; afternoons are for experts.

Essaouira, p140

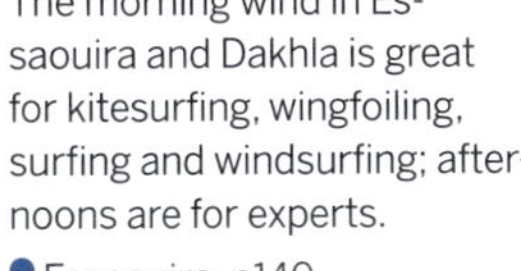

Book surfing and windsurfing equipment well in advance.

ion-club.net

Average daytime max: 30°C
Days of rainfall: 0 (Atlantic Coast)

AUGUST

Average daytime max: 30°C
Days of rainfall: 0 (Atlantic Coast)

Packing Notes

A hat, sunglasses and lots of sunscreen to protect against the fierce African sun.

Marrakesh is usually about 5°C warmer than the rest of Morocco, with less rainfall too.

↙ Tanjazz

Tangier rocks for four days in September at Tanjazz. Expect local and international stars in the streets, concert halls and intimate venues.

Tangier, p159

▸ tanjazz.org

→ Sufi Festival

The Fes Festival of Sufi Culture runs in Fez over a week in October. Lectures are in French, but concerts are well worth attending.

Fez, p174

▸ festivalculturesoufie.com

SEPTEMBER

Average daytime max: 30°C
Days of rainfall: 3 (Fez)

OCTOBER

Morocco in AUTUMN

FROM LEFT: GEOFF GOLDSWAIN/SHUTTERSTOCK, GODONG/ALAMY, ELENA MOISEEVA/SHUTTERSTOCK, RYBARMAREKK/SHUTTERSTOCK BACKGROUND: JULIA LAV/SHUTTERSTOCK

↘ A Moveable Feast

Taliouine's Saffron Festival happens within the first two weeks of November, but dates depend on the harvest.

▶ souktanadusafran.com

↗ Best for Surfing

Morocco's surf is at its very best in winter. Try Taghazout, Imsouane and Sidi Kaouki.

Taghazout, Imsouane, Sidi Kaouki; p222

The end of October European school holidays make this peak season in Morocco. Book everything well in advance.

Average daytime max: 27°C
Days of rainfall: 7 (Fez)

NOVEMBER

Average daytime max: 21°C
Days of rainfall: 7 (Marrakesh)

Wrap up – it can be cold and wintry in Morocco in November.

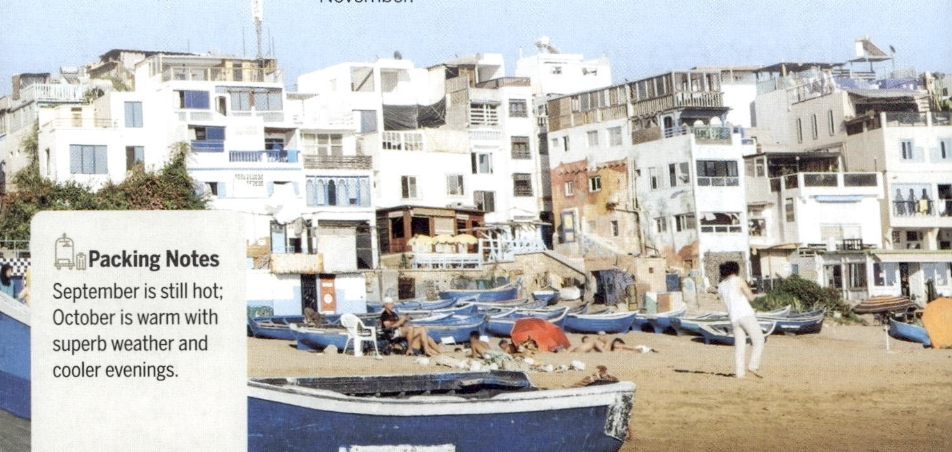

Packing Notes

September is still hot; October is warm with superb weather and cooler evenings.

Rainfall is limited in Sahara regions to two days per month, and it's a chilly 7°C at night.

Expect snow in the High and Middle Atlas Mountains, occasionally with road closures.

→ The Big Screen

Marrakesh's International Film Festival wows audiences with cinema and outdoor screenings in late November/ early December.

Marrakesh (p42)

▸ marrakech-festival.com

Christmas and New Year are peak season, especially in Marrakesh where hotels often demand a minimum stay.

DECEMBER

Average daytime max: 19°C
Days of rainfall: 7 (Marrakesh)

JANUARY

Morocco in WINTER

FROM LEFT: ANADOLU/GETTY IMAGES, CHRISTIAN ASLUND/GETTY IMAGES, BACKGROUND: FRANTICOO/SHUTTERSTOCK

Tell Me a Story

The Marrakech International World Storytelling Festival takes place in the city at the end of January.

Marrakesh (p42)

▸ worldstorytellingcafe.com/marrakech-international-storytelling-festival

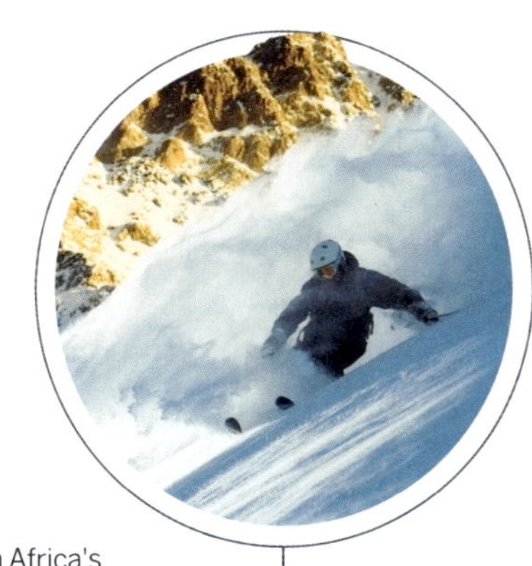

→ On-Piste High Atlas

Oukaimeden is a modest ski resort with Africa's highest slopes. Snow is erratic so check lifts are open.

Oukaimeden, p95

FEBRUARY

Average daytime max: 19°C
Days of rainfall: 8 (Marrakesh)

Average daytime max: 20°C
Days of rainfall: 7 (Marrakesh)

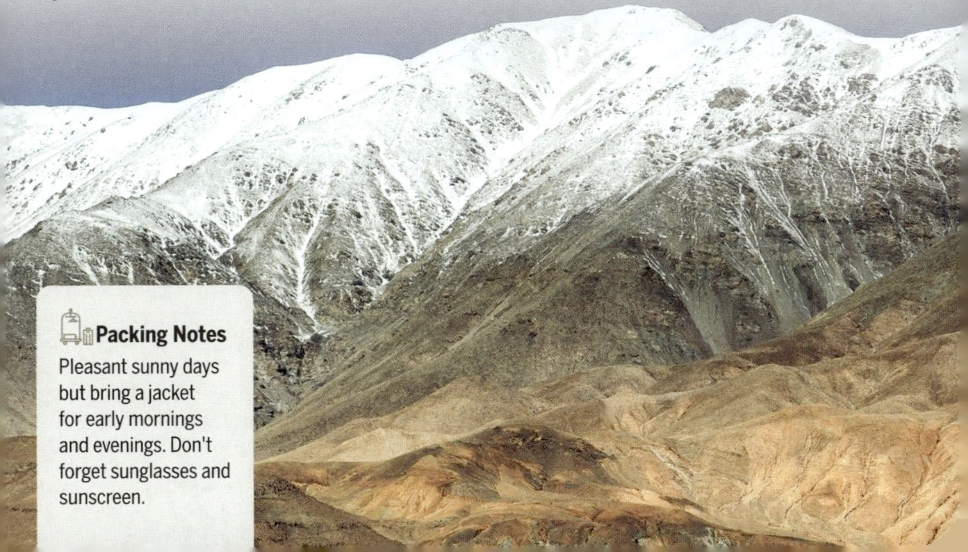

Packing Notes

Pleasant sunny days but bring a jacket for early mornings and evenings. Don't forget sunglasses and sunscreen.

Chefchaouen gets the most spring rain, with 11 umbrella days each month. Fez comes second with 10 in March and April.

↘ Bloomin' Marvelous

Spring flowers abound in the countryside, and are especially colourful between Meknes and Moulay Idriss Zerhoun.

Meknes, p198

Moulay Idriss Zerhoun, p201

↖ Scented Souqs

Fez's medina is deliciously fragrant in March when orange blossoms appear in the souqs for distilling orange flower water.

Fez, p174

MARCH

APRIL

Average daytime max: 22°C
Days of rainfall: 10 (Marrakesh)

Morocco in SPRING

FROM LEFT: NATURE'S CLICKS/SHUTTERSTOCK, BILDAGENTUR ZOONAR GMBH/SHUTTERSTOCK, TERRY137/SHUTTERSTOCK, CHRIS GRIFFITHS/GETTY IMAGES. BACKGROUND: A JOHN RUSSELL/SHUTTERSTOCK

Easter

European school holidays make Easter extra busy. Be sure to book everything well in advance.

↘ Darling Buds of May

Huge baskets of rosebuds follow in May, to make rose water. Buy a bag to delight your nose.

← Rose Festival

See the Rose Queen crowned at Kelaa M'Gouna's Rose Festival, usually the second weekend in May, depending on the harvest.

▸ foruminternationalroses59@gmail.com

Average daytime max: 23°C
Days of rainfall: 8 (Marrakesh)

MAY

Average daytime max: 26°C
Days of rainfall: 7 (Marrakesh)

Packing Notes

Layers for this lovely spring weather, that you can peel off come May.

MARRAKESH & THE HIGH ATLAS MOUNTAINS

Trip Builder

TAKE YOUR PICK OF MUST-SEES AND HIDDEN GEMS

From the exciting Red City, you can see the lofty, snow-covered peaks of the High Atlas that rise between Marrakesh and the Sahara. They invite you to leave the frenzy of the souqs and wander into green valleys, winding passes and imposing mountains for some respite and some adventure.

Trip Notes

Hub towns Marrakesh, Ouarzazate

How long Allow seven days

Getting around Marrakesh has good air, train and bus links. Ouarzazate has fewer flights but good bus links. Hire a car or arrange transfers with your accommodation. If you're trekking, a mule and its handler will carry your luggage.

Tips Driving can be slow; most roads are sealed, and there's often only one lane in each direction on twisty mountain roads.

Ourika
Take a strenuous hike up to the highest waterfall; attend the lively Setti Fetma *moussem* (festival); stroll through a saffron farm; stay in a valley lodge or mountain-top kasbah (pictured above).
1hr from Marrakesh

Aït Ben Haddou
Capture this well-preserved UNESCO Heritage Site (pictured right) in early-morning light; ask a local to show you around inside; have lunch with the women artisans at Timouzounin.
3½hrs from Marrakesh

Imlil
Hire a guide for a day's hike in the Toubkal National Park; set off for the six-day Toubkal Circuit or climb North Africa's highest peak; stay in a luxurious kasbah hotel.
1½hrs from Marrakesh

Ouarzazate
Imagine you're an action hero at the Atlas Studios; admire the crumbling former glory of the Glaoui family at Taourirt Kasbah; spot migrating birds from a kayak on the lake.
3½hrs from Marrakesh

Ouirgane
Browse the Wednesday souq; savour lake views (pictured left) over lunch; get some action horse riding, mountain biking or river rafting; cook in an organic garden; be pampered at a country lodge.
1½hrs from Marrakesh

Oued Oum Er Rbia
Oued Tessaout
El Kelaa des Sraghna
Bin El Ouidane
Ouzoud
Oude Tissakht
Azilal
Zaouiat Ahansal Valley
Oued el Akhdar
Demnate
Imi n'Ifri
Tizi n'Tirghist
Sidi Rahal
Aït Bououli
Assif Rbat
Aït Bougmez Valley
M'Goun Massif
HIGH ATLAS
Jebel M'Goun
Oued Ourika
Oued Tessaout
Toufrine
Ourika
Yaggour Plateau
Taddert
Tnine
Ourika Valley
High Atlas
Tizi n'Tichka
kaimeden
Setti Fatma
Ounila Valley
Agouim
oubkal ational Park
Aït Ben Haddou
Skoura
Dadès Valley
Ouarzazate
Oued Drâa
Tizi n'Tinififft
Jebel Kissane
Jebel Siroua

SAHARAN DUNES & KASBAHS
Trip Builder

TAKE YOUR PICK OF MUST-SEES AND HIDDEN GEMS

Exploring towns along the Dadès River reveals kasbahs in oases thick with palm trees, spectacular gorges and glorious views of the High Atlas and Jebel Sahro Mountains. In Erfoud you can hunt for fossils from the dinosaur age while around Merzouga the Saharan dunes are accessible; or venture to the more remote Erg Chigaga from M'Hamid.

Trip Notes

Hub towns M'Hamid; Merzouga

How long Allow six days

Getting around Hire a car in Marrakesh or Fez to go at your own pace. There's a daily CTM bus service along the N10 (Ouarzazate to Errachidia), but to get further south, you'll need a *grand taxi* or your own transport.

Tips Roads are sealed, but mostly one lane in either direction. Look out for nomad tents on the lower slopes in winter.

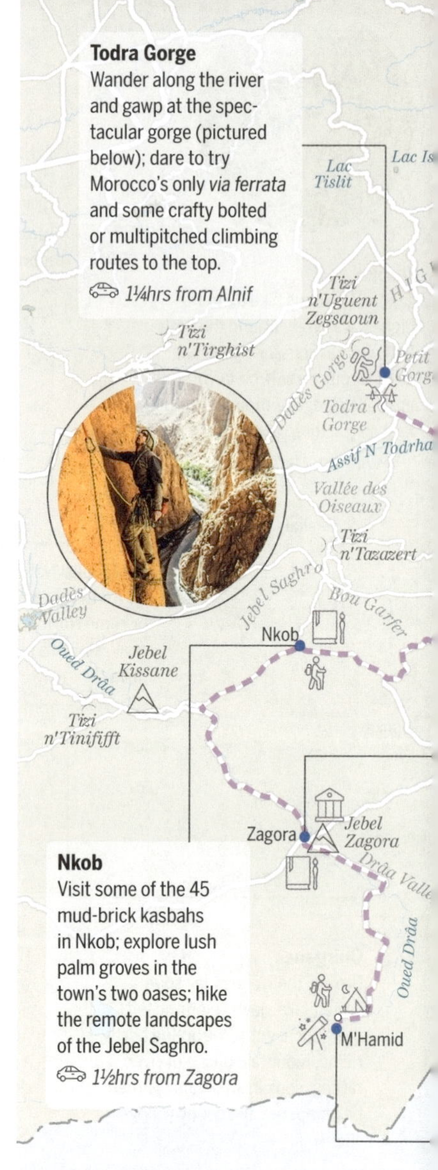

FROM LEFT: EWA CIE_LIKIEWICZ/AURORA PHOTOS/GETTY IMAGES, ART4STOCK/SHUTTERSTOCK, ART KONOVALOV/SHUTTERSTOCK

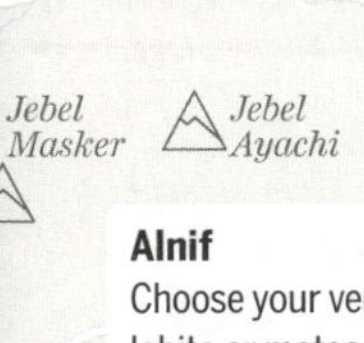

Alnif
Choose your very own trilobite or meteorite at the Ihmadi Trilobites Centre; pick up some local cumin for your next tajine.

1½hrs from Nkob

Erfoud
Look out for life-sized replicas of dinosaur skeletons just south of Erfoud, welcoming you to the Tahiri Museum of Fossils & Minerals.

2¼hrs from Todra Gorge

Merzouga
Check out some ancient 4WD vehicles at the Morocco National Auto Museum (pictured left); climb aboard your camel and lope off into the Sahara to watch the sun rise or set across the dunes.

1hr from Erfoud

Zagora
Explore crumbling 16th-century Ksar Tissergate; find out about local tribes at the Musée des Arts et Traditions.

1½hrs from M'Hamid

M'Hamid
Take a nomad-style multiday trek with local guides and camel herders; stay in a luxurious tented camp; try sandboarding and watch the night sky in Morocco's most remote dunes.

7½hrs from Marrakesh

NORTHERN MOROCCO
Trip Builder

TAKE YOUR PICK OF MUST-SEES AND HIDDEN GEMS

Soak up the international vibe of Tangier, explore little-visited Tetouan and delight in Chefchaouen blue. Enjoy views from Moulay Idriss Zerhoun before admiring Roman mosaics at Volubilis. Meknes is a charming imperial city, while majestic Fez awaits with its magnificent monuments. Sefrou is full of crafts, and Ifrane's cedar forests are enchanting.

Trip Notes

Hub towns Fez, Tangier

How long Allow seven days

Getting around Hire a car in Tangier or Fez to go at your own pace. There's a regular CTM bus service from Tangier to Tetouan and from Tetouan to Chefchaouen and Meknes. From Meknes take a *grand taxi* or your own transport to Moulay Idriss Zerhoun and Fez. Buses serve Sefrou and Ifrane.

Tips Road are good, but mountainous between Tetouan and Meknes; there's a motorway from Meknes to Fez.

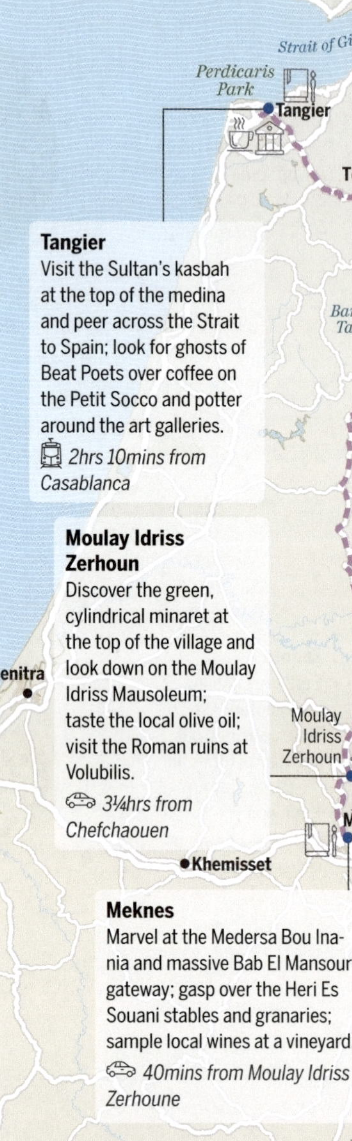

Tangier
Visit the Sultan's kasbah at the top of the medina and peer across the Strait to Spain; look for ghosts of Beat Poets over coffee on the Petit Socco and potter around the art galleries.
2hrs 10mins from Casablanca

Moulay Idriss Zerhoun
Discover the green, cylindrical minaret at the top of the village and look down on the Moulay Idriss Mausoleum; taste the local olive oil; visit the Roman ruins at Volubilis.
3¼hrs from Chefchaouen

Meknes
Marvel at the Medersa Bou Inania and massive Bab El Mansour gateway; gasp over the Heri Es Souani stables and granaries; sample local wines at a vineyard.
40mins from Moulay Idriss Zerhoune

Tetouan

Practise your Spanish in Tetouan; don't miss a visit to the Royal Artisan School followed by an artisanal tour; see the art at the old Spanish station, now the excellent Centro de Arte Moderno.

1½hrs from Tangier

Chefchaouen

Venture out early with your camera to capture the blue streets (pictured right), a few cats and no tourists; watch women doing their washing at Ras El Maa; walk up to the old Spanish mosque.

1½hrs from Tetouan

Fez

Get lost in the medina; wonder at the stunning Bou Inania and El Attarine *medersas* (pictured right; theological schools); watch the coppersmiths at work under the plane tree on Place Seffarine; dip into the famous Fassi cuisine.

1hr from Meknes

Sefrou

Take an artisanal tour in the medina; have lunch to the tune of the blacksmith's hammer; visit the tiny Museum of Multiculturalism.

40mins from Fez

Azrou

Join the locals at the huge Tuesday market; shop for pure wool rugs hand-woven by Middle Atlas women (pictured right); eat mountain trout for lunch. If you have more time, hike through ancient cedar forests in Ifrane National Park to the south.

1½hrs from Sefrou

euta
Oued Laou
Ghorghiz Peak
Jebel El Kelaa
Chefchaouen
Isla de Tierra
Isla de Mar
Nador
El Peñón de Alhucemas
Jbel Tidirhine (2456m)
Tarquist
Berkane
Beni-Snassen Mountains
Tizi n' Touahar
Taza
Tazekka National Park
Jebel Tazekka
Fez
Oued Sebou
Sefrou
Oued Moulouya
Jebel Bou Iblane
Dayet Aoua
Dayet Ifrah
Azrou
Guigou River
MIDDLE ATLAS
Ifrane National Park

ATLANTIC COAST
Trip Builder

TAKE YOUR PICK OF MUST-SEES AND HIDDEN GEMS

Follow the Atlantic Coast from laid-back Essaouira through dreamy coastal resorts that time forgot, to the surprisingly chilled capital, a birding paradise lagoon and on to arty Asilah.

Trip Notes

Hub towns Essaouira, Asilah

How long Allow four days

Getting around Take a *grand taxi* from town to town, or hire your own car for greater flexibility.

Tips Roads are good, though usually single-lane, except around Rabat.

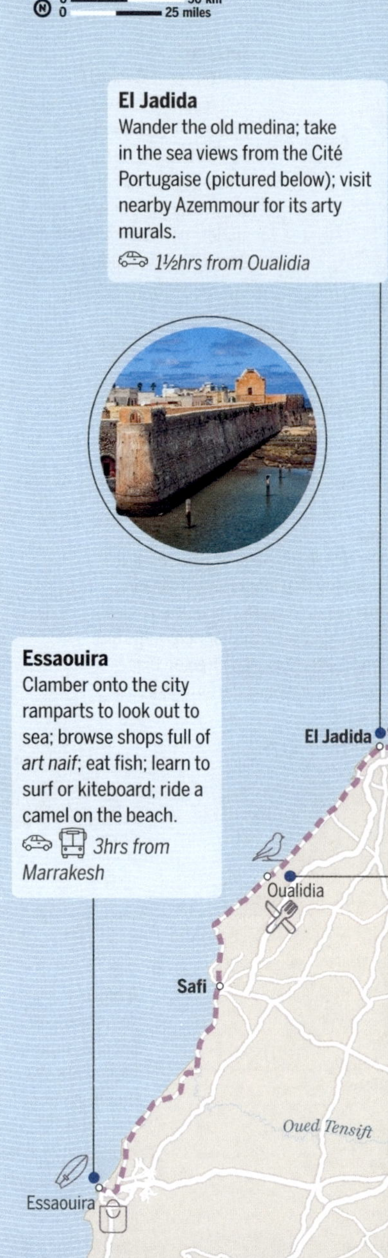

FROM LEFT: MADRUGADA VERDE/SHUTTERSTOCK, JOSE Y YO ESTUDIO/SHUTTERSTOCK, SAIKO3P/SHUTTERSTOCK

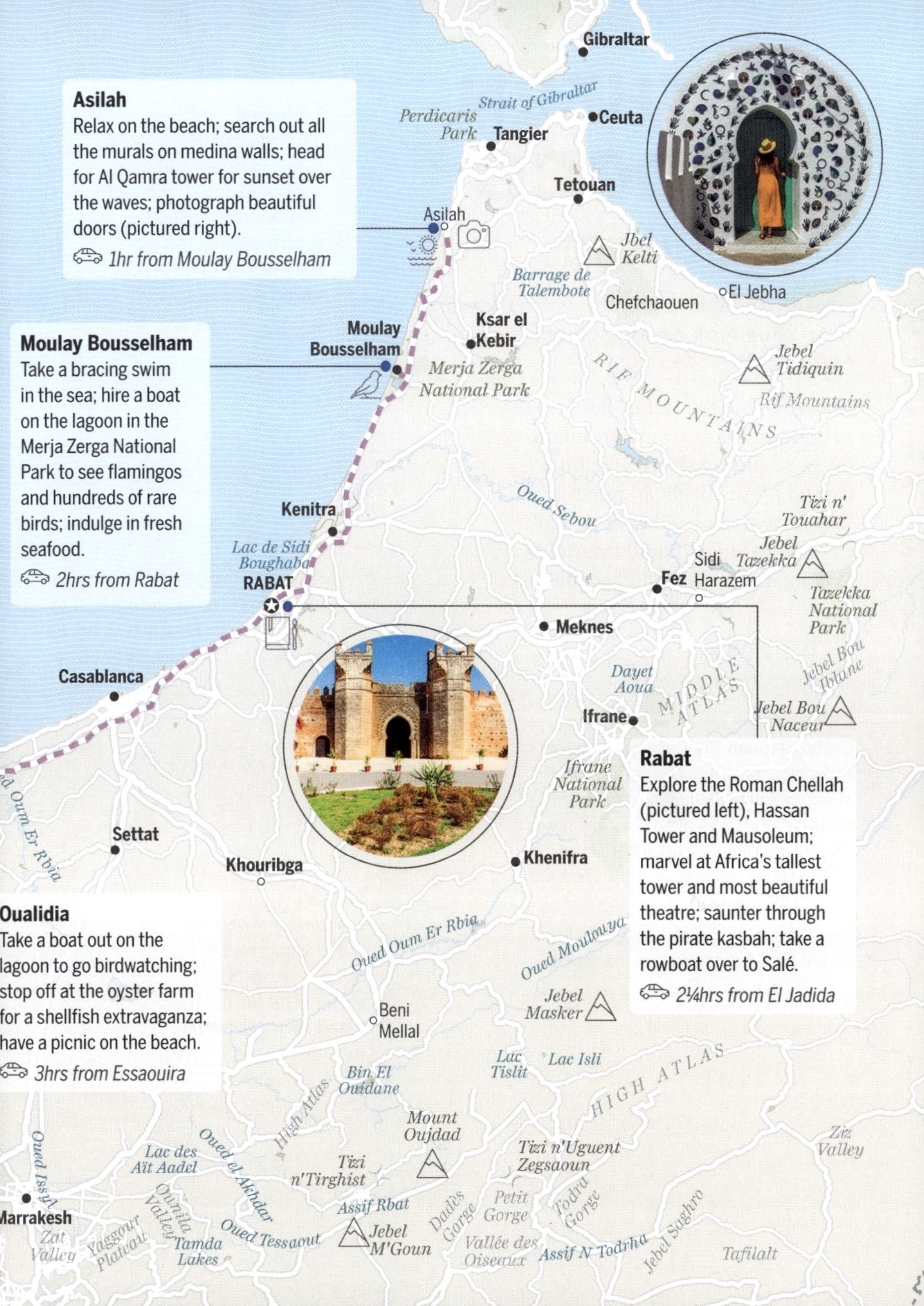
Gibraltar
Strait of Gibraltar
Ceuta
Perdicaris Park
Tangier
Tetouan
Asilah
Relax on the beach; search out all the murals on medina walls; head for Al Qamra tower for sunset over the waves; photograph beautiful doors (pictured right).
1hr from Moulay Bousselham
Asilah
Jbel Kelti
Barrage de Talembote
Chefchaouen
El Jebha
Moulay Bousselham
Take a bracing swim in the sea; hire a boat on the lagoon in the Merja Zerga National Park to see flamingos and hundreds of rare birds; indulge in fresh seafood.
2hrs from Rabat
Moulay Bousselham
Ksar el Kebir
Merja Zerga National Park
Jebel Tidiquin
RIF MOUNTAINS
Rif Mountains
Oued Sebou
Kenitra
Lac de Sidi Boughaba
RABAT
Tizi n' Touahar
Jebel Tazekka
Sidi Harazem
Fez
Tazekka National Park
Meknes
Casablanca
Dayet Aoua
MIDDLE ATLAS
Jebel Bou Iblane
Jebel Bou Naceur
Ifrane
Rabat
Explore the Roman Chellah (pictured left), Hassan Tower and Mausoleum; marvel at Africa's tallest tower and most beautiful theatre; saunter through the pirate kasbah; take a rowboat over to Salé.
2¼hrs from El Jadida
Ifrane National Park
Oued Oum Er Rbia
Settat
Khouribga
Khenifra
Oualidia
Take a boat out on the lagoon to go birdwatching; stop off at the oyster farm for a shellfish extravaganza; have a picnic on the beach.
3hrs from Essaouira
Oued Oum Er Rbia
Oued Moulouya
Jebel Masker
Beni Mellal
Lac Tislit
Lac Isli
Bin El Ouidane
HIGH ATLAS
High Atlas
Mount Oujdad
Tizi n'Uguent Zegsaoun
Ziz Valley
Oued Issyl
Lac des Aït Aadel
Oued el Akhdar
Tizi n'Tirghist
Marrakesh
Ounila Valley
Assif Rbat
Dadès Gorge
Petit Gorge
Todra Gorge
Jebel Saghro
Zat Valley
Yaggour Plateau
Tamda Lakes
Oued Tessaout
Jebel M'Goun
Vallée des Oiseaux
Assif N Todrha
Tafilalt

SOUTHERN MOROCCO
Trip Builder

TAKE YOUR PICK OF MUST-SEES AND HIDDEN GEMS

Follow the last of the Anti-Atlas Mountains from Taroudant down to the coast and sunshine capital of Agadir; head north to laid-back surfing villages, or south to dreamy Sidi Ifni and eventually, Dakhla, the perfect kiteboarding spot.

Trip Notes

Hub towns Taroudant, Agadir

How long Allow seven days

Getting around There are regular buses to Taroudant and Agadir from all over Morocco. A **shuttle bus** (souktosurf.com) takes surfers from Agadir to surfing towns. Hire a car for the long drive from Agadir to Dakhla (14hrs) or fly Royal Air Maroc from Agadir (1hr50mins).

Tips Roads in this region are good. Hire a 4WD if you intend to drive in the desert.

KINGMA PHOTOS/SHUTTERSTOCK

Taghazout
Surf Taghazout's long peeling right-hander; stretch into a yoga asana on the rooftop of your beachfront stay; relax with an argan-oil massage; enjoy freshly grilled seafood while the sun sets.
 *30mins from Agadir*

Agadir
Get up close and personal to the crocs in the Crocopark; shop at Souq Al Had; laze on the wide, sandy beach.
1½hrs from Taroudant

Sidi Ifni
Soak up the relaxed vibe of this remote region; notice the Hispanic flavour of the food and the art deco architecture; try paragliding or learn to surf in gentle waves.
1½hrs from Tiznit

Timslit
Mirleft
Sidi Ifni

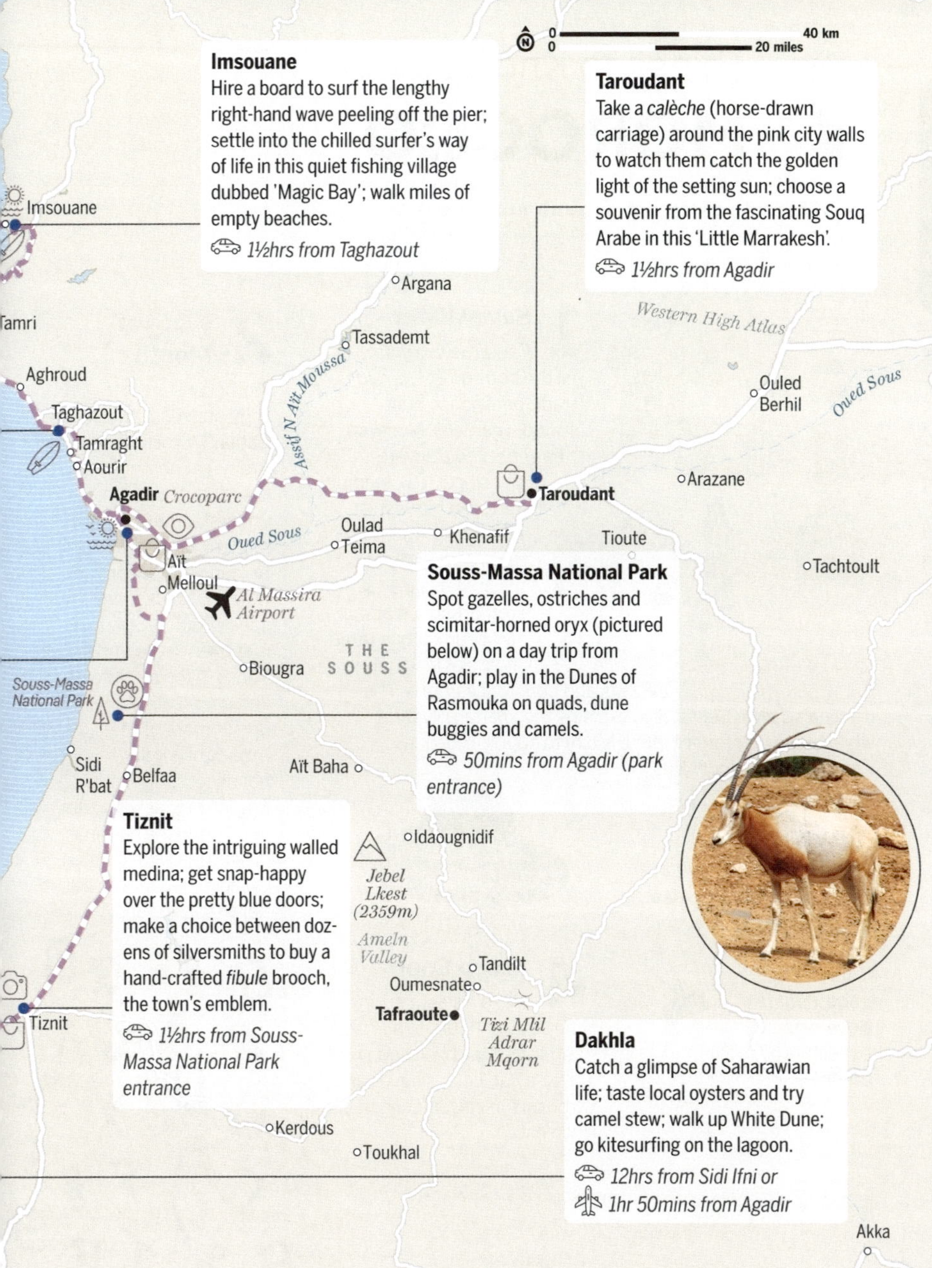

0
0
40 km
20 miles
Imsouane
Hire a board to surf the lengthy right-hand wave peeling off the pier; settle into the chilled surfer's way of life in this quiet fishing village dubbed 'Magic Bay'; walk miles of empty beaches.
1½hrs from Taghazout
Taroudant
Take a calèche (horse-drawn carriage) around the pink city walls to watch them catch the golden light of the setting sun; choose a souvenir from the fascinating Souq Arabe in this 'Little Marrakesh'.
1½hrs from Agadir
Imsouane
Argana
Tamri
Tassademt
Western High Atlas
Aghroud
Assif N Aït Moussa
Ouled Berhil
Oued Sous
Taghazout
Tamraght
Aourir
Arazane
Agadir
Crocoparc
Taroudant
Oulad Teima
Khenafif
Tioute
Oued Sous
Aït Melloul
Tachtoult
Souss-Massa National Park
Spot gazelles, ostriches and scimitar-horned oryx (pictured below) on a day trip from Agadir; play in the Dunes of Rasmouka on quads, dune buggies and camels.
50mins from Agadir (park entrance)
Al Massira Airport
THE SOUSS
Biougra
Souss-Massa National Park
Sidi R'bat
Belfaa
Aït Baha
Tiznit
Explore the intriguing walled medina; get snap-happy over the pretty blue doors; make a choice between dozens of silversmiths to buy a hand-crafted fibule brooch, the town's emblem.
1½hrs from Souss-Massa National Park entrance
Idaougnidif
Jebel Lkest (2359m)
Ameln Valley
Tandilt
Oumesnate
Tafraoute
Tizi Mlil
Adrar Mqorn
Tiznit
Dakhla
Catch a glimpse of Saharawian life; taste local oysters and try camel stew; walk up White Dune; go kitesurfing on the lagoon.
12hrs from Sidi Ifni or
1hr 50mins from Agadir
Kerdous
Toukhal
Akka

Things to Know About MOROCCO

INSIDER TIPS TO HIT THE GROUND RUNNING

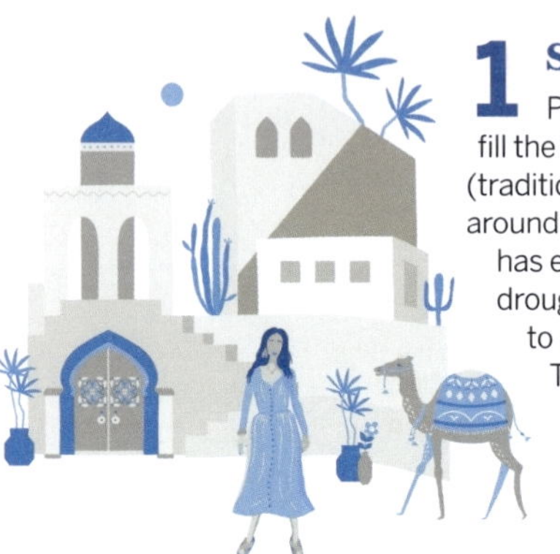

1 Save Water

Pause before you fill the bathtub at the *riad* (traditional house built around a garden). Morocco has endured a severe drought since 2017, leading to reduced harvests. To see how water can be managed, visit Marrakesh's remarkable Water Museum. It has three floors of fascinating exhibits and beautiful gardens. The medina's Jardin Secret also explains the *khettara* system where water is brought into the city to supply mosques, hammams and fountains.

2 Word of Mouth

Moroccans are talented linguists: most speak Darija (Moroccan Arabic) at home, some Classical Arabic to understand the Quran, Modern Standard Arabic to read newspapers and watch TV, plus many speak French. Spanish is spoken in the north. Those in the mountains and countryside speak one or more of the Amazigh languages, not necessarily Darija. English is widely spoken, and kids in the medina pick up enough German, Chinese, Japanese and Italian to earn tips.

3 When to Tip

Tip everyone who helps you. Ten percent in a restaurant is fine. Guides and private drivers expect a tip, but give only if service was good. *Petit taxi* drivers don't expect anything.

4 Keep Cool

Take a siesta during the sizzling hours of high summer. Stay hydrated and wear a hat. Long sleeves and trousers in cotton or linen are coolest.

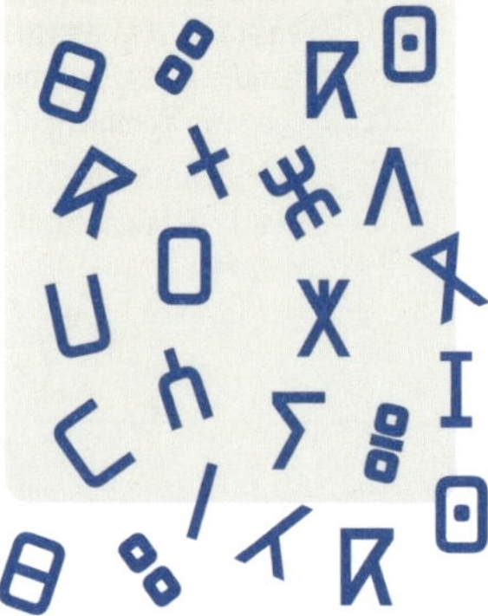

CLOCKWISE FROM LEFT: KSENIA LOKKO/SHUTTERSTOCK, TASNIM AHMAD/SHUTTERSTOCK, SENTAVIO/SHUTTERSTOCK, ETACARINAE89/SHUTTERSTOCK, VERONIKA108/SHUTTERSTOCK, KUTUZOVADESIGN/SHUTTERSTOCK

5 Visit During Ramadan

Visiting Morocco during Ramadan gives a fascinating insight into local culture. For four weeks every year (dates change in accordance with the Islamic calendar), Moroccans don't eat, drink or smoke between sun-up and sunset. Exempt are young children, the sick, pregnant people, travellers and non-Muslim visitors – though be discreet (don't eat or drink on the street). It's a happy, family-oriented time when people reconnect with their spiritual life and emphasise helping the poor. They tend to wear traditional clothes more often, eat special dishes and, in the evenings, take the children to the funfair or out for ice cream, and chat with neighbours in the square. Shops, offices and banks have different hours as people sleep later; some cafes close but places catering to tourists remain open. Grab the chance to break the fast – called *ftour* or *iftar* (a delicious meal with specific foods) – with locals.

▶ See more about Ramadan on p74

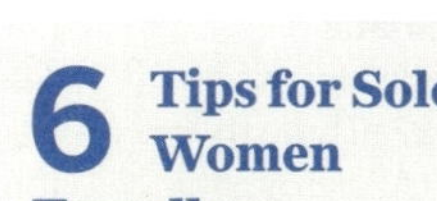

6 Tips for Solo Women Travellers

Dress modestly and wear sunglasses to avoid eye contact. Take trains in day time and taxis at night. Eat in places that are busy with locals or frequented by international residents. Choose accommodation where you can relax and retreat. Seek out female guides. If someone is uncomfortably persistent, do not engage. Stay calm and look around for help; it's never far away.

7 Entering Mosques

French colonisers banned non-Muslims from entering mosques in Morocco, but everyone can visit the magnificent Hassan II Mosque in Casablanca for a 40-minute tour. Once post-earthquake renovations on the High Atlas Tinmel Mosque are completed, all will be able to visit that too as it's no longer used for worship.

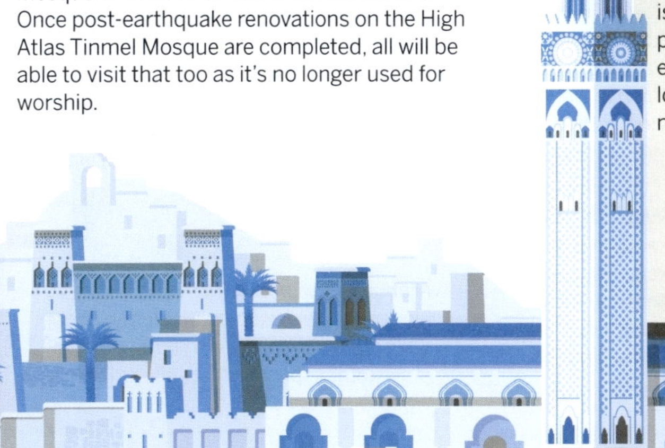

Read, Listen, Watch & Follow

READ

Walking with Nomads (Alice Morrison; 2022) Through the Atlas from the Sahara to the sea.

In Arabian Nights (Tahir Shah; 2009) Tales of wisdom from a journey through Morocco.

Dreams of Trespass: Tales of a Harem Girlhood (Fatima Mernissi; 1994) Sociologist Mernissi's childhood in 1950s Fez.

The Country of Others (Leila Slimani; 2022) Slimani's French grandmother's life in post-WWII Morocco.

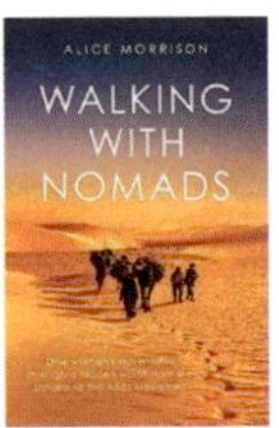

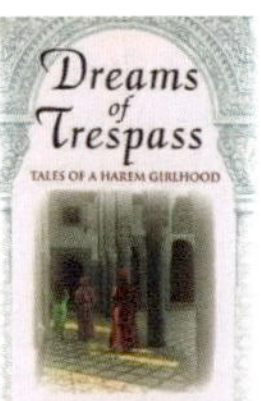

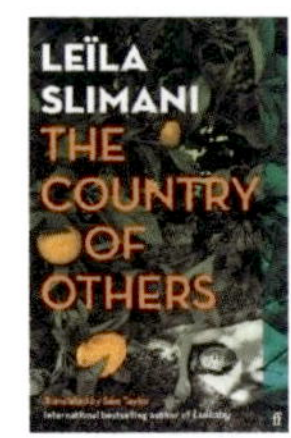

LISTEN

Sigham Olinw (Tasuta N-Ima; 2019) Laid-back Amazigh desert blues from Ouarzazate. The band's name means 'future generation'.

Inas Inas (Mohamed Rouicha; 1983) Beloved Amazigh poet, singer, composer and musician, now deceased.

Maghadnich Frakek (Cheb Kader Wahrani; 2022) Algerian singer/songwriter of Rai music; very popular in Morocco.

Reggada (Majda Raoui; 2023) Reggada is Arab/Amazigh dance music from the far north of Morocco.

RICHARD HEATHCOTE/GETTY IMAGES

Arabian Heartbreak (Manal; 2024) Singer/songwriter of rap and urban pop. Sang *Light Up the Sky* with three other Arab women (pictured) at Qatar's FIFA World Cup 2022.

WATCH

House In The Fields (Tala Hadid; 2017) Life in an isolated village in the Atlas.

Fragments from Heaven (Adnane Baraka, 2022) A nomad and a scientist search for meteorites.

Lalla Aïcha (Mohamed El Badaoui, 2019) A strong mother keeps her family together.

The Blue Caftan (pictured right; Maryam Touzani; 2022) A Salé couple running a caftan store hire a young apprentice.

A Short History of the Moors (Ian Cross, 2018) Moorish dynasties and their cultural legacy.

LIFESTYLE PICTURES/ALAMY

FOLLOW

moroccoworldnews.com Moroccan news in English.

@visit_morocco_ Official site of Moroccan Tourism.

@maison.blaoui Moroccan interiors to dream about.

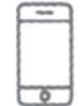

alicemorrison.co.uk Follow Alice's blog of her life in Imlil.

@leonie.marrakech For inspiring photos of Morocco.

MARRAKESH

PALACES | MUSEUMS | CULTURE

RESEARCHED BY HELEN RANGER

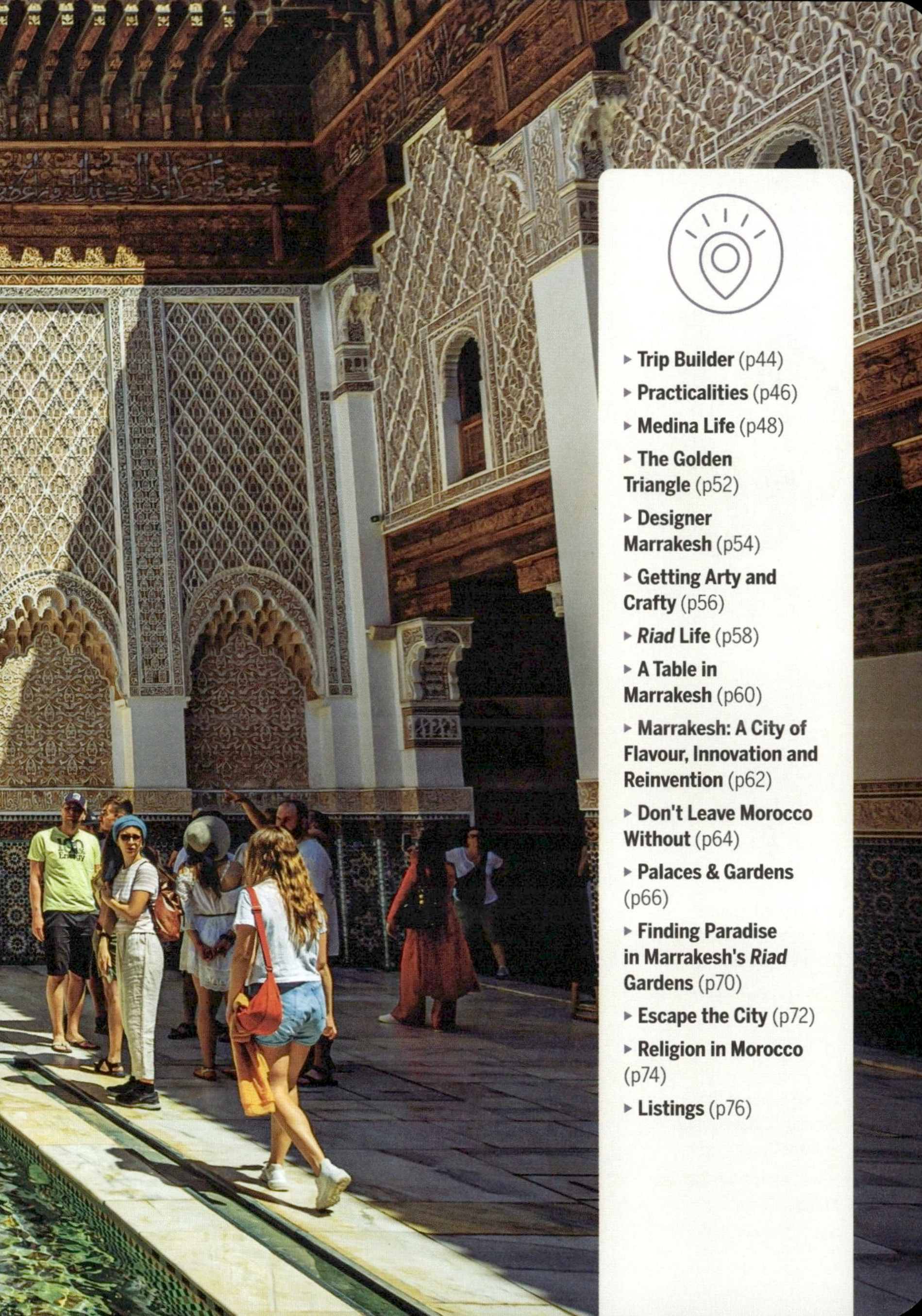

FROM LEFT: GARDENS BY DESIGN/SHUTTERSTOCK, AURALAURA/SHUTTERSTOCK,MARIAKOVALEVA/SHUTTERSTOCK PREVIOUS SPREAD: PARADISE AT RISK/SHUTTERSTOCK

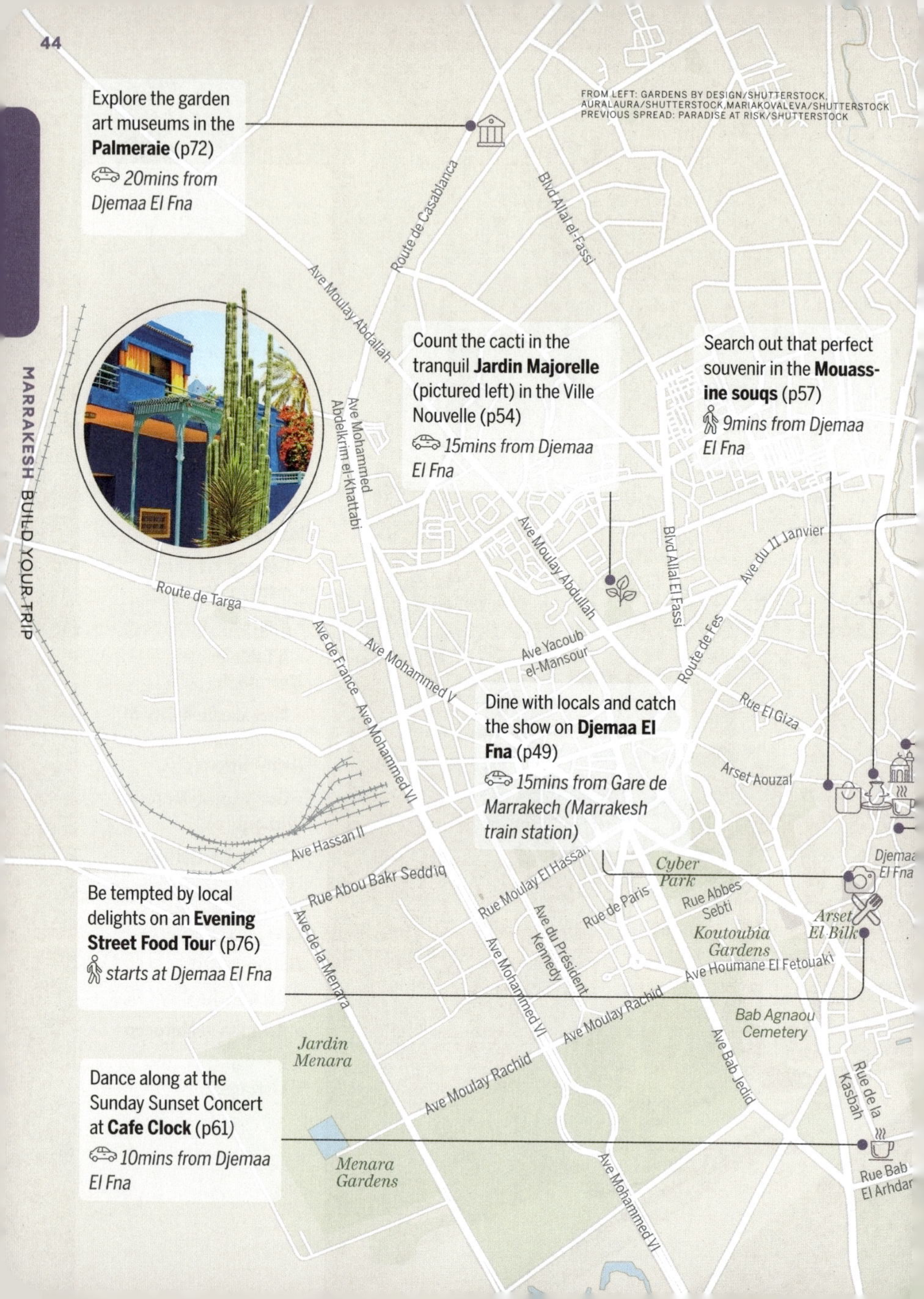

Explore the garden art museums in the **Palmeraie** (p72)

20mins from Djemaa El Fna

Count the cacti in the tranquil **Jardin Majorelle** (pictured left) in the Ville Nouvelle (p54)

15mins from Djemaa El Fna

Search out that perfect souvenir in the **Mouassine souqs** (p57)

9mins from Djemaa El Fna

Dine with locals and catch the show on **Djemaa El Fna** (p49)

15mins from Gare de Marrakech (Marrakesh train station)

Be tempted by local delights on an **Evening Street Food Tour** (p76)

starts at Djemaa El Fna

Dance along at the Sunday Sunset Concert at **Cafe Clock** (p61)

10mins from Djemaa El Fna

Route de Casablanca
Blvd Allal el-Fassi
Ave Moulay Abdallah
Ave Mohammed Abdelkrim el-Khattabi
Ave Moulay Abdullah
Blvd Allal El Fassi
Ave du 11 Janvier
Route de Targa
Ave Yacoub el-Mansour
Route de Fes
Ave de France
Ave Mohammed V
Rue El Giza
Ave Mohammed VI
Arset Aouzal
Ave Hassan II
Djemaa El Fna
Rue Abou Bakr Seddiq
Rue Moulay El Hassan
Cyber Park
Rue de Paris
Rue Abbes Sebti
Arset El Bilk
Ave de la Menara
Ave du Président Kennedy
Koutoubia Gardens
Ave Houmane El Fetouaki
Ave Moulay Rachid
Bab Agnaou Cemetery
Jardin Menara
Ave Bab Jedid
Rue de la Kasbah
Menara Gardens
Rue Bab El Arhdar

Marvel at the glorious medieval **Ben Youssef Medersa** (pictured left; p52)
11mins from Djemaa El Fna

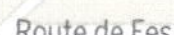

Try your hand at a traditional painting workshop at **Zwaq Art** (p57)
11mins from Djemaa El Fna

Sample regional teas from across Morocco at **1112 Marrakech** (p59)
11mins from Djemaa El Fna

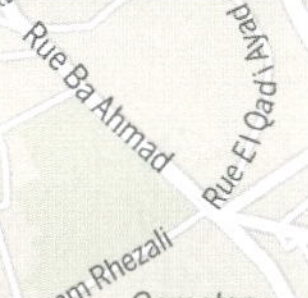

MARRAKESH
Trip Builder

Marrakesh oozes drama and excitement, from sizzling nights on Djemaa El Fna to museums grand and small, stately monuments and palaces, glorious *riads* (traditional houses built around gardens), entrancing souqs, tranquil gardens, a vibrant food scene and a dash of new city glamour.

Practicalities

ANDRZEJ LISOWSKI TRAVEL/SHUTTERSTOCK

ARRIVING

Menara Airport (pictured) is a 20-minute drive to the medina. Pay in advance (day/night Dh80/120) at the airport kiosk or ask your *riad* to send a taxi so you'll be dropped close to where you're staying. The L19 shuttle bus (Dh30) runs from the airport to Djemaa El Fna and to the Ville Nouvelle.

Gare de Marrakech (train station) is located in Gueliz in the Ville Nouvelle, a 13-minute taxi ride (about Dh12) from Djemaa El Fna.

HOW MUCH FOR A

Orange juice on Djemaa El Fna Dh8

Scrub and steam at Hammam Mouassine Dh170

***Tanjia* for two Dh160**

WHEN TO GO

JAN–MAR
Chilly mornings and evenings, blue skies

APR–JUNE
Ideal weather with warm to hot days

JUL–AUG
Very high temperatures

SEP–DEC
Still sunny and warm, but getting cooler later

GETTING AROUND

Walking Apart from pesky motorcycles and the odd tuk-tuk, there's no vehicular traffic inside the medina, so you'll do a lot of walking.

Petits taxis Hire one on the street and check the meter is on. If you take a taxi from a stand, the driver is not obliged to use the meter and it will cost more. They're not allowed on Djemaa El Fna after 1pm so will drop you nearby.

Tuk-tuk Small enough to ply medina streets and useful when you get tired. **Tuk Tuk Marrakech** is a city initiative providing employment for disabled people; some vehicles are electric. Hire one on Djemaa El Fna or WhatsApp (0641887553) for a pick-up.

TOP: GLEN BERLIN/SHUTTERSTOCK
BOTTOM: GLEN BERLIN/SHUTTERSTOCK

EATING & DRINKING

Join locals on Djemaa El Fna by night and sample snails in broth (pictured bottom right), steamed sheep's heads (pictured top right) or Marrakesh's favourite, beef or mutton *tanjia* stew slow-cooked with preserved lemon and saffron. Exploring deeper into the medina will reveal more classics: mounds of buttery couscous, subtly spiced lamb shank, chicken and olive tajine, all served with mint tea. The Ville Nouvelle is the epicentre of Morocco's modern food scene, where innovative chefs meld traditional flavours with global influences in a raft of hip restaurants.

Must-try *tanjia*
Chez Lamine Hadj Mustapha (p50)

Best laid-back cocktails
Les Jardins du Lotus (p78)

CONNECT & FIND YOUR WAY

Wi-fi Most cafes and restaurants offer free wi-fi, as will your hotel, though medina *riads'* ancient, thick walls sometimes mean connections are weak. The best way to stay connected is to buy a SIM card at the airport or an eSIM in advance.

Navigation Using GPS is usually efficient, though tiny medina streets are sometimes not visible.

WHERE TO STAY

Stay in a *riad* in the medina for the best Moroccan experience: you'll spend most of your time here. Western-style hotels can be found in the Ville Nouvelle.

Neighbourhood	Pro/Con
Around Djemaa El Fna	Central hub; action until late. Busy and noisy.
Mouassine	Souq central; easily accessible.
Bab Doukkala & Riad Laarous	More residential with small markets and street food. Quieter streets.
Kasbah and Mellah	Small area easy to navigate. 25-minute walk to Djemaa El Fna.
Kaât Ben Nahid & Bab Debbagh	Central for major monuments, museums. Busy streets.
Ville Nouvelle	Architecture, galleries, modern restaurants. 12-minute taxi ride to the medina.

TAKE A BREAK

When the medina gets overwhelming, grab a juice or ice cream from the square and escape to the gardens around the Koutoubia Mosque.

MONEY

Cash is king: you can't always pay by card in shops and restaurants. Have coins and small-denomination notes for tips in cafes, taxis and to tip street performers on Djemaa El Fna by night.

01 Medina LIFE

SQUARES | STREET FOOD | HISTORY

Experience life in the medina: the vibrant squares and narrow streets humming with activity all day and into the night. Here you'll see artisans in their tiny workshops, shopkeepers keen to make a deal, and people busy shopping, going to the hammam, to school or to bake bread in the community oven.

PAVLIHA/GETTY IMAGES

How to

Getting around You'll be on foot in the medina, so wear comfortable shoes to cope with the cobbles. If you get too tired (or lost), call a tuk-tuk (0641887553).

When to go Early morning is a great time to grab some breakfast at a pavement cafe and watch the medina waking up. In the afternoons, crowds thicken in medina streets. On Djemaa El Fna, vendors start setting up their food stalls from 5pm and the square bursts into life at sunset.

Take a break If the pace gets too busy, head for the gardens around the Koutoubia for some respite.

MALEO PHOTOGRAPHY/SHUTTERSTOCK

History & Heritage

When UNESCO inscribed Djemaa El Fna as representing intangible cultural heritage of humanity, it defined the square as being a unique concentration of popular Moroccan cultural traditions performed through musical, religious and artistic expressions. To understand the importance of the square, start at the excellent **Musée du Patrimoine Immatériel** (Museum of Intangible Heritage) showcasing water-carriers, storytellers, Amazigh musicians, Gnaoua bands, traditional healers, fortune-tellers, henna tattooists and traditional food vendors. Set in a gracious art deco building right on the square, it's well organised with good signage, art exhibitions, interactive screens with puzzles and quizzes for children, and movie posters from all the films made on or around the square.

SAATON/SHUTTERSTOCK

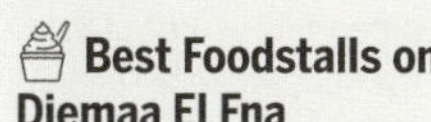

Best Foodstalls on Djemaa El Fna

Stall 75 is a good start for *harira* soup with pretzel-like *chebakia*, or barley soup.

Head to **Stall 14** for fried fish, calamari and salads.

Aicha on **Stall 1** serves brochettes and tajines.

End with **Stall 71**'s smiley Si Mohamed for spiced tea and ginger cake.

Far left and above Stalls at Djemaa El Fna
Left Musée du Patrimoine Immatériel

Dominating the displays are two enormous paintings by Jacques Majorelle. Some of those depicted in the paintings are looking straight at the viewer: their faces are so familiar that you feel you've just seen them on the square.

Carnival on the Square

Stroll Djemaa El Fna as it wakes up to catch the plaza at its least frenetic. Fruit juice vendors are first on the scene, then you'll hear the piercing pipes of the few remaining snake charmers. Have coffee high up above the square at **Café de France** to watch the herbalists set out their wares on the pavement and the henna artists arrange their stools. Shops selling baskets and souvenirs encircle the square, and by 11am it's packed with visitors.

Evenings

Evenings are dinner and a show, Marrakesh-style. Approach it like the locals: pick what you want to eat from the busiest stalls. The great favourite is *tanjia*, a Marrakesh speciality of beef with preserved lemon and

Mechoui Alley

Just before noon, the vendors at these stalls start carving up steaming sides of *mechoui* (slow-roasted lamb). Munch falling-from-the-bone lamb with fresh-baked bread, cumin and salt sitting behind the counter, next to the hot hole in the floor where the lamb is cooked.

The alley's southern entrance is famous for **Chez Lamine Hadj Mustapha** where the speciality is the paper-sealed crockpots of *tanjia,* Morocco's famed 'bachelor's stew'. Use bread as your utensil to scoop up the butter-soft meat.

Nearby is the **olive souq**, with a dozen stalls specialising in glistening Moroccan olives: green, black, pink, dried, stuffed or marinated. Ask to taste before you buy.

Left *Tanjia* (slow-cooked beef or mutton stew) preparation
Below Café des Épices overlooking market

saffron, slow-cooked in a terracotta urn left to braise for hours in the ashes of the hammam fire. Try sheep's' heads, fried fish, grilled brochettes, egg-stuffed rolls, *harira* soup and snails in their spicy broth, and top it off with spicy tea and ginger cake.

Next, wander around the musicians, singers, acrobats, belly-dancing men, boxers and comedians. Have some coins ready for tips, or notes if you take photos. Cafe rooftops are just the place for taking photos of the square and nearby Koutoubia minaret.

Seek out Other Squares

Over in Mouassine, **Place Rahba Kedima** is a fascinating mix of gentrification and traditional wares. You'll find basketware stalls and apothecaries alongside swish boutiques, and a carpet auction house. Climb to the top terrace of **Ayaso** or **Café des Épices** for lunch with amazing views of the market below.

Place des Ferblantiers used to house tinsmiths and metalworkers, and you'll still find a few shops here that sell metal lanterns and homeware. The pretty square is surrounded by pavement cafes – try **Mazel Streetfood Coffee** for falafel bowls or **Kosybar** for a glass of wine at sunset.

02 The Golden TRIANGLE

ARCHITECTURE | MONUMENTS | ARTISTRY

Kaat Ben Nahid is the heart of the old medina, home to the important Ben Youssef Mosque, its spectacular Medersa (Quranic school), the delightful Koubba and the Musée de Marrakech. Tiny alleyways hide 17th-century *riads* built by the wealthy Saadian dynasty. Some are now museums worth visiting for the beauty of their architecture as well as the contents.

XAMNESIACX84/SHUTTERSTOCK

How to

Getting here As the Medersa and Koubba are in the centre of the medina, a visit is going to involve a walk of 10 to 20 minutes, but there is a lot to see in this neighbourhood. You can always call a tuk-tuk (0641887553).

How long to spend here Plan to spend a couple of hours visiting the Medersa, Koubba and Marrakech Museum, and more for the other museums around here.

KATE DOUGHERTY PHOTOGRAPH/SHUTTERSTOCK

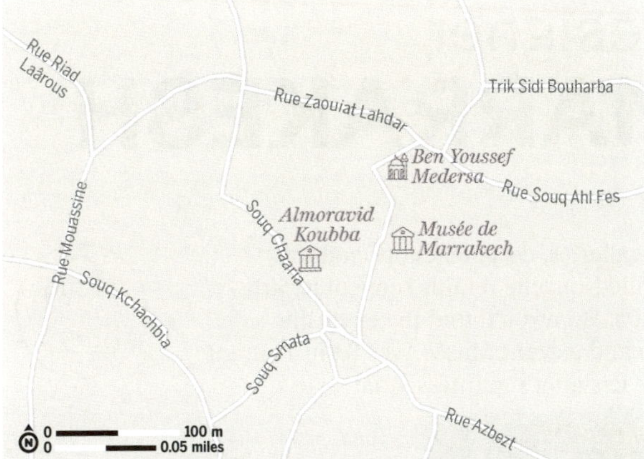

'You who enter my door, may your highest hopes be exceeded' is written above the entryway of the **Ben Youssef Medersa** (Quranic school), and if you want to see an example of Moroccan medieval architecture and artisanship, then your hopes will indeed be exceeded. First built in the 14th century, the Medersa was embellished with carved and painted cedarwood, carved plaster, *zellige* (colourful geometric mosaic) tiles and calligraphy by the Saadians, a dynasty of the 16th century. It was entirely renovated in the early 2020s and is probably the most remarkable building you will see in Morocco. Look out for the water system that you can see revealed in a wall.

Almost adjacent is the **Musée de Marrakech**, set in the Palais Mnebhi. The central internal courtyard, with its riot of cedar archways, stained-glass windows, intricate painted door panels and, of course, lashings of *zellige*, is the highlight, though don't miss the display of exquisite Fez ceramics in the main room off the courtyard, and the palace's hammam. This is one of Marrakesh's oldest museums and looks dated compared with some others.

Nearby is the **Koubba**, built by the Almoravid Dynasty in 1117. Inside it's richly decorated with floral patterns, calligraphy and exquisite *muqarnas* (decorative plaster vaulting). The dome covers a pool used for ablutions before prayer, and *khettaras* (traditional underground irrigation systems) supply latrines and drinking-water taps.

Far left Ben Youssef Medersa
Left Dome underside, the Koubba

Glory of the Golden Age

Most of all it is the Ben Youssef Medersa that I love visiting myself and showing to visitors. It is the most important monument. Everybody gasps when they see what is inside. The very best artisans worked on it almost 500 years ago; it's Saadian art from the golden age of Marrakesh and of Morocco.

The Medersa has real significance – it celebrates the thirst for knowledge, science and theology. Go upstairs to see the rooms the students used – how lucky they were to have such a marvellous place to study!

Omar Chouiyakh, expert registered guide and tour manager. *@moroccobyomar*

03 Designer MARRAKESH

ART | ART DECO | DESIGN

Home to numerous galleries, designer shops and top restaurants, Marrakesh's Ville Nouvelle retains some of its art deco glamour from the 1930s. Here you'll find the exquisite Jardin Majorelle (pictured) and elegant Musée Yves Saint Laurent Marrakech, showing off the designer's quintessential style.

ALEXANDER_MAGNUM/SHUTTERSTOCK

How to

Getting here Take a taxi from the medina to the Jardin Majorelle and Musée YSL, or to Rue Yougoslavie in Gueliz for easy access to the galleries.

Tips Tickets must be bought online (jardinmajorelle.com) in advance for **Jardin Majorelle** and for **Musée Yves Saint Laurent Marrakech**. Combined tickets are cheaper. Go early to avoid the crowds. The Pierre Bergé Museum of Berber Art is inside the garden and well worth a visit. Book for lunch at Café Le Studio at the Musée YSL.

Creative Collective

We Arty (we-arty.com) is a collective of some 20 galleries, museums and art institutions in Marrakesh that come together to organise weekends of openings in Gueliz, and exhibitions and performances in Hivernage, the medina and Sidi Ghanem. Check out the website for the next arty weekend.

01 In Passage Ghandouri off Rue Yougoslavie, you'll find the **Matisse Art Gallery** (contemporary Moroccan art), **Yahya** (lighting), **Fadila El Gadi** (bespoke clothing) and Musée d'Art et Culture Marrakech (**MACMA**; photography).

02 Elegant art deco **Comptoir des Mines Galerie** and nearby **Loft Art Gallery** both show contemporary Moroccan artists. On Rue de la Liberté, **Habib Kibari Gallery** celebrates the local contemporary art scene.

03 On Rue Tariq Bnou Ziad, **Galerie Siniya28** promotes emerging Moroccan artists; **Yasalam** has art prints and jewellery from North Africa, the Levant and the Gulf; **Norya Ayron** designs exquisite caftans.

04 Hop in a taxi or walk to Rue Yves Saint Laurent (pictured below) where tempting shops await like **33 Rue Majorelle**, offering clothing, jewellery, homeware and perfume.

05 End with that most sublime designer, **Yves Saint Laurent**, and the exciting museum (pictured below) dedicated to his work. For garden design and landscaping, **Jardin Majorelle** is adjacent.

FROM LEFT: MOONSTONE IMAGES/GETTY IMAGES, NOYANYALCIN/SHUTTERSTOCK

04 Getting Arty & CRAFTY

SOUQS | ARTISANS | WORKSHOPS

After a day or two in Marrakesh, you soon realise you're surrounded by beautiful crafts. It could be your breakfast bowl, a mesmerising floor of *zellige* tiles at your guesthouse, pretty baskets that catch your eye at Rahba Kedima or a pierced metal lantern that you know will work well in your home. Venture into the souqs and learn how to create some of these artefacts yourself.

CHECCO2/SHUTTERSTOCK

How to

How to book Contact the company direct rather than using a guiding platform so you're sure of getting a place.

How long Most courses take half a day, and many include lunch too. If you're painting on wood, you'll need to return later to pick up your treasure.

What to wear Don't wear your best clothes: you're likely to get dusty or splashed with paint. Aprons are often provided.

ANA IACOB PHOTOGRAPHY/SHUTTERSTOCK

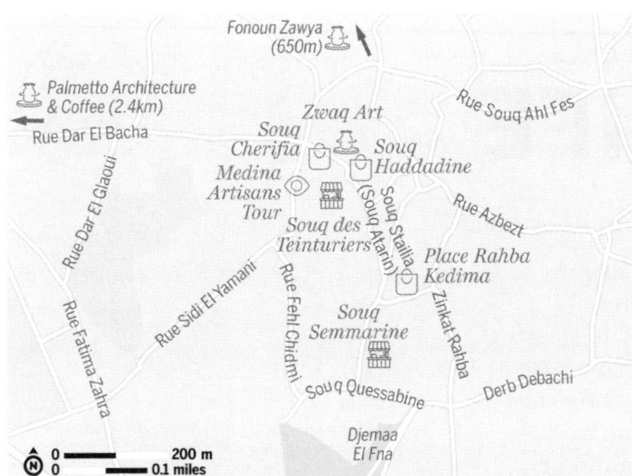

If you look in awe at the painted wood in Bahia Palace, a technique known as *zouak*, here's your chance to try it yourself. Head to the beautifully restored Funduq Moulay Boubkar in Souk Jeld. Abdelhaq Doulaki at **Zwaq Art** (@zwaq_art) will show you how to paint a tray, tile, or hand of Fatima using stencils. Once you're done, it has to dry and is then varnished to give it more durability. Leather work and *zellige* courses are also available.

Fonoun Zawya (zawyaty.com) has half-day courses run by experienced craftsmen: try metalwork to make jewellery, wood carving, leather work or make a *zellige* mosaic tile. A buffet lunch is served on the rooftop after class. In the afternoons, they encourage local kids to work with the *mâalems* (masters) to keep the arts alive.

Put together a *tanjia* and drop it off to cook in the coals at the hammam before visiting three workshops on the hands-on **Medina Artisans Tour** (marrakech.moroccanfoodadventures.com/tour/marrakech-artisan-day). Chat to the *mâalems* and learn about traditional Moroccan crafts. Eat your *tanjia* at the end of the tour.

It's not all about the medina: head to **Palmetto Architecture & Coffee** (@palmettocoffeemarrakech) in the Ville Nouvelle, a small coffee shop that's part of an architectural practice. Here you can take part in workshops to learn painting on canvas, pottery, embroidery, bakery and even facial yoga.

Top left Souq Haddadine
Bottom left Doorway embellished with the *zouak* technique, Bahia Palace (p67)

Souqs & More Souqs

Wander the souqs between Djemaa El Fna and Mouassine: **Souq Semmarine** is chock-full of merchandise aimed squarely at tourists. Products have been made in the surrounding neighbourhoods (and are usually cheaper there). You'll find pierced metal lanterns, burnished copper basins, metal-framed mirrors and silky bed-throws.

Mouassine is souq central with both chic concept stores and old-fashioned souqs selling everything from clothing to argan oil. Spice shops line **Place Rahba Kedima**, and metalwork can be found in **Souq Haddadine** (blacksmiths' souq). **Souq des Teinturiers** (Dyers' Souq) is still functioning, with just a few artisans dying wool and textiles. **Souq Cherifia** has young designers on the first floor.

05 Riad LIFE

GUESTHOUSES | COURTYARDS | ROOFTOPS

It's one thing to visit historic monuments, but it's an entirely different thing to actually go to sleep in one at night. Wake up in a room with a magnificently carved ceiling, breakfast under orange trees, and listen to the call to prayer from a panoramic terrace. And there are some sumptuous *riads* you can visit during your stay.

How to

How much does it cost? From around €85 (Dh894) to €1000 (Dh10515) per double room per night, including breakfast.

Where are the *riads*? You'll find *riads* in all parts of the medina but not in the Ville Nouvelle.

Find your way While taxis can't drive you to the door, they can take you to the nearest drop-off point and *riad* staff will come to meet you and walk you to the house, helping you with your luggage.

Ave du 11 Janvier
Rue de Bab El Khemis
Les Jardins du Lotus
The Moroccan Botanist
1112 Marrakech
Musée de la Musique
Rue Ba Ahmad
El Fenn
Cyber Park
Ave Mohammed V
Djemaa El Fna
Ave El Yarmouk
Koutoubia Gardens
Arset El Bilk
Ave Houmane El Fetouaki
Le Monde des Arts de la Parure
Ave Bab Jedid
Rue de la Kasbah
La Sultana Spa
Rue Bab El Arhdar
Agdal Garden
0 500 m
0 0.25 miles

You never can tell what lies behind that wooden door down a tiny medina street. Step into the house (with your right foot, preferably) and prepare for a surprise: a wide courtyard open to the sky will be revealed, perhaps with a colourful *zellige* floor, citrus trees and a marble fountain. This traditional house has rooms arranged around the courtyard on two or three levels, and the rooftop views can be spectacular. A *dar* (house) is similar but doesn't have a garden in the courtyard. These days, the word *riad* has come to mean 'guesthouse'.

In Marrakesh there are hundreds of *riads* to choose from, all of them old houses that have been restored. Most have a swimming pool, some have a hammam. They have just a few rooms, all different, so are very intimate, though some comprise multiple *riads* joined together, with several courtyards. Bathrooms often have a *tadelakt* (satiny, hand-polished lime plaster) finish.

IMAGE PROFESSIONALS GMBH/ALAMY

Come for Tea

When tea began arriving in significant quantities in the mid-19th century, Moroccans simply added it to their extensive existing traditions of herbal infusions. The spectacular **1112 Marrakech** teahouse showcases a dozen regional variations beyond just mint, including one from Fez with fresh verbena, geranium, absinthe, sage and various mints.

Leading the trend of local, high-end blends, **The Moroccan Botanist** offers 14 luxury options. Try the Sultan's Orchard, containing oolong, mint and orange blossom; an original, perfect combination. For the 100th anniversary of Jardin Majorelle, they created a melange of green tea with – what else? – four varieties of mint.

Jeff Koehler is the James Beard Award–winning author of 11 books, including *The North African Cookbook*. @jeff_koehler

You can visit these beautiful riads even if you don't stay here:

El Fenn for cocktails on the rooftop and to wonder at the amazing decor and art.

Le Monde des Arts de la Parure, the jewellery museum, for its architecture and superb exhibits.

La Sultana Spa in the Kasbah for the most romantic decoration.

Musée de la Musique for a concert.

1112 Marrakech for tea in the leafy courtyard.

Les Jardins du Lotus for lunch.

Above La Sultana Spa

06 A Table IN MARRAKESH

CUISINE | FLAVOURS | INNOVATION

Taste the flavours of Morocco at hundreds of cafes and restaurants in the medina offering irresistible dishes. At its heart, Djemaa El Fna boasts dozens of stalls every evening for an exciting foray into local street food. In the Ville Nouvelle (new city), stylish restaurants and bars showcase a modern approach to cooking with Moroccan panache.

IMAGEBROKER.COM/ALAMY

How to

Get a table Pick the busiest **Djemaa El Fna Food Stalls** and sit down with locals. You might have to queue. Book in advance at fashionable medina or Ville Nouvelle restaurants.

Time your trip Moroccans love their couscous for Friday lunch. Some of the best is at **Naima**'s hole-in-the-wall.

Take a tour Sign up for a **Moroccan Food Adventures** (moroccanfoodadventures.com) street food tour and dive into medina streets to find delicious dishes you might otherwise miss.

ILPO MUSTO/ALAMY

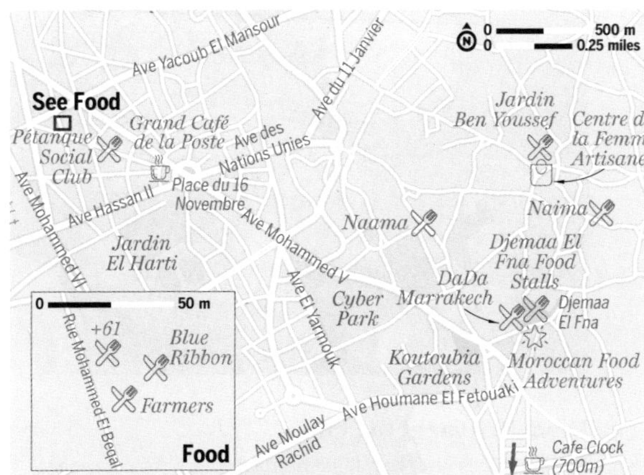

Morocco is famous for its delicious cuisine and you don't have to go far – or spend a fortune – to find it. The medina buzzes with pavement cafes and restaurants where a pot of mint tea is refreshing on a hot day as you watch the world go by. Seek out a rooftop restaurant for views while you eat, and try a tajine or a couscous. If you like art with your meal, head to **DaDa Marrakech** next to Djemaa El Fna with its enormous exhibition space and fabulous art bookshop. Another repurposed space is a former school where you can have a simple lunch in the pretty **Jardin Ben Youssef** after exploring the delightful **Centre de la Femme Artisane** with its numerous craft outlets. To find out where Moroccan cuisine is heading, try the innovative **Naama** for sublime food and architecture.

Over in the Ville Nouvelle, restaurants tend to take a more modern approach to traditional Moroccan fare, while making the most of superb local produce. Several excellent examples can be found together on Rue Mohamed El Beqal in Gueliz: the perennial favourite **+61** alongside the superb **Farmers**, supplied by a Permaculture farm outside town, and **Blue Ribbon**, a good idea for brunch. An aperitif at **Grand Café de la Poste** or in the lovely garden at the **Pétanque Social Club** could be the start of a gourmet evening.

Top left Camel burger and food platter, Cafe Clock
Bottom left Dessert, Grand Café de la Poste

Cafe Clock

Cafe Clock (cafeclock.com) in the Kasbah has a mission to provide easy access to the exciting and diverse culture of Morocco and attracts locals and visitors alike.

Saturday evenings feature Houariyat, a lively band of five women from the countryside who perform traditional music, while a Gnaoua group entertains at the Sunday Sunset concerts. Weekday evenings showcase different types of music and Thursdays are set aside for traditional storytelling in English and Moroccan Arabic (Moroccan Darija).

Clock Kitchen cooking classes are very popular, and you can try your hand at Arabic calligraphy. All this and good food too – the camel burgers are legendary.

■ By Tara Stevens
Tara is the founder of Courtyard Kitchen Fez. @tarastevenswrites

Marrakesh: A City of Flavour, Innovation and Reinvention

FROM SMOKY GRILLS TO GILDED RIAD TABLES

Marrakesh has always known how to eat well. Charcoal pits smoulder, grills hiss with spice-rubbed meat, and mint tea is poured from great heights. Age-old food stalls sit beside sleek bistros, and tajines bubble just streets from *harissa*-spiked cocktails. This is a city where tradition meets bold, brilliant reinvention.

Left Tajine
Centre Bacha Coffee
Right *Bastilla* (a savoury-sweet pie)

TATIANA BRALNINA/SHUTTERSTOCK

From Pavement to Plate

By day, locals grab breakfast on the move – fresh orange juice, cumin-scented *bissara* (fava-bean and garlic soup) ladled from steaming pots, and *msemen* pancakes sizzling on griddles, flaky and hot with honey and butter. Lunch is quick and filling: lentil stews at nameless canteens, or urns of *tanjia* (slow-cooked meat with a handful of spices) left to bubble for hours in the hammam embers. Roast-chicken stalls churn out golden-skinned, lemon-stuffed birds, best eaten with chips and a slick of chilli sauce. As night falls, the square comes alive with grill smoke and mayhem. Snails arrive in peppery broth, crisp-fried fish is handed out in paper cones, and sheep's heads – eyes and all – are carved to order by men with cleavers and a loyal queue.

The Moroccan Feast

Moroccan food takes its time. It's a cuisine of long braises, hand-rolled couscous and deeply layered spice. The most memorable meals unfold in *riads,* where a proper *diffa* (feast) stretches over multiple courses: orange-blossom salads, chermoula-stuffed sardines, cinnamon-dusted *bastilla* (a savoury-sweet pie), and tajines bubbling with quince and lamb. At **La Maison Arabe**, pigeon *bastilla* shatters at the fork; at **Dar Zellij**, a 17th-century merchant's house, the setting is all candlelight and carved cedar. **Sahbi Sahbi**, powered by an all-female kitchen, leans into seasonal produce and revives lesser-known dishes from across the country. For something more rustic, **Chez Lamine Hadj Mustapha** is a medina classic. Whole lambs roast in underground clay pits, the meat pulled apart by hand, dusted with cumin salt, and eaten elbow-to-elbow with the lunchtime crowd.

ESCAPETHEOFFICE/JOB/ALAMY

KONSTANTIN KOPACHINSKY/SHUTTERSTOCK

The New Wave

A new guard of chefs is reshaping the city's food culture, fusing Moroccan ingredients with global technique. Tucked in the medina, **La Famille** serves zucchini carpaccio with argan-oil-and-*harissa*-roasted carrots; **Mazel Streetfood Coffee** dishes up falafel with turmeric tahini on charred flatbreads; **Les Jardins du Lotus** throws shrimp tacos and ceviche into the mix. And fancy new tearooms and coffee shops are adding a splash of glamour. At **Bacha Coffee**, inside a restored palace, waiters in white jackets serve single-origin brews in golden pots, while **1112 Marrakech** teahouse offers a different tea for each of Morocco's 12 regions.

> Moroccan food takes its time. It's a cuisine of long braises, hand-rolled couscous and deeply layered spice.

But the Ville Nouvelle is the true home of the modern Moroccan bistro. At **Farmers**, *fritto misto* comes with foraged greens, and glazed aubergines sit under a swirl of tahini-smoked onion. **+61** turns out clever Mediterranean-inspired riffs on local organic produce, while **Cantine Mouton Noir** does great steaks, frites and brunch. Moroccan wine is finally having a moment too, championed by sommeliers across the city. Crisp whites counter preserved lemon; bold reds anchor lamb tajine. And cocktail culture is catching up – **Baromètre** does *harissa* margaritas and saffron gin in a dark and sultry setting; **Kabana** rocks the medina from its rooftop perch over spritzes infused with lavender, hibiscus and bitter orange.

Marrakesh Joins the Big League

In 2025, four Marrakesh restaurants earned spots on the World's 50 Best Middle East and North Africa (MENA) Restaurants list. At Royal Mansour, **La Grande Table Marocaine** elevates traditional dishes with haute gastronomy flair – meticulous *bastilla*, spice-rich tajines and elegant pastries in an opulent *riad*. Sister restaurant **Sesamo** delivers polished Italian fine dining.

Over in Gueliz, **+61** takes a modern, Mediterranean-inspired approach, showcasing seasonal produce, fresh seafood and clean, unfussy flavours. Meanwhile, **Le Petit Cornichon** blends French technique with Moroccan ingredients in refined plates like duck breast with beetroot jus. Marrakesh has always known how to feed people – now the rest of the world is taking note.

DON'T LEAVE
Morocco Without...

01

02

03

04

05

01 Teapot
And a box of gunpowder tea. Now all you need is the spearmint – and sugar.

02 Caftan
Think of all those summer parties when you can waft around in it.

03 Lantern
Made of pierced metal, these give a beautiful glow. Put a candle inside, or get one that can be plugged in.

04 Dried Rose Buds
Use as pot pourri or grind into spice rubs for a floral touch

05 Barbary Fig Face Cream
Move over argan oil – this is sublime for your skin.

06 Henna Tattoo
Pretty arabesques winding over your hands and up your arms. The tattoos will last up to three weeks.

07 Recipes from a Cooking Class
Recreate that delicious meal you made when you get home and impress your friends and family.

08 Edible Argan Oil
Superb finishing touch to gravlax, smoked salmon, salad greens and vegetables. Make a dip for bread with cumin, garlic and chili mixed into the oil.

09 Straw Basket
For carrying home all your souvenirs. For the best choice, browse the shops surrounding Djemaa El Fna.

10 Ras Al Hanout Spice Mixture
Rub into cubes of meat or vegetables for kebabs, or try a dusting on top of chocolate mousse.

01 KAJZRPHOTOGRAPHY/SHUTTERSTOCK, **02** MS JAKIA/SHUTTERSTOCK, **03** DALEEN LOEST/SHUTTERSTOCK, **04** PICTURE PARTNERS/SHUTTERSTOCK, **05** XPIXEL/SHUTTERSTOCK, **06** EMILY MARIE WILSON/SHUTTERSTOCK, **07** NATALLIA YAUMENENKA/SHUTTERSTOCK, **08** PICTURE PARTNERS/SHUTTERSTOCK, **09** DESIGN WORLDS/SHUTTERSTOCK, **10** TIMOTHY NEUMANN/SHUTTERSTOCK

Palaces & GARDENS

HISTORY | MUSEUMS | ARTISANSHIP

The remarkable palaces and gardens of Marrakesh are worth seeking out. They exude a sense of tranquillity, perhaps because of the trance-like state that master artisans are said to achieve when they are carving plaster or placing a *zellige* tile in a mosaic pattern.

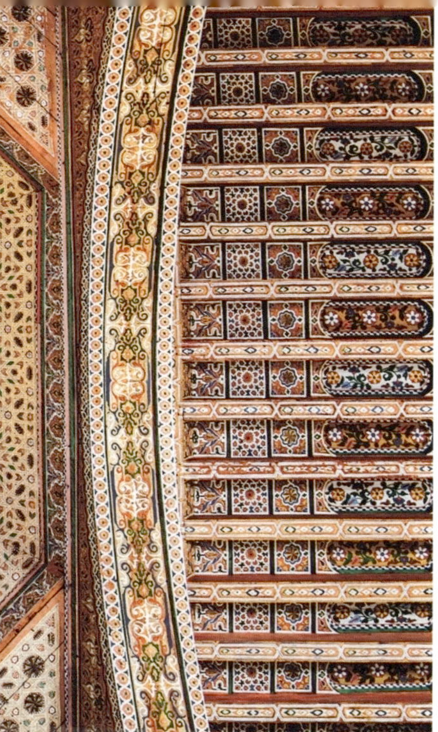

SAIKO3P/SHUTTERSTOCK

How to

Getting here The Bahia Palace is near the Mellah, within easy walking distance of Place des Ferblantiers. To reach Le Jardin Secret in Mouassine, walk from Dar El Bacha. The Musée des Confluences Dar El Bacha is at a taxi drop-off point, or a short walk from Djemaa El Fna.

How long to spend here Expect to take about one to two hours to wander rooms and gardens at each location.

ANDRZEJ LISOWSKI TRAVEL/SHUTTERSTOCK

Brilliant Bahia Palace

When the Almohads conquered Marrakesh in 1147, they built the Kasbah to keep the Sultan safe, and today the palace in the Kasbah is still an official residence of King Mohamed VI. Courtiers built themselves fine palaces and houses round about to be close to the Sultan. The finest is the **Bahia Palace**, first built in the 1860s by Si Moussa, the grand vizier, and expanded by his son Ba Ahmed, also grand vizier, between 1894 and 1900. Bahia means 'brilliance', and it's aptly named. The 150 rooms, courtyards, fountains and lush gardens feature intricate woodwork, beautiful *zellige* and ornate painted ceilings. During the Protectorate years (1912–56), the palace housed the Resident General Hubert Lyautey, who added electricity and central heating. Go late afternoon when all the tour groups have gone.

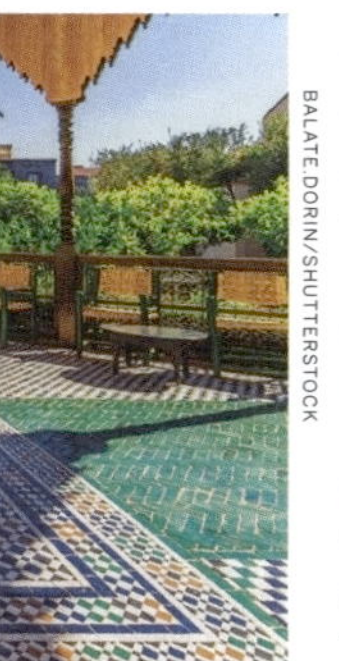

BALATE.DORIN/SHUTTERSTOCK

Bacha Coffee

Bacha Coffee is a very elegant coffee shop at the Musée des Confluences Dar Al Bacha and the perfect rest stop. When you enter the museum, book a table that will await you once you've finished exploring the house. They serve pastries, brunch and lunch, and offer some 200 varieties of coffee.

Far left Bahia Palace
Left Le Jardin Secret (p68)
Above Bacha Coffee

Just up the street you'll find the *riad* that is now the **Musée de l'Art Culinaire Marocain** (Moroccan Culinary Arts Museum), an enormous palace with courtyards, *zellige*, hand-painted cedarwood, fountains and columns built by the Zniber family. Close by is **Dar Si Saïd**, now the Museum of Weaving and Carpets. This splendid *riad* has a lovely central garden with fountain. Badly damaged in the 2023 earthquake, the museum is due to reopen in late 2025 or early 2026.

Water Garden

Le Jardin Secret (Secret Garden) in Mouassine combines two riads and their gardens. The buildings are pleasant enough, but here it's the traditional Islamic garden that is of particular interest. The paths are constructed of *bejmat* (terracotta bricks) and green *zellige* tiles from Fez, and there are a series of water channels, pools and fountains. This layout, found in Morocco since the 12th century, represents heaven and is considered a sacred space. The

Saadian Sultan

Signage at the entrance to the **Badi Palace** helps you imagine what this enormous complex once was. Though now in ruins, it had spectacular sunken gardens and pools, marble columns, intricate *zellige* and 360 rooms. It was built by the Saadian Sultan Ahmad Al Mansur in the 16th century as a show of wealth and power.

Sultan Al Mansur also built the highly decorated mausoleums in the nearby **Saadian tombs**. He lies buried in the Chamber of the Twelve Columns which you can't enter, but you can peer through a narrow passage at the stupendous carvings, pillars, *zellige* and skylights. In the garden are graves of courtiers. Go late afternoon for the light on the marble.

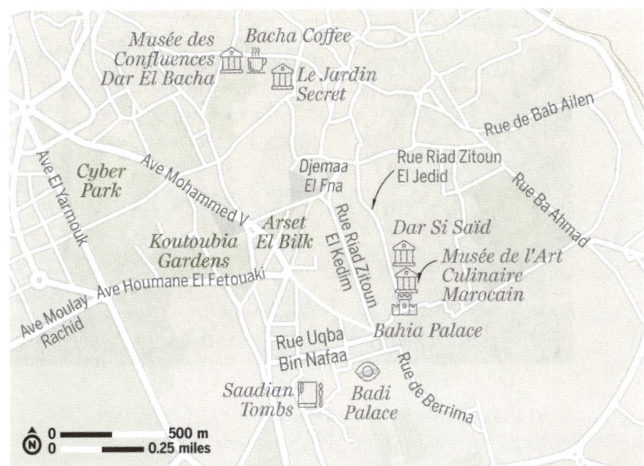

Left Badi Palace
Below Musée des Confluences Dar El Bacha

gardens are fed by a restored original *khettara* (underground irrigation system) and designed to demonstrate the ancient waterworks. High-tech screens use CGI to show the flow of water around the site and a fascinating documentary details the restoration process. You can also climb the tower for outstanding views over the medina. Le Jardin is a peaceful spot full of birdsong, olive and citrus trees and seemingly far from the busy medina outside. Chill out in the cafes in the garden and on the rooftop.

A Warlord's Palace

Catch a glimpse into the world of fabulously wealthy Moroccan warlord Thami El Glaoui, Pasha of Marrakesh from 1912 to 1956. He was one of the world's richest men, building this magnificent residence, and Palais Glaoui in Fez. Built in 1910, **Musée des Confluences Dar El Bacha** is a superb example of traditional Moroccan architecture. It has round columns covered in *zellige* topped with carved plaster and heavily carved cedarwood lintels, plus a shady garden intersected by walkways and full of orange trees. The six salons surrounding the courtyard house temporary exhibits featuring different facets of Moroccan culture, including ceramics, jewellery, brassware and items from the three monotheistic faiths.

FROM LEFT: ZARUBA ONDREJ/SHUTTERSTOCK, CKTRAVELS.COM/SHUTTERSTOCK

■ By Paula Hardy
Paula is a freelance journalist who has been working in North Africa for over 20 years. @paulahardy

Finding Paradise in Marrakesh's Riad Gardens

BEHIND THE CITY'S CEDAR DOORS YOU'LL FIND A LABYRINTH OF SECRET GARDENS

It might not look like it in the dusty streets, but the Marrakesh medina with its earthen ramparts is an enormous walled garden intricately divided by a jigsaw of dwellings. This model of a garden city reflects deeply held Islamic beliefs about privacy, pleasure and the restorative power of nature.

Left Bahia Palace (p67)
Centre Badi Palace (p68)
Right Le Jardin Secret (p68)

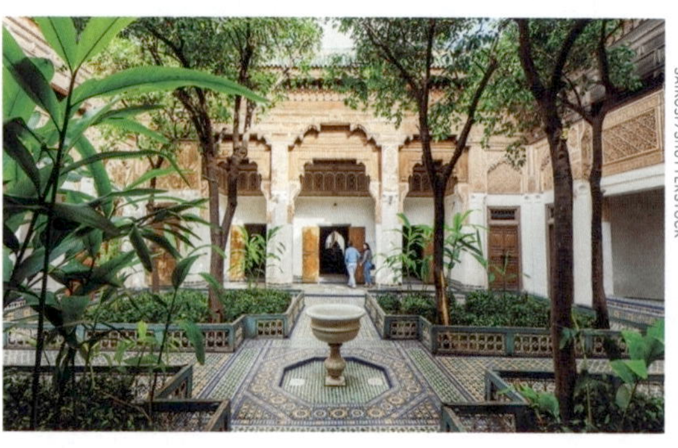

SAIKO3P/SHUTTERSTOCK

Marrakesh summers regularly top 40°C. In such an unforgiving environment, the greenery of a garden is an incomparable luxury. *Riads* like Riad Mena, Riad Berbere and L'Hotel are exemplar *riads*. Their courtyards are divided into four planted quadrants, known as *chahar bagh*, which mirror the Quranic vision of the fourfold universe while the paths in between represent the four rivers of Paradise. In the centre is the *sahrîdj*, a shallow basin with a fountain. It is the most important element of the garden, because as the Quran states: Allah 'created from water every living thing,' making it the basis of all creation (Surah Al Anbiya 21:30).

The Art of Living in the Islamic World

These *riad* gardens have both a functional and spiritual dimension. Fruit trees such as orange, date palm, pomegranate and olive offer sustenance and symbolise happiness, abundance, prosperity and peace. They are under-planted by aromatic herbs, prized for their medicinal properties, such as mint, rosemary and aloe. The garden is mostly green – the colour of Islam – although a few fragrant flowers such as jasmine perfume the air. All of it is irrigated by the fountain, reminding visitors of the life-giving force of water.

Riads, which strictly speaking means 'gardens', aren't just a feature of domestic homes. The Koutoubia Mosque has one. There's one at the heart of the **Bahia Palace** (p67), where VIPs were once received. In **Dar Si Saïd** (p68) paths of glossy green-and-white tiles mimic the rivers of paradise while the central fountain is shaded by a pergola covered in hand-painted blooms. According to scholars, the epic ruins of the 16th-century **Badi Palace** (p68) are the epitome of the style. Here the four gardens are sunken 2.5m below

FRANCESCO BONINO/SHUTTERSTOCK

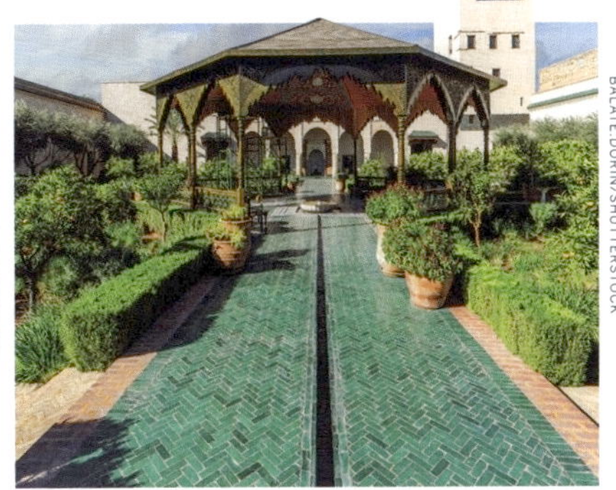
BALATE.DORIN/SHUTTERSTOCK

the walkways so visitors can enjoy the orange blossom on the treetops and inhale the rising scent.

Balancing Tradition & Modernity

The presence of *riad* gardens in Marrakesh's finest palaces indicates the wealth and power of their inhabitants. But more than that, in the desert, gardens are a blessing and speak to a central Islamic tenet that sees humanity occupy the position of *khalifa* (guardians of nature). Chancellor Mohammed Loukrissi, the last owner of **Le Jardin Secret** (p68), acquitted himself admirably as a steward of his magnificent garden. Reopened to the public in 2016 following extensive restoration, it is the only *riad* in the medina to retain its ingenious gravitational flow irrigation system. Two interlinked gardens symbolise two different versions of paradise. While the main Islamic garden follows Quranic precepts, the smaller Exotic garden is planted with drought-resistant global species sporting unusual shapes, textures and colours that are meant to soothe and inspire. This fits with the Islamic concept of gardens as sanctuary spaces, but in an era when restorative conservation is believed to be the foundation of ecological resilience, it raises questions as to the appropriateness of introducing non-native species in such a symbolic context. The gardens highlight a growing debate in Marrakesh over the need to preserve local traditions versus adopting global trends and combating the increasing effects of desertification caused by climate change.

> *Riad* gardens have both a functional and spiritual dimension.

Paradise on Earth

In the desert, an oasis means life itself, and as Islam emerged in the desert, an Islamic garden represents an earthly analogue for paradise. Even the word paradise comes from the Persian *pairidaeza*, which means 'enclosed garden'. This ancient concept of paradise, which dates back 5000 years, combined with Quranic references to Paradise as a garden flowing with four rivers of water, wine, milk and honey to become a central element of Muslim culture.

08 Escape the CITY

ART | COUNTRY CLUBS | GARDENS

There are times when medina madness overtakes you, and you just have to get out of the city for a refresh. Luckily, within 20 minutes' drive north or south of the city are several art museums set in lush gardens, a remarkable water museum, a fun park perfect for the kids, a rustic country club or two, and one of Morocco's best interior design outlets. What are you waiting for?

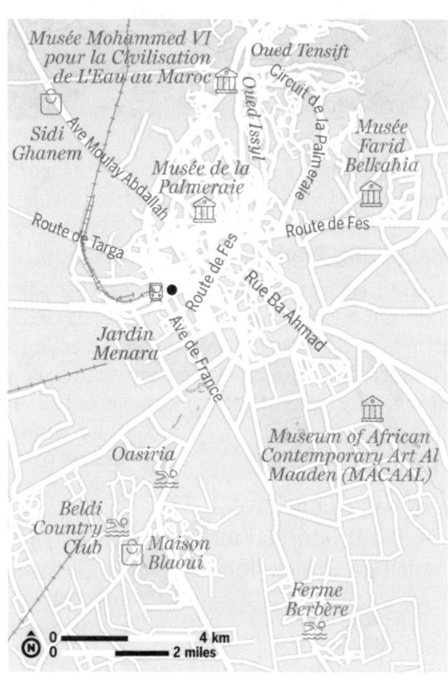

How to

Getting here To visit the museums and Maison Blaoui, organise transport through your accommodation or negotiate with a *grand taxi* driver. Expect to pay about Dh600/1000 for a half/full day. There's nowhere for refreshments, so take water and perhaps a picnic.

The country clubs offer transport when you book, and the waterpark has a free shuttle service from Djemaa El Fna and Gueliz Post Office throughout the day.

The Palmeraie

The palm groves north of the city are home to major museums. **Musée de la Palmeraie** houses a private collection of contemporary art. The gardens are dotted with sculptures. **Musée Farid Belkahia** celebrates the eponymous artist with his paintings and copper sculptures. The lovely gardens have a conference room, shop and studio. **Museum of African Contemporary Art Al Maaden** (MACAAL) is a private, non-profit museum promoting African art, set in a monumental sculpture park. **Musée Mohammed VI pour la Civilisation de L'Eau au Maroc**, or Water Museum, offers a fascinating display of hydraulic innovations, urban architecture and ecology. The 7.5-acre park showcases the revitalisation of palm groves.

Down South

Resorts include the forever-chic eco-lodge **Beldi Country Club** (beldicountry club.com) where the air is

COLINMTHOMPSON/SHUTTERSTOCK

scented with thousands of rose bushes. Choose between several pools, have lunch, a hammam and visit the smart shops. **Ferme Berbère** (lafermeberbere.ellohaweb.com) is a rustic retreat with lunch sourced from its gardens. Loungers surround the pool, and there's a hammam. It's for adults only. **Oasiria** (oasiria.com) is perfect for kids: a waterpark with slides, a wave pool, river tubing and a pirates' lagoon. There's also petanque, padel courts and a gym. Free shuttles run from Djemaa El Fna and Gueliz. To make your home look like that dreamy Moroccan *riad,* don't miss the fabulous decor collection at Maison Blaoui arranged as in a real house.

Browsing the Market

A little further out of the city (a 30-minute drive) is the industrial quarter of Sidi Ghanem. Unprepossessing it might be, but it does house dozens of interior designers and artists who have large showrooms.

Here you'll find Hassan Hajjaj, internationally renowned contemporary artist and photographer, and his quirky teashop and restaurant; ceramicist and designer LRNCE; furniture and homewear outlets such as Le Marrakchoise, Kessy Beldi, Studio Lid and many more.

Prices are fixed and credit cards widely accepted, so it's easier than bargaining in the souqs. Hire a *grand taxi* and expect to spend at least half a day here.

Above Oasiria

■ By Tharik Hussain
Tharik is the author of the award-winning Minarets in the Mountains: a Journey into Muslim Europe, *@tharik_hussain*

Religion in Morocco

HOME OF SUFI SAINTS AND MYSTICAL LODGES

With Islam being the state religion, much of Moroccan society is dictated by the Islamic calendar and festivals like Ramadan and Eid. Most Moroccans are Sunnis and follow the Maliki school of theology as well as some form of Sufism (the mystical branch of Islam).

Left Ramadan foods
Centre Eid Al Fitr prayer, Salé (p134)
Right Eid sweet pastries

FEVZIE/SHUTTERSTOCK

Christians in Morocco tend to be foreign residents, and though the country had a large Jewish community historically – **Fez** was home to one of the most influential (p190) – almost all of them have now moved abroad. Whilst a tiny minority of Moroccan Muslims – less than 1% – are Shia, the religious events and activities observed across the country tend to fall within the Sunni, Maliki and Sufi traditions.

The Islamic Calendar

Known as the Hijri calendar because it starts from the famous migration – *hijrah* in Arabic – by the Prophet Muhammad in 622 CE from Makkah to Madinah, the Islamic calendar is a lunar calendar dependent on actual sightings of the moon to determine the start and end of each month. This means the timings of all the country's Islamic festivals can appear to 'change' year upon year when placed alongside the Gregorian calendar, which is also used for civic matters in Morocco.

Important Religious Festivals

Rabi al-Awwal The 12th day of Rabi al-Awwal is the birthday of the Prophet Muhammad, known as Eid al-Mawlid when mosques and *zawiyas* (Sufi lodges) observe supererogatory and *dhikr* (repetitive) prayers to honour the Prophet.

Ramadan Sees Moroccans fasting during daylight with special foods and meals prepared for the start and end of each day. Society slows down as working hours are altered accordingly. Evenings are vibrant with mosques full for the special Ramadan prayers called *tarawih*, observed late into the night, and cafes and restaurants are busy until sunrise.

ANADOLU/GETTY IMAGES

MOHA EL-JAW/SHUTTERSTOCK

Shawwal Marks the end of Ramadan and the days of Eid Al Fitr, known locally as Eid as-Saghir (the 'small feast'). The night before this Eid, Moroccans across the country will try to sight the new moon to confirm the start of Shawwal. Eid begins with a special prayer performed in mosques and outdoor spaces. Most Moroccans then head to the local cemetery to honour their ancestors. Afterwards children receive gifts or money to spend at Eid markets and everyone puts on special outfits. Eid baked sweet treats and pastries are prepared, and delicious Eid dinners like couscous with beef and prunes are eaten at night.

It is important to remember that not all mosques or *zawiyas* allow non-Muslim visitors.

Dhu al-Hijjah This is a month of pilgrimage (the hajj) and when Eid Al Adha, known locally as Eid al-Kabir, is observed. This feast commemorates the Prophet Ibrahim's willingness to sacrifice his son Ishmael, and sees Moroccans everywhere purchasing a sheep or goat, and sacrificing it ahead of Eid to feed the needy in society and themselves. Eid Al Adha falls on the 10th of the month and is again observed with a special prayer, grave visitations, gifts and much feasting.

It is important to remember that not all mosques or *zawiyas* allow non-Muslim visitors. If they do, men and women should use their respective entrances (not all will have a female space); dress modestly (no shorts or sleeveless tops), and women should cover their heads with a scarf.

Travelling in Morocco During Ramadan

Travellers should sleep in the day and stay up through the night to enjoy the unique nocturnal culture that emerges, with cafes, shisha lounges and restaurants open until the early hours serving unique Ramadan foods and special *iftar* meals that break the fast.

Ramadan in Morocco is particularly rewarding for Muslim travellers who can take part in spiritually nourishing *tarawih* and *dhikr* prayers observed in every mosque and *zawiya* across the country long into the night.

Ramadan is also when many sights and monuments observe reduced hours and they may even close, so do research ahead of making any travel plans.

Listings

BEST OF THE REST

Cooking up a Feast Moroccan-Style

Cafe Clock

Shop in the souq for ingredients, then head back to the ever-popular Clock Kitchen to cook up a storm. The workshop ends with the lunch you made, around 2.30pm.

La Maison Arabe Cooking School

A state-of-the-art teaching kitchen at two locations: the medina hotel or their Country Club where you can pick herbs for your dishes. Half-day course, one-hour express demonstration, Jewish cooking or five-day immersive.

Faim d'Epices

Fun, hands-on cooking courses with an accent on spices are held on a farm just outside the city. Transport is provided. Stop en route for ingredient shopping in a village souq. Class ends with a long, lazy lunch.

Best Medina Tours

Evening Street Food Tour

Explore out-of-the-way restaurants that you probably wouldn't find yourself, or wouldn't dare try. This is a fun evening of about 3½ hours, in a small group.

Marrakech Artisan Day

Visit three different workshops for a hands-on experience with traditional Moroccan craftspeople. This immersive tour ends with enjoying a *tanjia* made at the start of the tour.

Marrakech Green Wheels

This non-profit outfit offers exciting tours on two wheels: city discovery tour, city night tour, Marrakesh gardens tour and a photography tour. You can even design your own tour.

Designs on You

Marrakech Henna Art Cafe

This arty cafe just south of Djemaa El Fna offers good quality, safe henna designs from Dh50. Have a healthy drink or meal while you're waiting for it to dry.

Henna Art Discovery

Siham offers the biggest range of henna designs, from Dh200 per person. Organise a henna party for a group, or take the henna class and learn how to do it yourself.

Best Art-Filled Riads

El Fenn

This stylish *riad* is home to a remarkable collection of art belonging to Vanessa Branson. Visit the *riad* for a drink or dinner on the roof terrace to see some of the works.

Riad Linda

The large contemporary abstract paintings on the walls here are by the owner's husband Gordon Davis, and are all for sale.

Riad Rosemary

Marrakesh designer Laurence Leenaert is behind this elegant *riad* that features her ceramics and decorative touches.

Clean Up in a Hammam

Hammam Mouassine

Have a scrub and steam session followed by a massage at this public hammam that has been sensitively restored. It has separate facilities and entrances for men and women.

Hammam de la Rose

Come out smelling of roses at this tranquil place in Mouassine. Various massages and treatments are available in addition to the hammam.

La Mamounia

For a 1001-nights experience, book at this sumptuous spa. After your hammam, you'll be hard-pressed to choose between all the gorgeous treatments on offer.

In Fashion

Sarah Maj

This tiny shop with blue doors is a bijou Moroccan/Italian boutique in Mouassine (with another branch in Gueliz). The marriage of Italian fabrics with Moroccan design makes for particularly good long shirt-dresses.

Norya Ayron

This Algerian designer counts film stars among her clientele who love her contemporary take on traditional silky caftans. Located in Gueliz, with a tiny branch at restaurant Le Jardin in the medina.

Sissi Morocco

This tiny shop on Place Rahba Kedima, stocks dresses, shirts, cushions and bags, many printed with old sepia photos of Amazigh tribal women.

Best Restaurants in the Ville Nouvelle

Farmers €€€

Quickly establishing itself as one of the top restaurants in Marrakesh, the lovely Farmers is supplied by a farm just outside the city. It serves organic and natural wines too.

+61 €€€

A favourite, this Australian-influenced restaurant is still doing good things with bountiful

BTWIMAGES/SHUTTERSTOCK

Craftsperson, Marrakesh's medina (p48)

fresh produce and innovative dishes. They make their own bread, pasta, cheese and yoghurt daily.

Amal Center €€

Dine in a pretty garden and enjoy delicious fare at Amal Center. The organisation trains women on their journey towards empowerment and financial independence.

Where to Buy Your Rugs & Carpets

Soufiane Zarib

Knock on the huge brown door to be admitted to this spectacular showroom of rugs in Riad Laarous. Soufiane Zarib buys his own wool and employs weavers in the Atlas Mountains to create his designs.

Les Nomades de Marrakech

Know exactly what you want when you enter this emporium close to the Ben Youssef Medersa – the towering piles of beautiful rugs in room after room will be confusing if you don't.

Bibi Art

Rabii and Abdel at Bibi Art in Mouassine buy their own wool and work with women all over the Atlas Mountains to produce quality carpets, all handcrafted using traditional looms and stitching.

Best Homeware Stores

Maison Blaoui

You'll need to hire transport to get 6km south of Marrakesh. But oh, is it worth it. Just the place to find that special *objet*, or to turn your home into a veritable Moroccan *riad*.

Corinne Bensimon Maison

Conjure up an entire look at this stylish gem of a shop in the Mouassine neighbourhood, where you can pick up clothes, accessories, tableware and textiles.

33 Rue Majorelle

Despite its name, this large concept store is on Rue Yves Saint Laurent near Jardin Majorelle, selling clothing, accessories and homeware from various top Marrakesh designers.

Best for Cocktails

Les Jardins du Lotus €€€

You could plump for The Billionaire's Beverage of Tequila Don Julio 1942 at Dh1400 a pop, or one of the classic cocktails at more reasonable prices at pretty-in-pink Les Jardins du Lotus in Riad Laarous.

Kabana €€€

Order a signature cocktail at super-cool Kabana, kick back and enjoy the music, good food and great views from this leafy rooftop near the Koutoubia Mosque.

Pétanque Social Club €€€

For a very chilled way to spend an hour or two, head to Pétanque Social Club in the Ville Nouvelle where you can choose a cocktail to enjoy in the tree-filled garden.

Essential Oils & Cosmetics

Naturom

The go-to place near Bahia Palace for handmade natural bath products and cosmetics based on 100% organic argan oil. There's Barbary fig oil too, the latest skin-care product.

Aromatimri

Pretty wooden dressers and tables display high-quality perfumes and fragrant skincare products made from natural ingredients, presented in collectable bottles.

Green Spaces

Koutoubia Gardens

Just to the south of the mosque itself, these gardens offer a welcome respite, especially on a hot day. There are paths through the palm trees, benches to rest on and photo opportunities for the minaret.

Jardin Majorelle

The Jardin Majorelle is one of the most visited places in Morocco. Go early – they open at 8.30am – and you'll avoid the crowds. The pools and soaring palm trees are most restful.

Top-End Medina Restaurants

Naama €€€

Naama is part of Riad 72 so you can expect the same exquisite architecture and attention to detail. The food is superb thanks to chef Aniss Meski.

Koutoubia Gardens

La Maison Arabe €€€

At Trois Saveurs restaurant in this smart hotel, choose from French, Moroccan and Asian dishes prepared by three chefs. Eat inside or on the terrace overlooking the gardens.

Dar Zellij €€€

This restaurant can be found in a romantic 17th-century *riad.* Look out for the signature dishes of *trid* (stewed chicken) or *mechoui* (slow-roasted lamb). A belly dancer entertains on Thursdays and Sundays.

Sweet Treats

Pâtisserie des Princes €€

When the medina gets overwhelming, treat yourself to a box of traditional Moroccan cookies and retire to the Koutoubia gardens for a break.

Bacha Coffee €€

It's hard to resist the gourmet sweet croissants and pastries at Bacha Coffee that so perfectly complement the superb coffees on offer here in the Musée des Confluences Dar El Bacha.

1112 Marrakech €€

Elevenses is a tradition at 1112 near Ben Youssef Medersa. Pop in for 11 o'clock *atay* (tea) with classic pastries – the pistachio-stuffed gazelle horns dipped in chocolate are sublime.

Favourite Medina Restaurants

L'Mida €€

Be sure to book here or you'll have to queue in the street. On offer is a modern look at Moroccan fare: try the pokē bowl with tuna in a sweet-and-sour chermoula or a vegetarian *bastilla.*

Mandala Society €€

Heading south from Djemaa El Fna, find Mandala Society for brunch. A fusion between Morocco and Iceland, this meat-free zone promises delicious, healthy dishes. A speciality tea or coffee alongside a savoury brunch board for two is the way to go.

Nomad €€€

This multitiered rooftop near Medersa Ben Youssef is one of the medina's buzziest venues. The small menu adds contemporary twists to North African ingredients and flavours. There's plenty for vegetarians and vegans too.

Le Trou Au Mur €€€

Here is a classy joint near the Musée de Marrakech serving unusual Moroccan dishes, fusion (think Amazigh shepherd's pie) and house speciality *mechoui*.

Le Jardin €€

Close to all the concept stores of Mouassine, Le Jardin is a pretty oasis where you can lunch beneath a canopy of banana trees. The Agadir octopus with romesco sauce or fish fillet with preserved lemon sauce are recommended.

Medina Action

Marrakech Green Wheels

Hire a bike or take a cycling tour with this non-profit organisation that teaches kids to ride bikes. An interesting option is the night ride.

Pikala Bikes

At another non-profit community project, you can join a group cycling tour from Riad Laârous that includes a backstreet tea break and interesting cultural insights.

Dar Anis Yoga Studio

Try a daily drop-in yoga class near Dar El Bacha. Stef specialises in flow yoga, sound-bath meditations and restorative yoga. A half-day retreat with lunch and a massage costs €95.

09 Escape to AGAFAY

VISTAS | ACTION | ROMANCE

Wave goodbye to the Marrakech medina and unwind in the lunar-like landscape of stony desert framed by spectacular High Atlas peaks. Ride a camel or get a thrill on a dune buggy or quad, and enjoy lunch overlooking the desert on a day excursion. Glamping in luxurious tents and dinner under a spectacular starry sky await those staying the night.

THOMAS M BARWICK INC/GETTY IMAGES

How to

Getting here Go on a tour or arrive on a motorbike and sidecar. All accommodation and excursion options organise transport to and from Marrakesh.

When to go Avoid the intense summer heat. For the best stargazing, avoid the full moon.

How long to stay Combine with a day trip into the High Atlas foothills, or come for dinner and stargazing. Stay for a night or two to try more activities.

THOMAS BARWICK/GETTY IMAGES

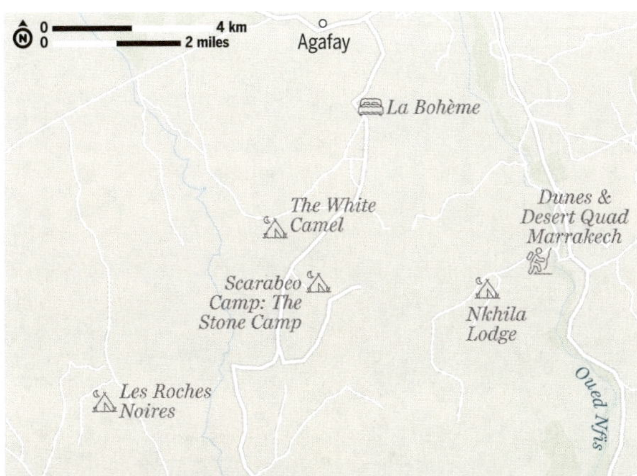

Top left Camel ride, Agafay
Bottom left Desert camp, Agafay

Off for the day Offering a startling change from the city, coming to Agafay for the day means riding a camel or a hair-raising ride on a dune buggy or quad, or simply relaxing by the pool. Outfits such as **Dunes & Desert Quad Marrakech** (dunesdesert.com) have packages that include rides and lunch in an Amazigh village over a half or full day. **Insiders Experience** (insidersexperience.com) will take you to visit the small town of Tameslouht on the way, then to one of the camps for rides and lunch. If you prefer two wheels under your own steam, there are desert biking adventures that include Agafay such as **Mountain Bike Morocco** (mtbmorocco.com) or **Marrakech Green Wheels** (marrakechgreenwheels.com). Note that while quad biking is popular in the desert regions, there is ongoing discussion of the noise pollution and ecological damage it creates.

Desert glamour The camps offer luxurious glamping – tents come tastefully furnished and have a private bathroom. In winter, a wood-burning stove keeps you warm. On hot summer days, you can cool off in the pool. Choose your camp according to your requirements: as well as quad, buggy and camel rides, **The White Camel** (thewhitecamel.com) offers astronomy evenings and yoga; **Scarabeo Camp: The Stone Camp** (scarabeocamp.com) suggests pottery workshops and has a massage cottage; and **Nkhila Lodge** (nkhilalodge.com) is great for children, offering a kids' menu and family tents or cabins. **Les Roches Noires** (scarabeocamp.com/les-roches-noires) is the most secluded. Binoculars for bird-watching and telescopes for star-gazing are available. **La Bohème** has evening parties with dinner, dancing and entertainment.

But It's Not the 'Real' Desert...

No, Agafay is not the Sahara and doesn't have sand dunes. Underfoot are small, sharp stones, the terrain is hilly with dry riverbeds and the often snow-covered High Atlas Mountains rise in the distance. Agafay's apparent remoteness and barren, lunar landscape make it perfect for quad biking, dune buggies and camel riding. Camps have sprung up, providing a sense of adventure alongside accommodation in luxurious, safari-type tents. Agafay makes a great break from the frenetic intensity of Marrakesh, offering a taste of desert life without the long journey to the Sahara (a minimum of 450km best done over two days).

Here are a few tips...

- Be sure to book your tour through a bona fide company rather than a guiding platform. Ask your accommodation for recommendations.
- Take a scarf to wear across your face in a buggy or on a quad to protect against the dust.
- Teenagers 16 and up can drive buggies and quads. Children over 6 ride their own camel if they're big enough.

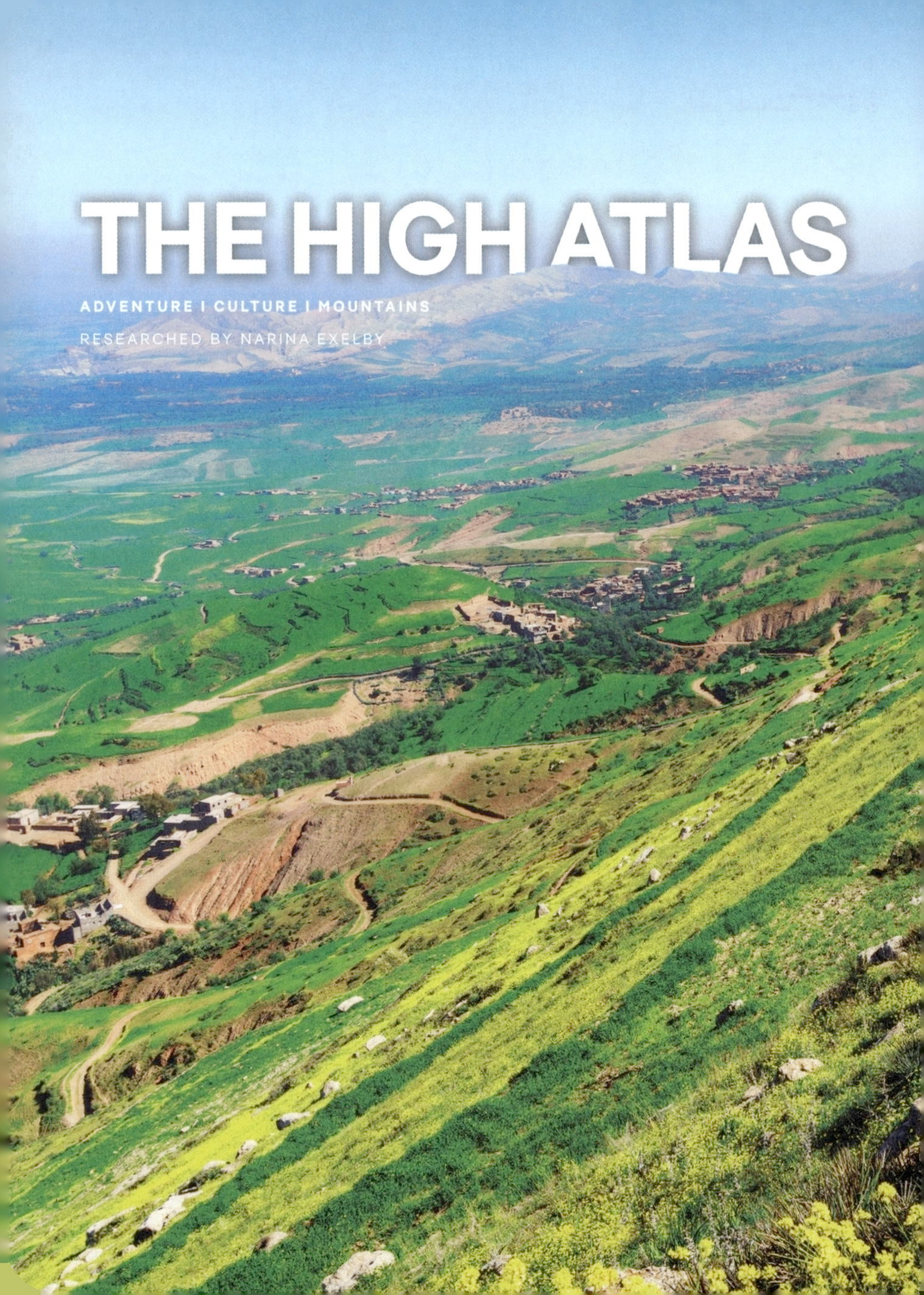
THE HIGH ATLAS
ADVENTURE | CULTURE | MOUNTAINS
RESEARCHED BY NARINA EXELBY

THE HIGH ATLAS
Trip Builder

Boasting the tallest peak in North Africa, the majestic High Atlas Mountains provide ample opportunity to connect with the wilder side of Morocco. From lonely mule trails winding across steep, rugged slopes to hair-raising passes, bucolic valleys and traditional Amazigh villages, it's a region of incredible diversity.

Learn about the geological history of the High Atlas Mountains at the **Azilal Museum** (p93)

3hrs from Marrakesh

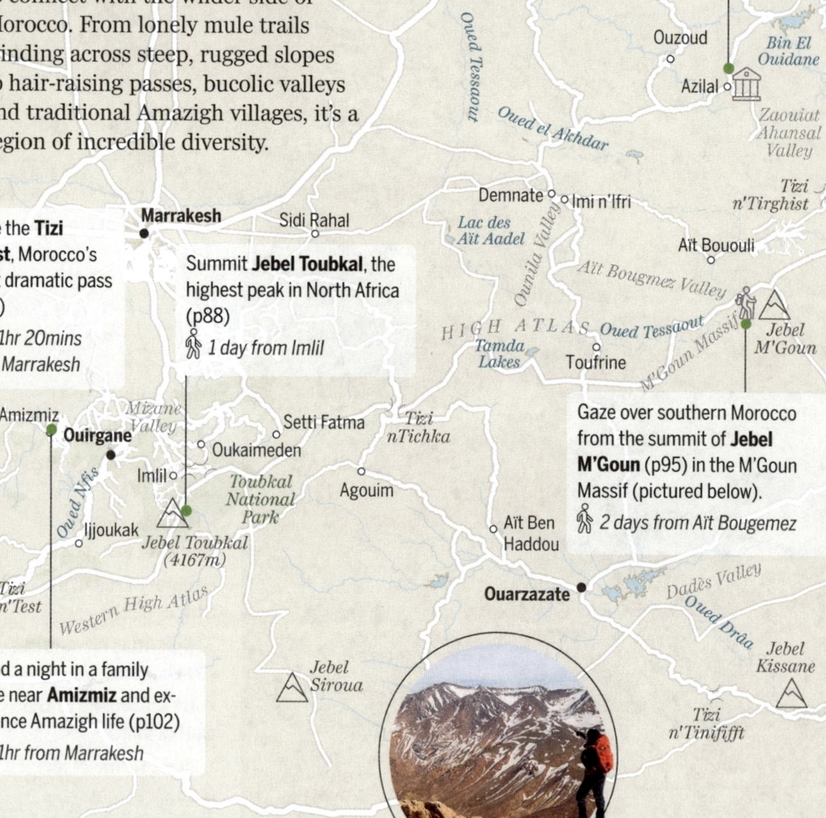

Drive the **Tizi n'Test**, Morocco's most dramatic pass (p99)

1hr 20mins from Marrakesh

Summit **Jebel Toubkal**, the highest peak in North Africa (p88)

1 day from Imlil

Gaze over southern Morocco from the summit of **Jebel M'Goun** (p95) in the M'Goun Massif (pictured below).

2 days from Aït Bougemez

Spend a night in a family home near **Amizmiz** and experience Amazigh life (p102)

1hr from Marrakesh

TOLOBALAGUER.COM/SHUTTERSTOCK
PREVIOUS SPREAD: FRANCOIS SEURET/SHUTTERSTOCK

Practicalities

ARRIVING

The High Atlas Mountains can be accessed fairly easily from Marrakesh by *grand taxi* via the transport hubs of Asni (for Imlil/Toubkal National Park and Ouirgane) and Azilal (Central High Atlas).

FIND YOUR WAY

As internet mobile phone data is generally reliable in the High Atlas, it's easy to navigate using Google Maps.

MONEY

You'll need cash in the villages as cards are rarely accepted. ATMs are available in larger towns like Amizmiz, Asni, Ourika and Azilal.

WHERE TO STAY

Place	Pros
Ouirgane	An excellent base for trekking in the Ouirgane Valley area.
Imlil	Gateway to Toubkal National Park; there's a variety of accommodation here.
Ourika	A pleasant valley with a range of luxury and mid-range guesthouses.
Aït Bougmez Valley	Stay here for scenic day walks and to begin Central High Atlas treks.

GETTING AROUND

Car The easiest way to explore the High Atlas independently is to have your own car/driver.

Taxi Taxis run regularly between the larger towns in the High Atlas, and depart when full.

Foot Trekking across mountains and between villages is the best way to experience High Atlas life.

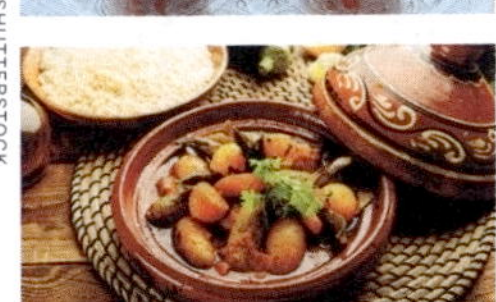

TOP: OUMAIMA BACHIRI/SHUTTERSTOCK
BOTTOM: FOOD SHOP/SHUTTERSTOCK

EATING & DRINKING

Tajines (pictured bottom left) are the norm and in the High Atlas, along with the usual lamb or chicken, you might find goat or rabbit on the menu. Vegetarians: try tchicha (soup made with barley, olive oil and mint).

Best tajine (with a view) Ouirgane Discovery Lodge (p102)

Must-try saffron tea (pictured top left) Le Jardine du Safran (p97)

APR–JUN
Beautiful, warm days; the wildflowers and fruit trees are in bloom

JUL–SEPT
The mountains are a refuge from lowland heat

OCT–NOV
Expect autumnal colours; the cooler weather means prime trekking conditions

DEC–MAR
Skies are blue; there's usually snow on the ground at higher altitudes

10 Connect with AMAZIGH CULTURE

FOOD I MARKETS I HOMESTAYS

The mountains of the High Atlas are home to the Imazighen (formerly Berber), proud people with a distinct culture whose roots in the region can be traced back thousands of years. Amazigh people are revered for their hospitality and time spent in High Atlas villages and homes provides an unforgettable chance to experience their authentic, age-old culture.

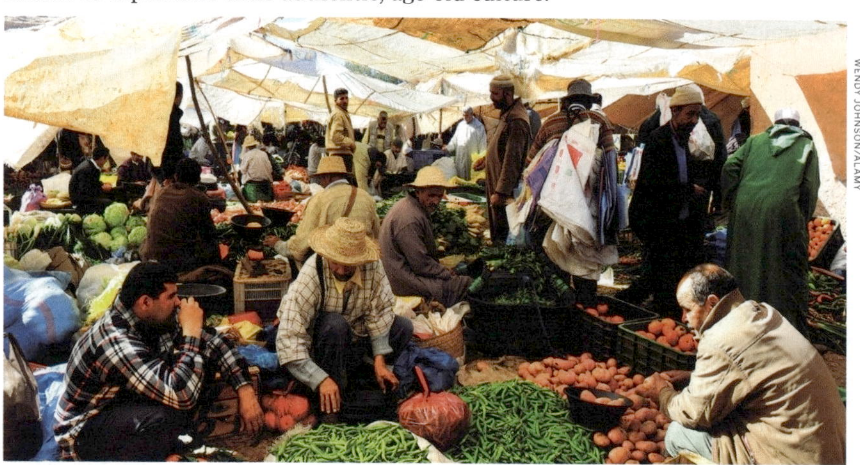

WENDY JOHNSON/ALAMY

How to

Getting here/around Take buses or *grands taxis* between towns to really get a feel for local life.

When to go Plan your trip around weekly markets in the big towns – and be sure to stop at the market for lunch (or even just mint tea), or to buy some fruit and dates.

Get connected Most guides (p103) will be able to arrange an overnight stay in a village somewhere in the High Atlas, and most guesthouses will be able to set up a cooking class.

AMANDA COGAN BARBER/SHUTTERSTOCK

ANA GAAS/SHUTTERSTOCK

Far left Friday market, Aghmat
Bottom left Amazigh village, the HIgh Atlas region
Left Interior of an Amazigh home

Stay with an Amazigh family Spend a night with a family in the High Atlas Mountains and you'll experience first-hand the incredible warmth and generosity of Amazigh hospitality. An overnight stay usually involves a walk through the hills to a mountain village and dinner with your host family; it also gives you the opportunity to be part of everyday village life – from feeding livestock to enjoying casual visits (and plenty of mint tea) with neighbours and friends.

Take a cooking class Sharing meals is an important part of Amazigh culture, and a lot of preparation and care goes into crafting the meals. Take a cooking class in someone's home and you'll not only learn the secrets of baking bread and making a tasty tajine, but you'll likely also find out how to brew the perfect pot of mint tea. For a hands-on, how-to focused session in the kitchen, book a cooking class hosted at a hotel; for more of a cultural experience, take a cooking class in someone's home.

Trawl a weekly market Weekly markets provide not only the chance for locals to shop for everything from meat and vegetables to clothes, farming implements and household goods, but also to visit a healer, get a haircut and socialise with friends. Wander between the stalls and sit down for a meal, and you'll soak up the frenzied atmosphere of market day. Markets usually run from sunrise to sunset; among the biggest in the High Atlas region are Tuesdays in Amizmiz, Thursdays in Azilal, Fridays in Aghmat and Mondays in Ourika.

Etiquette for Visiting an Amazigh Home

Always ask permission before taking someone's photo. Women will often refuse; *oho oho* means 'no'.

Public displays of affection are disrespectful of local traditions. In public, it's considered good manners for men and women to leave space between one another.

Dress conservatively, and remove shoes when entering a carpeted room.

Wash your hands before each meal. The typical Moroccan way is to eat from one communal dish, and to use bread as a substitute for cutlery. Bread can be taken with the left hand, but it should be dipped into the bowl only with the right hand.

Registered guide **Jamal Ait Lachegar** is the founder of Berber Travel Adventures. *berberadventures.com*

11 Hike North Africa's HIGHEST PEAK

MOUNTAINS I VIEWS I VILLAGES

At 4167m, Jebel Toubkal is the highest peak in North Africa. To hike up here is to adventure across rugged landscapes and savour outrageous views, dramatic peaks and pretty valleys. It's an invigorating hike that passes through traditional villages and reveals the raw beauty of nature.

LUKAS HODON/SHUTTERSTOCK

How to

Getting around You'll need a guide to hike in Toubkal National Park. Contact the **Bureau des Guides d'Imlil** (bureaudesguidesimlil.com) or stop in at their office in Imlil to hire a guide (about Dh700 a day) and mule (about Dh200 a day).

When to go Jebel Toubkal can be summited year-round, but during winter you'll need to have previous snow-trekking experience.

Gear up You can hire everything from jackets to boots to trekking poles and crampons at many stores in Imlil.

MALEO PHOTOGRAPHY/SHUTTERSTOCK

Head Out for One Day

You won't get to the summit of **Jebel Toubkal**, but one day is enough to experience the absolute thrill of walking in the rugged High Atlas Mountains. A classic day hike in the Imlil Valley is the beginning of the Toubkal summit trek: start just above Imlil in the village of Aroumd (1900m), and follow the trail to the tiny Amazigh village and historic shrine of Sidi Chamharouch (2310m). It's a four- to six-hour hike up to the shrine and back down again, and you'll need to have a guide with you (there's a check point just south of Aroumd). If you're daunted by the thought of the walk (and weigh less than 75kg), you can hire a mule to help you on your way.

ONDREJ BUCEK/SHUTTERSTOCK

Be Aware of Altitude Sickness

Hike slowly to avoid altitude sickness (nausea, headaches, dizziness and shortness of breath). To help adjust to lower oxygen levels, drink plenty of water in the days before your trek, and avoid caffeine and alcohol (which can exacerbate symptoms). Rest as soon as you begin to feel unwell; if symptoms worsen, descend immediately.

Far left View from Jebel Toubkal
Left Checkpoint, Jebel Toubkal trek
Above Hiker's lunch, Sidi Chamharouch

Summit Toubkal in Two Days

The summit of **Jebel Toubkal** has long drawn hikers who dream of looking down on Africa from this highest peak in the High Atlas Mountains. There are various routes to the top: the quieter one begins to the southeast of Jebel Toubkal in the village of Amsouzart and can be done in two days. The classic ascent of Toubkal can also be done in two days; it begins in the village of Aroumd (1900m), just up the valley from Imlil. The first day is a 10km hike that leads past the Sidi Chamharouch shrine (2330m) to the overnight stop at either the Refuge du Toubkal or the adjacent Refuge Toubkal Les Mouflons (3207m). From here, it's a four- or five-hour climb to the summit – but this second day is long and you'll need to begin the ascent of Toubkal before sunrise in order to make the 17km (nine-hour) hike from the refuge point to the summit and back down to Aroumd in daylight. If you have the time, add another day to your trip and stay in

Local Knowledge

You need to be prepared for anything in the High Atlas Mountains, because the weather can change in an instant and, even in summer, the nights can be very cold. Always carry warm clothing and wear good shoes. You can walk alone in the villages and valleys around Imlil, but to walk into the mountains it's essential to go with a guide; all those connected with **Bureau des Guides d'Imlil** (bureaudesguidesimlil.com) are local, accredited mountain guides and they know Toubkal very well.

Advice from Brahim Toudaoui, who heads up the Bureau des Guides Imlil and has been a mountain guide for 49 years. *trekkinginmorocco.com*

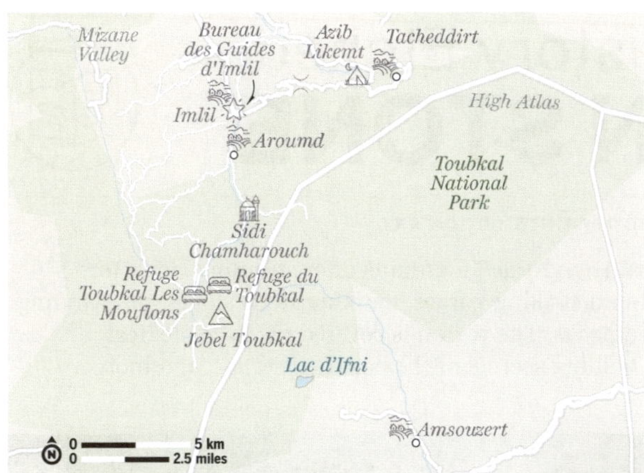

one of the refuges a second night, then continue to Aroumd or Imlil on the third day.

Hike the Six-Day Toubkal Circuit

Turn your summit of Toubkal into a majestic mountain adventure that unfolds over six days, with the grand finale of summiting North Africa's highest peak on your final morning in the mountains. Walk a six-day, 77km loop by zigzagging from Imlil to Tacchedirt (night one); then hike a long, steep climb to a goat shelter above Azib Likemt (night two); walk through a stunning gorge to a *gite* at Amsouzert (night three); take an easy hike to Lac d'Ifni (night four); and cross dramatic gorges to reach Refuge du Toubkal (night five) before summiting Toubkal and hiking down to Imlil (day six). Your guide will arrange mules to carry food and bedding.

Left Hike to the summit of Jebel Toubkal
Below Lac d'Ifni

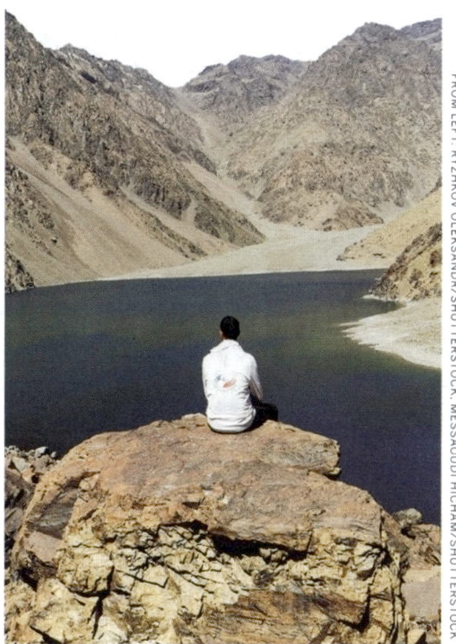

FROM LEFT: RYZHKOV OLEKSANDR/SHUTTERSTOCK, MESSAOUDI HICHAM/SHUTTERSTOCK

12 History Etched IN STONE

WATERFALLS I DINOSAUR FOOTPRINTS I ROCK ART

The dramatic Central High Atlas Mountains offer stunning views for travellers: roads sweep around striking gorges, flanking steep slopes and winding towards often-snow-capped peaks. The region is revered for its geological wonders, with landscapes holding secrets of the earth's distant – and more recent – past.

ALBERTOLOYO/GETTY IMAGES

Trip Notes

Getting around Hire a car, or a guide and driver.

When to go Avoid the crowds at Cascades d'Ouzoud by going on a weekday.

Need to know Begin with a visit to the Azilal Museum (closed Tuesdays) – it'll put everything else in context.

Picture this You'll get the best photos of Cascades d'Ouzoud around midday, and of Imi n'Ifri natural bridge in the afternoon.

Stretch Your Legs

Aït Bougmez Valley Wander the beautiful valley, through orchards farmed for generations.

Sidi Moussa Walk up to this centuries-old shrine from the village of Timit for exceptional valley views.

Tanaghmelt From Cascades d'Ouzoud, walk the 5km trail to Tanaghmelt, an historic village where most homes are made from earth.

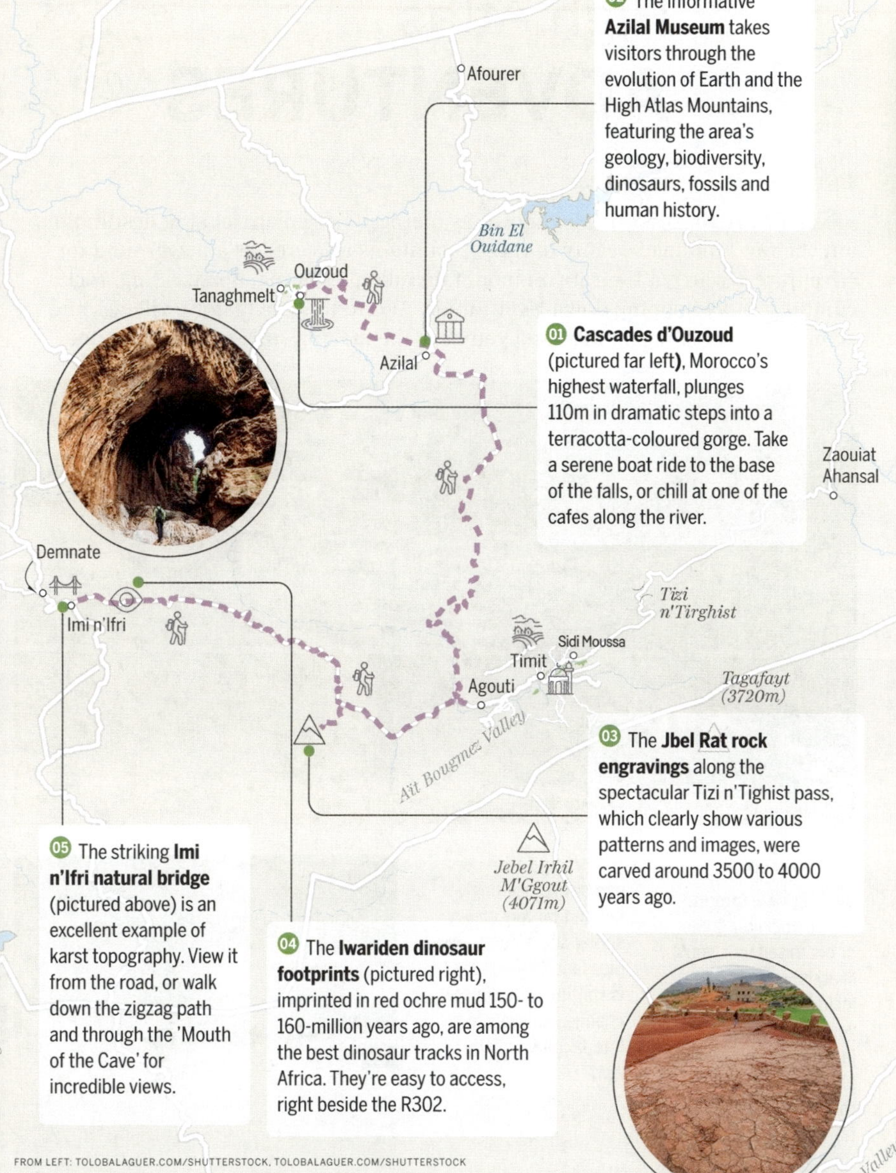

02 The informative **Azilal Museum** takes visitors through the evolution of Earth and the High Atlas Mountains, featuring the area's geology, biodiversity, dinosaurs, fossils and human history.

01 **Cascades d'Ouzoud** (pictured far left**)**, Morocco's highest waterfall, plunges 110m in dramatic steps into a terracotta-coloured gorge. Take a serene boat ride to the base of the falls, or chill at one of the cafes along the river.

03 The **Jbel Rat rock engravings** along the spectacular Tizi n'Tighist pass, which clearly show various patterns and images, were carved around 3500 to 4000 years ago.

05 The striking **Imi n'Ifri natural bridge** (pictured above) is an excellent example of karst topography. View it from the road, or walk down the zigzag path and through the 'Mouth of the Cave' for incredible views.

04 The **Iwariden dinosaur footprints** (pictured right), imprinted in red ochre mud 150- to 160-million years ago, are among the best dinosaur tracks in North Africa. They're easy to access, right beside the R302.

FROM LEFT: TOLOBALAGUER.COM/SHUTTERSTOCK, TOLOBALAGUER.COM/SHUTTERSTOCK

13 High Atlas ADVENTURES

SUMMITS I VALLEYS I TRAILS

The High Atlas may be known as Morocco's premier trekking destination, but the raw, untamed beauty of these mountains also creates a playground for adventurers who get their fix on mountain bikes, by skiing, horse riding, rock climbing and whooping down river rapids. Add to this the historic villages and genuine Amazigh hospitality, and you have the makings of a trip of a lifetime.

FRANCOIS SEURET/SHUTTERSTOCK

How to

Getting here/around If you've booked a guide or organised tour, you'll likely have transport included or arranged for you. If you're travelling independently, you'll be able to travel easily on the network of public transport that runs through the High Atlas.

When to go Summers can be excruciatingly hot and winters snowy; spring and autumn are pleasant. The ski season is shifting with climate change, but likely to be late January to early April.

ALAN CURRIE/GETTY IMAGES

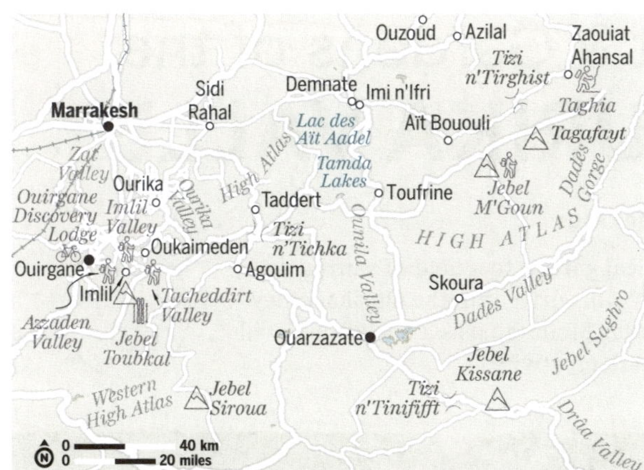

Adventures on two wheels The mule paths that for generations have connected the villages of the High Atlas Mountains make for exceptional mountain biking. The trails can cross steep slopes and be very technical, so some areas (like Imlil Valley) are better suited to experienced riders while others (like the Ouirgane Valley) are brilliant for easy day rides. Let a company such as **Bike Adventures in Morocco** (bikeadventuresinmorocco.com) suggest a destination based on your skills.

Adventures on skis Morocco is an unlikely skiing destination, but the 10km of runs at Oukaimeden present a fun opportunity to carve some powder on African slopes. You can rent all gear from one of the many small stores in the village. The ski lift was closed for upgrade in early 2025, but mules are available to transport skiers up the slopes. An adventurous option for experienced skiers: head out on a multiday skiing and trekking tour around **Jebel Toubkal** (trekkinginmorocco.com).

Adventures on four hooves An unforgettable way to get to know the slopes, valleys and villages of the High Atlas is to explore them on horseback (cavaliersdelatlas.com). A multiday ride will get you off the beaten track and give you the opportunity to do some cantering as well as steep climbs. If you're not comfortable on a horse, a short, sedentary mule ride might suit you better – and this can be arranged by almost any guesthouse or guide.

Top left Bike tour
Bottom left Jebel Toubkal hike

Mountain Highs

Taghia, near Zaouiat Ahansal, is my favourite area for rock climbing. The small, peaceful village is surrounded by impressive limestone walls suited to experienced climbers.

For a challenging trek, hike from Happy Valley to the summit of **Jebel M'Goun**. It takes four to eight days through a diverse landscape, and gives you a chance to disconnect completely. You'll camp overnight with a team of muleteers and a cook: a special way to learn more about Amazigh culture, and create jobs for villagers.

To connect deeply with Amazigh culture and hospitality, hike from village to village through the **Azzaden Valley** to **Imlil Valley** and **Tacheddirt Valley**.

Mountaineer **Sara Chakir** is a guide at Intrepid Travel and also leads their women's expeditions. *intrepidtravel.com*

14 Art & Gardens of the OURIKA VALLEY

SCULPTURE I SAFFRON I CERAMICS

From a surreal tropical garden to a field of saffron and a traditional potters' village, this drive into the Ourika Valley – with views of the High Atlas Mountains as a backdrop – will delight your senses and spark creativity.

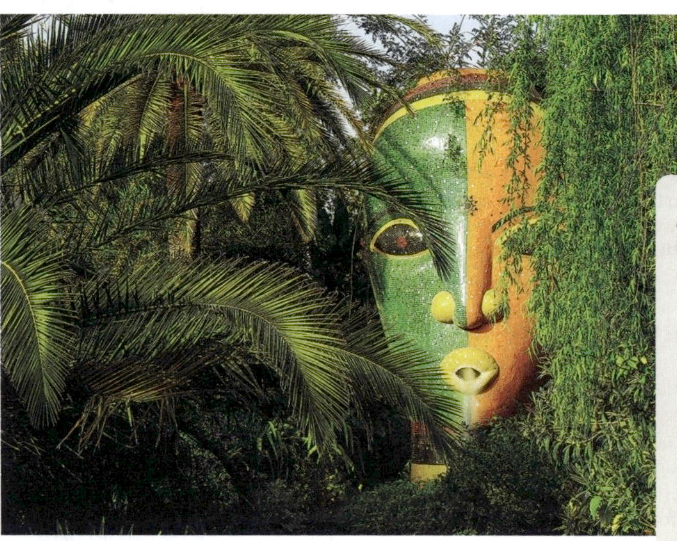

Trip Notes

Getting around Travelling by taxi between the first three stops will be tricky. You'll have the freedom you need to enjoy this route if you have your own vehicle.

When to go The saffron flowers are usually in bloom between late October and the end of November.

On a budget? Entrance to Anima Garden is expensive, but they do have a free shuttle from Marrakesh (book in advance).

Get Your Hands Dirty

Make a full day of this itinerary by booking a pottery class in Tafza with registered guide Khalid Ben Youssef (WhatsApp +212 657471151), whose family has lived in this village of potters for generations. During the two-hour session he'll take you around a traditional workshop where you can see the masters at work; he'll then teach you the basic techniques of wheel work, and give you time to put them into practice.

01 Nature and culture collide in the lush **Anima Garden** (pictured left and right; anima-garden.com). Designed by multimedia artist André Heller, it's filled with exotic blooms, cacti, trees and hidden sculptures.

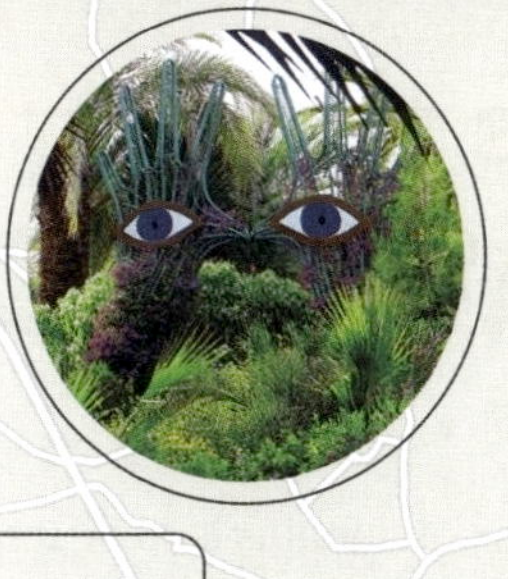

03 Stroll the herb gardens at **Jardin Bio-Aromatique d'Ourika** (jardine-bioaromatique-ourika.com). Indulge in a relaxing foot bath, or a bread-making, cooking or henna tattoo workshop (book ahead).

02 Take a guided tour through the saffron cultivating process at **Le Jardine du Safran**, and explore the garden in which the bulbs grow. End with saffron tea served under an old mulberry tree.

04 The road through **Tafza village** (p96) is lined with ceramic stores. Tajines, platters, pots and vases of all shapes and sizes are handcrafted here from red clay gathered nearby.

05 At **Le Savo'Art Fer**, Moroccan artist and sculptor Abdelhaq Elyoussi recycles iron to create sought-after, one-of-a-kind sculptures. He's happy to down tools and chat about his work.

FROM TOP: ALBINA BAUER/ANIMA ©, KALINA GEORGIEVA/SHUTTERSTOCK, BALATE.DORIN/SHUTTERSTOCK

15 Views to TRAVEL FOR

STARS I MOUNTAINS I VALLEYS

To spend time in the High Atlas Mountains is to be treated to some of the most exquisite views in North Africa. Majestic mountains, dramatic valleys, traditional Amazigh villages and lush orchards with towering peaks – often snow-capped – looming in the background make for truly unforgettable views. From one hilltop to the next, the scenery is ever changing.

TOLOBALAGUER.COM/SHUTTERSTOCK

How to

Getting here/around You could travel between bigger towns by public transport, but it's easier to hire a car or driver.

When to go The air is usually clearer – and views therefore better – during winter. But winters are chilly in the High Atlas so wrap up. If you're wanting to see the Milky Way, you'll need to be in Morocco during the summer months.

Top tip Carry cash. There are no ATMs outside the bigger towns, and cards are rarely accepted.

PÉTER MOCSONOKY/500PX

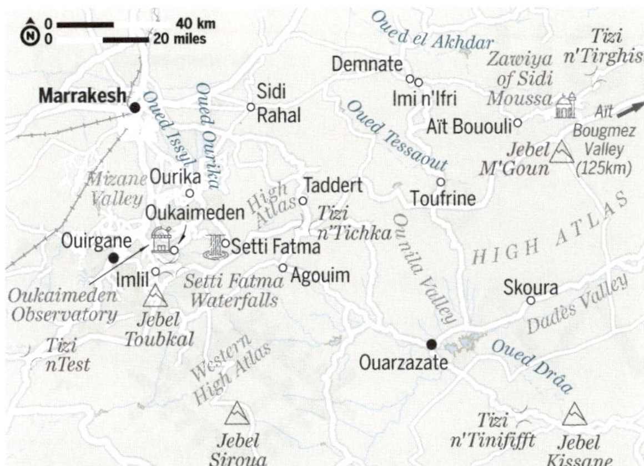

By telescope Low levels of light pollution around the High Atlas peaks translate into exceptional viewing of the night skies – especially when using a powerful telescope. Take a guided tour of the **Oukaimeden Observatory** (book through intrepid travel.com), and spend an evening in the ski-resort village with an astronomer, gazing at planets and far-off constellations.

By car You'll need to keep your wits about you to enjoy the gob-smacking mountain and valley views from the **Tizi n'Test** pass, Morocco's most dramatic road. The pass, which connects Ouirgane with Taroudant, cuts through the High Atlas in a series of outrageous hairpin bends. It's one-car wide in some places, and without a safety barrier in many. The road was built almost a century ago and is currently being upgraded; navigating the roadworks adds to the thrill – and the time it'll take to drive the 161km route.

Hiking Take a three-day hike from the Aït Bougmez Valley to the summit of **Jebel M'Goun** (4071m), Morocco's third-highest mountain, and you'll be rewarded with magnificent views across southern Morocco. You'll need to hike with an experienced mountain guide.

On foot The bucolic Aït Bougmez Valley (aka Happy Valley) – a patchwork of fruit trees, fringed with village clusters – is best seen from the **Zawiya of Sidi Moussa**, a historic hilltop granary above Timit village. It's a steep but easy walk up a paved pathway; be sure to climb to the roof of the *zawiya* (Sufi lodge) for the exquisite views, which are best in the late afternoon.

Top left Jebel M'Goun hike
Bottom left Tizi n'Test pass

Chasing Waterfalls

The biggest attractions in the Ourika Valley (less than an hour from Marrakesh) are the **Setti Fatma waterfalls**. This series of seven waterfalls drops down through a dramatic gorge; most people visit only the first one, and the crowded trail to its base is lined with souvenir shops and cafes. From the first waterfall the path loops right back to town – but if you walk left instead, the rocky trail will take you higher into the gorge and you'll have amazing views of the ravine and waterfalls almost all to yourself. You can walk as far as the fifth waterfall.

Registered guide **Ait Ali Abdelkarim**, owner of Ourika Lodge, grew up in the Ourika Valley. *@karim.certified.guide*

AMAZIGH
Symbols

01 Diamond
Perhaps the most prominent of all symbols in Amazigh culture, the diamond represents femininity, fertility and protection, and is often used to ward off evil spirits.

02 Zigzag
Water, a vital resource (of course) is shown with a zigzag. These jagged lines can also sometimes signify mountains and valleys.

03 Triangle
The triangle, associated with fertility and womanhood, often represents family and the cycle of life. In some parts of the High Atlas the triangle is associated with men, not women.

04 Eye
An eye is usually shown as a diamond with a dot in its centre. It wards off the evil eye, and symbolises protection and caution.

05 Cross
The cross can sometimes be seen as a body; it also shows a connection to ancestors and spiritual guidance.

06 Zigzag

These four angled lines show masculinity, and are used to symbolise the strength and power of men.

07 Bird

Bird symbols typically represent freedom, or a connection to higher realms. They are also used to show guidance and transformation.

08 Yaz

Arguably the most important symbol to the Imazighen, this shape represents freedom and the free spirit of the Amazigh people.

09 Chevron

This pattern shows movement, and implies ambition, progress and movement in life. In some areas the symbol also represents the feminine.

10 Hourglass

The two opposing triangles that create an hourglass shape are often used to show the time between life and death.

YULIA MOTINOVA/SHUTTERSTOCK

Listings

BEST OF THE REST

 Restaurants with a View

Kasbah du Toubkal €€

The historic Kasbah du Toubkal – originally built in the 1920s – sits on a hilltop and has extraordinary views of Jebel Toubkal. Book ahead and enjoy a traditional Moroccan lunch on the terrace.

Bouche de la Source €€

Setti Fatma has an abundance of cafes and restaurants strung all along the Ourika River. At Bouche de la Source you can lounge beside the stream on floor cushions, under a parasol.

Chez Mohamed Tafdnae €€

Enjoy the very best view of Cascade d'Ouzoud from the terrace of this rustic riverside cafe with campsite. The chicken tajine is exceptional.

Ouirgane Discovery Lodge €€

From the terrace, look across the river to the lake and Ouirgane village, and the mountains beyond. There's accommodation here too, and the restaurant is among the best in the area.

 Classic Coffee Cafes

Café Paul Bowles €

Come for the sculpture garden, stay for the coffee. The menu at this cafe in Amina Garden near Ourika is bursting with coffee options, as well as smoothies, cakes, salads and pizzas.

Café 38 Concept €

Pop in for a cappuccino (or, highly recommended, an Amazigh omelette) while visiting neighbouring ceramic shops in Tafza – or book ahead to do an alfresco cooking class.

 Cooking Classes

Dar Tassa

Learn the secrets of Moroccan cooking during a hands-on cooking class with Ourika Organic Kitchen at this guesthouse with exceptional views over the Ouirgane Valley.

Ouirgane

Settle into an Amazigh kitchen with a glass of fresh mint tea and watch as bread and tajine are made the way they have been for generations. Guide Mohamed Ait Mhand (WhatsApp +212 662645555) sets up classes at family homes around the Ouirgane area.

Authentic Toubkal Lodge

There is a depth to the tradition of mint tea. Learn how to make it, and how to bake bread, at Authentic Toubkal Lodge near Imlil.

Saida Berber House

At Saida Berber House near Amizmiz you'll not only learn how to prepare a traditional meal, but you'll also have a chance to explore the village. Saida works hard to share her culture, and to empower women in her community.

Ultrarunners, the HIgh Atlas

Make a Difference

Asni area

The Eve Branson Foundation runs a number of training, healthcare, education and sustainability programmes in the High Atlas. In partnership with Kasbah Tamadot, they arrange personalised visits to meet with artists and artisans in villages near Asni.

Education For All

Volunteer to assist girls with improving their language skills and school levels. Education For All provides housing and education for girls from remote High Atlas villages.

Amizmiz area

Walk through the High Atlas foothills around Amizmiz, the area worst hit by the devastating 2023 earthquake, and stay or have lunch with families in the area. Berber Travel Adventures sets up treks around here, and the money you spend goes straight into the communities.

Central High Atlas

Buy rugs directly from the women who made them. Many villages in the Central High Atlas (like Timit, Agouti and Tabant) have established women's cooperatives, where they sell their wares and make rugs to order.

Festivals & Events

Imilchil Marriage Mossem

In September thousands gather in Imilchil for the Marriage Mossem, a celebration of Amazigh marriage customs and mountain culture.

High Atlas Ultra Trail

This extreme endurance race through the rugged High Atlas covers various distances from 10km to 120km. It is one of North Africa's toughest endurance trails, with steep ascents, technical terrain and high-altitude conditions.

Atlas Mountain Race

Mountain bikers navigate 1300km of challenging off-road terrain, steep climbs and remote landscapes. The route runs from Marrakesh via the Atlas Mountains to Essaouira; there are no set stages, and each rider in this seven-day event must be self-supported.

Good Guides

Around Imlil

Lahcen Jellah, based in Imlil, has been leading MTB tours at **Bike Adventures in Morocco** for over 25 years. bikeadventuresinmorocco.com

Around Ouirgane

Registered Ouirgane-based mountain guide Mohamed Ait Mhand can arrange hikes, cooking classes and homestays in the Ouirgane region. ouirgane-trekking.com

Across the High Atlas

Registered mountain guide Ibrahim Ait Ouarab (WhatsApp +212 667690903) has been leading expeditions through the High Atlas for more than 30 years.

Around Ourika

Ait Ali Abdelkarim (WhatsApp +212 670721706), registered guide and owner of Ourika Lodge, grew up in the Ourika Valley and leads walks and tours in the area.

Around Amizmiz

Registered guide Jamal Ait Lachegar leads treks and sets up accommodation at homestays around Amizmiz and the High Atlas. berberadventures.com

Around Toubkal National Park

Mohamed Toudaoui, a leader at the Bureau des Guides Imlil, arranges trekking and skiing trips in the High Atlas Mountains. trekkinginmorocco.com

SOUTHERN OASES

DESERT | PALMERAIES | KASBAHS

RESEARCHED BY JADE BREMNER

SOUTHERN OASES
Trip Builder

Empty desert drives and tall sculpted Sahara dunes meet shimmering date-palm oases and copper-coloured kasbahs in this Moroccan region fit for the movies. Dubbed the 'Hollywood of Africa', it's scattered with filming locations rooted in Amazigh culture and opportunities for high-octane adventure – from quad biking in the desert to climbing soaring gorges and hiking though the Atlas Mountains.

CLOCKWISE FROM LEFT: THE VISUAL EXPLORER/SHUTTERSTOCK, JOSE A CONSTANTINO/SHUTTERSTOCK, JIRIK V/SHUTTERSTOCK
PREVIOUS SPREAD: DELBO ANDREA/SHUTTERSTOCK

Practicalities

SERGEY-73/SHUTTERSTOCK

ARRIVING

Tizi N' Tichka Driving is easy from Marrakesh over the pass. CTM buses also use this route. From here it's a four-hour drive to Erg Chigaga. Roads are easy in a 2WD, unless you go into the desert, where a 4WD is essential (expert drivers only).

Ouarzazate International Airport (pictured) If you're short on time, Ryanair operates routes direct from London to Ouarzazate. Royal Air Maroc offers direct flights from Casablanca to Ouarzazate.

HOW MUCH FOR A

Mint tea Dh10-21

Amazigh pizza Dh84-125

Sandboarding session Dh104-157

WHEN TO GO

JAN–MAR
Cold days in the desert and freezing at night – the Tizi N' Tichka may be closed due to snowfall

APR–JUN
A popular time to visit; roses are out in bloom, days are warm

JUL–SEP
The warmest months, with stiflingly hot desert days but ideal nights for stargazing

OCT–DEC
Ideal hiking and desert-exploring season; warm days and cooler nights drawing in

GETTING AROUND

Car Hiring a car – or a car and a driver – is the best way to discover the region's remote villages at your own pace. Parking is never an issue, but police road checks can slow you down (always carry the vehicle and rental documents, and your passport and driving licence).

Taxi and motorcycle Shared *grands taxis* ply the main roads, especially on market days, and the open roads around towns are made for motorcyclists.

Bus There's no shortage of budget-friendly buses town-hopping along the region's main arteries – the N9, N10, N12 and N13. You can get from Marrakesh to the dunes of M'hamid in 10 hours with CTM.

EATING & DRINKING

Good restaurants are few and far between. Most meals are Moroccan (tajines, couscous etc), which are home-cooked in kasbah accommodation. Quality is high, as fresh local produce is typically used. Meals should be booked ahead of time. Breakfast comes as standard in most guesthouses and hotels. It's possible to find a few upmarket dining experiences in Ouazazate, but small towns typically only have street food and snack options and very rustic spaces, though the food is usually good quality and homemade.

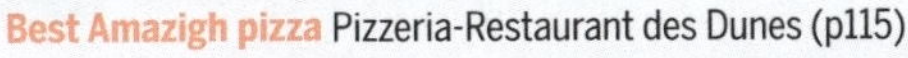

Best Amazigh pizza Pizzeria-Restaurant des Dunes (p115)

Must-try French/Moroccan dining Oz Palace Restaurant (p126)

TOP: PAWEL KAZMIERCZAK/SHUTTERSTOCK
BOTTOM: PALUMBO PHOTOGRAPHER/SHUTTERSTOCK

CONNECT & FIND YOUR WAY

Wi-fi Almost all guesthouses offer wi-fi during a stay; some desert camps even have it. A local SIM card has good coverage along major routes and in towns, with some black spots in the Atlas Mountains and quiet desert roads.

Tip Download offline maps for road trips and hikes before you set off.

WHERE TO STAY

Town/Village	Pro/Con
Ouarzazate	Transport hub. Good for supplies. Lots of accommodation options.
Fint Oasis	Quiet homestays near Ouarzazate in a lush palm grove. No facilities.
Skoura	Sleepy area, historic kasbahs, green palm oasis, a couple of good museums. No buzz.
Aït Ben Haddou	Well-preserved *ksar* (fortified village), lots of eating and drinking options. Touristy.
Merzouga	Gateway to the Sahara, home to Erg Chebbi. Lots of amenities. Unattractive town.
Zagora	Lots of facilities. An easy stop before the empty dunes of Erg Chigaga. Busy.

LOCAL GUIDES

When you arrive in each town it's easy to secure a local guide – many will simply wander up to you. Agree a price before setting off.

MONEY

Cash is king in these parts, with very few places (aside from larger accommodation) accepting cards. ATMs can be scarce in desert towns – make sure you carry cash.

16

Exploring Kasbahs & KSOUR

HISTORY | ARCHITECTURE | LOCAL LIFE

Derived from the Arabic word *qaṣaba* (fortress), around a thousand kasbahs are dotted around the remote Atlas Mountains, built using earth and stone in Amazigh and Arab styles, with passageways, geometric embellishments and central gardens. *Ksour* are fortified villages, protecting from invaders.

ROBERTO MOIOLA/ROBERTHARDING/GETTY IMAGES

How to

Getting here/around Buses N9, N10, N12 and N13 travel along the region's main arteries. Rental car is the easiest way to discover remote villages at your own pace.

When to go Kasbahs can be explored at any time of year – they can provide warmth in the winter and shelter from the summer heat.

Cash Carry it at all times. ATMs are hard to come by in smaller towns and villages, and cards are rarely accepted.

MATIAS PLANAS/SHUTTERSTOCK

Kasbah Amridil

One of the finest and best-preserved kasbahs in this part of the Morocco, the 17th-century **Kasbah Amridil** (facebook.com/thekasbahamridil, entry Dh20), once appeared on the Dh50 note. Now a museum, visitors can go on a self-guided or guided tour exploring traditional kasbah life over the centuries. Wander its well-preserved alleys, rooms and go up to the roof for wonderful views. Exhibitions throughout range from those on hand-carved door locks or how a traditional olive-oil press works, to those on traditional bread ovens. A satisfying adjacent restaurant serves up big bowls of couscous and tajines. Nearby, the **Musée Memoire de Ouarzazate**, inside Kasbah Dar Bahnini, has a smaller, more intimate exhibition on local craft, clothing and customs.

MARLENE VICENTE/GETTY IMAGES

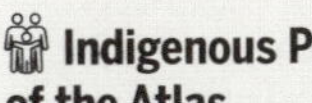

Indigenous People of the Atlas

Amazigh tribes have lived in this area for some 5000 years and retained their rule, even when colonising powers (such as the French and Arabs) occupied elsewhere. Amazigh/Tamazign is still commonly spoken throughout the region. Look for the blue, green and yellow Amazigh flag, with the 'free man' ⵣ symbol.

Far left and left Kasbah Amridil
Above Amazigh flag

Ksar Tissergate

Off the tourist trail, this abandoned *ksar* on the edge of Zagora's *palmeraie* (palm grove) is a fine example of southern Morocco's fortified villages. People still live in the village surrounding the crumbling 16th-century **Ksar Tissergate**, and children play in its passageways. Follow the signs from the car park to the rustic and maze-like **Musée des Arts et Traditions de la Valleé du Draa** (entry Dh25), documenting the traditions of the Drâa tribes via themed rooms, with artefacts including the wedding costumes of different ethnic groups and extravagant Amazigh jewellery. There's also farming equipment and early lamps, plus information about the area – such as that in the Drâa River, the longest in Morocco, running from the High Atlas Mountains to the Atlantic. Save time to explore the disorientating passageways surrounding the museum. **Kasbah Ziwana** inside the *ksar* has glorious views over the palms and smart rooms surrounding a gorgeous courtyard.

Village of 45 Kasbahs

The Drâa and Ziz valleys plus the Dadès and Todra Gorges are hot spots for kasbahs. The village of **Nkob** has 45 of these impressive red-hued mud and sand buildings, some standing for more than a century. Many are renovated and well-maintained guesthouses. **Kasbah Ennakhile** (kasbahennakhile.com) is a fine example, with gorgeous views over a *palmeraie* and oodles of traditional charm, while **Ksar Jenna** (ksarjenna.com) has an incredible ornate tiled ceiling and curved archways.

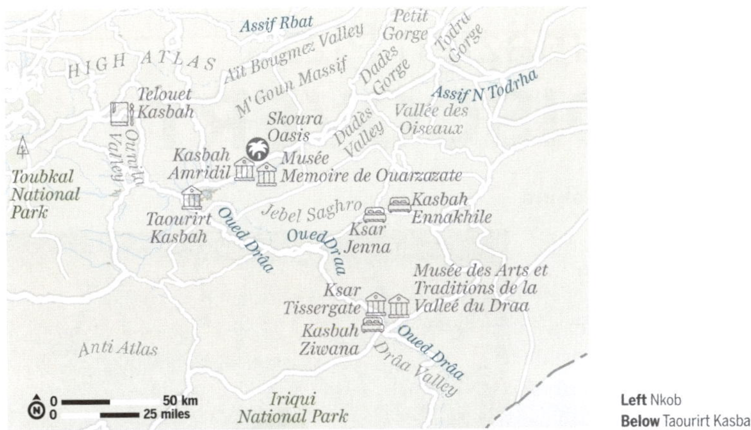

Left Nkob
Below Taourirt Kasbah

Taourirt Kasbah

The enormous **Taourirt Kasbah** (entry Dh20) on the edge of Ouarzazate had 300 rooms in its heyday. Taourirt was occupied by numerous relatives, along with a host of servants, craftsmen and merchants. Built by the prominent El Glaouis family in the 19th century, as a strategic location on Sahara trade routes between the Drâa and the Dadès, it was partially restored by UNESCO in the 1990s, and a section of ornate rooms on the upper floors with elaborate stucco, painted cedarwood and an original woven reed *(tataoui)* ceiling were made accessible to tourists. It also featured in the Hollywood films *Gladiator* and *The Sheltering Sky*.

Telouet Kasbah

Telouet was once a stronghold at the centre of a trans-Saharan trading empire, but these days it's a dusty town. A reminder of its former grandeur is **Telouet Kasbah** (also known as the Palace of Glaoui) constructed in the late 19th century. Owned by the El Glaoui family, who had some 300 artisans work to create salons faceted with stucco and thousands of colourful *zellige* tiles. In 2023 Telouet Kasbah was damaged by an earthquake and visitors are temporarily unable to go inside. Until then it's possible to view the outside of the grand building.

Amazigh Pizza DISCOVERY

DESERT PIZZA | FOOD | COOKING

Originating in the Atlas Mountains, 'Amazigh pizza' (or *madfouna* meaning 'buried' in Arabic) is made using a flaky dough from semolina flour. The thin flatbread is stuffed with fillings such as tomatoes, onions, herbs and spices (cumin, paprika and turmeric), plus olives and preserved lemons. It was traditionally baked in a clay oven or sand-baked in the Sahara ground.

IMAGEBROKER.COM/ALAMY

Trip Notes

Getting around The easiest way to explore this region is by car, but CTM buses run between the major towns.

When to go Amazigh pizza is available year-round. It's commonly sold as street food in the cooler months and evenings too.

Top tip Book ahead to try Amazigh pizzas at your guesthouse, kasbah or desert camp – many will make it if they have the time; some will use traditional methods (clay ovens).

Pair with Mint Tea

Dubbed 'Moroccan whiskey', fresh mint tea is typically served with Amazigh pizza to cleanse the palate and aid digestion. It's also a good source of calcium, magnesium and copper, aiding the immune system. Hosts theatrically pour tea from height from the spout of a silver pot. This aerates the tea and adds froth to the drink.

01 In the village of Nkob (pictured below left), the **Kasbah Imdoukal** (kasbahimdoukal.com) heritage hotel serves up a home-cooked Amazigh pizza bursting with flavour; call ahead to request it for dinner.

02 Next to the fascinating Tahiri Museum of Fossils & Minerals try Amazigh pizza at the **Dinorant Restaurant**. Book ahead so they can prepare the dough. Choose a meat or veggie-only pie.

04 In Erfoud, **Pizzeria-Restaurant des Dunes** (desduneserfoud.com) has a lovely courtyard garden where it serves puffy and golden *mad-founa* stuffed with herby chicken, beef or vegetables.

05 Join a *madfouna* cooking class at **Restaurant Nora** (pictured far left; Dh700, three hours) north of Khamlia. Using fresh local ingredients, students learn about Amazigh culture while devouring their creations.

03 Try the rich flavours of house-made flaky Amazigh pizza at the **Berber Palace Hotel Merzouga** (berberpalace.com) not far from Erg Chebbi, in a welcoming kasbah restaurant.

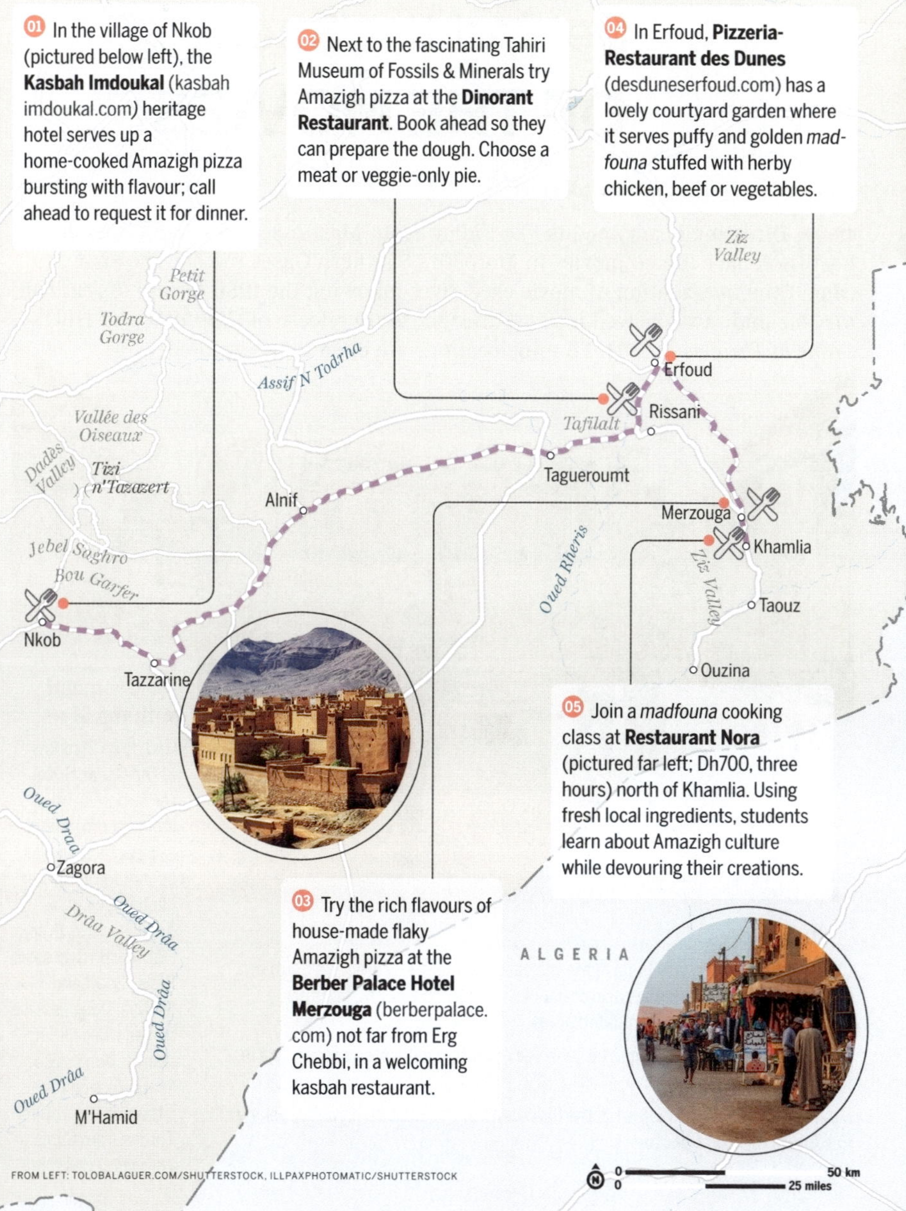

FROM LEFT: TOLOBALAGUER.COM/SHUTTERSTOCK, ILLPAXPHOTOMATIC/SHUTTERSTOCK

18 Behind the Scenes OF THE MOVIES

VILLAGES | FILMS | PHOTOGRAPHY

Directing heavyweights like Ridley Scott, Martin Scorsese and Clint Eastwood have filmed movies in Morocco's Southern Oases region. The area caught the imagination of movie executives following the 1986 release of *Jewel of the Nile* and saw renewed interest after the 2000 release of *Gladiator* and HBO's *Game of Thrones* in 2011. Filming locations are open to be explored.

KADAGAN/SHUTTERSTOCK

Trip Notes

Getting around It's easy to navigate the vast distances in Morocco's Southern Oases by car, but CTM buses also connect the major towns, and taxis are always available in more populated areas.

When to go Film locations can be seen year-round, but it's easier to explore in the cooler months.

Need to know Carry a picture of the film scene to the location if you're looking to capture the exact photo.

Overnight with the Stars

Bed down in rooms at the **Oscar Hotel** (oscarhotelbyatlas studios.com) where A-list actors such as Leonardo DiCaprio, Michael Douglas, Angelina Jolie, Brad Pitt, Martin Scorsese, Ridley Scott and Michael Douglas have stayed while filming nearby. Don't miss snapping a picture sitting on the Iron Throne from *Game of Thrones* series three.

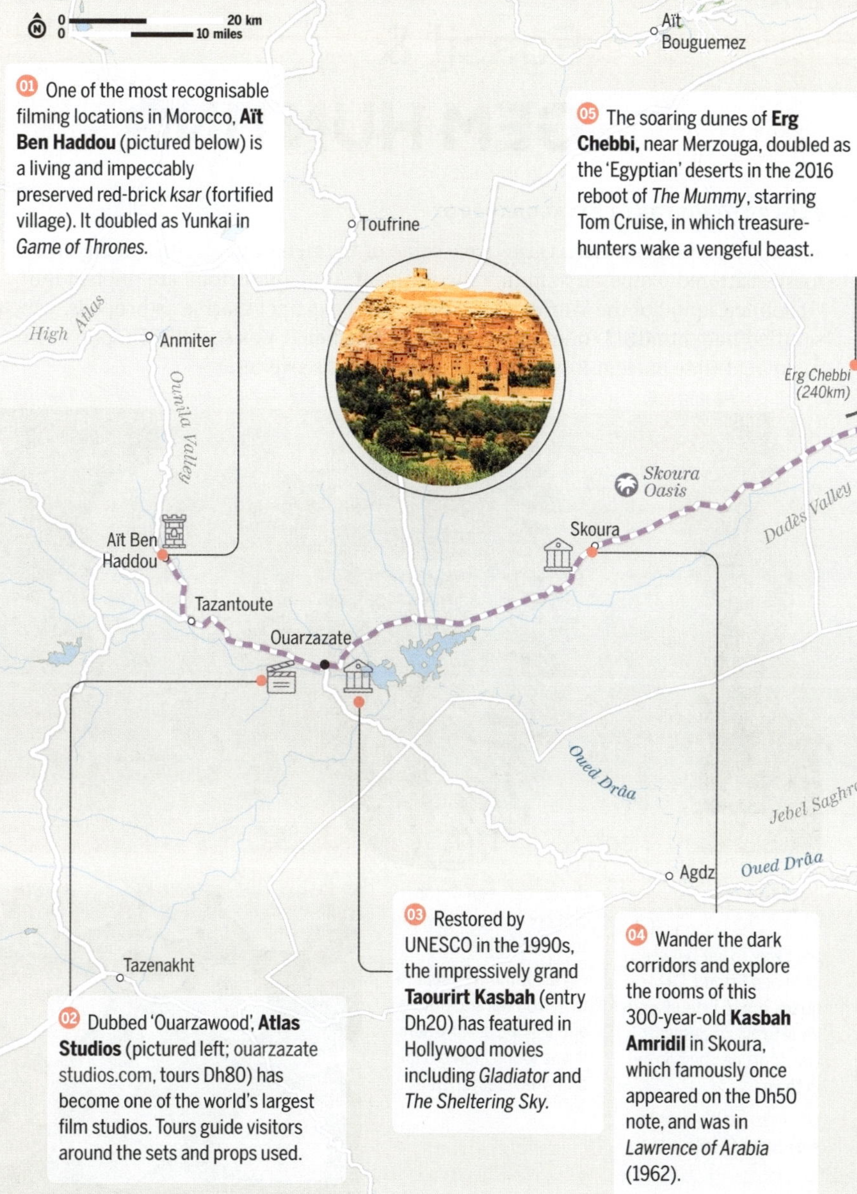

01 One of the most recognisable filming locations in Morocco, **Aït Ben Haddou** (pictured below) is a living and impeccably preserved red-brick *ksar* (fortified village). It doubled as Yunkai in *Game of Thrones*.

05 The soaring dunes of **Erg Chebbi,** near Merzouga, doubled as the 'Egyptian' deserts in the 2016 reboot of *The Mummy*, starring Tom Cruise, in which treasure-hunters wake a vengeful beast.

02 Dubbed 'Ouarzawood', **Atlas Studios** (pictured left; ouarzazatestudios.com, tours Dh80) has become one of the world's largest film studios. Tours guide visitors around the sets and props used.

03 Restored by UNESCO in the 1990s, the impressively grand **Taourirt Kasbah** (entry Dh20) has featured in Hollywood movies including *Gladiator* and *The Sheltering Sky*.

04 Wander the dark corridors and explore the rooms of this 300-year-old **Kasbah Amridil** in Skoura, which famously once appeared on the Dh50 note, and was in *Lawrence of Arabia* (1962).

RASPU/SHUTTERSTOCK

19 Fossil & GEM HUNTING

GEOLOGY | HISTORY | PALAEONTOLOGY

Morocco's Southern Oases have some of the richest fossil sites on Earth. The fossil-scattered plains surrounding the towns of Alnif and Erfoud are dubbed the 'Trilobite Capital of the World' – once home to the extinct marine arthropods, which scuttled here hundreds of millions of years ago when it was sea. It's still possible to make real-time ancient fossil and dinosaur bone discoveries.

GUIDO VERMEULEN-PERDAEN/SHUTTERSTOCK

How to

Getting here Car is the best way to get between Alnif and Erfoud. CTM buses run to Erfoud, and local fossil guides with transport can be booked in town.

When to go It's best to search for fossils in the desert between October and April, when temperatures are milder.

Fakes abound Research what you want to buy, and ask the seller where it was found, how old it is and what creature it is.

FRENTUSHA/GETTY IMAGES

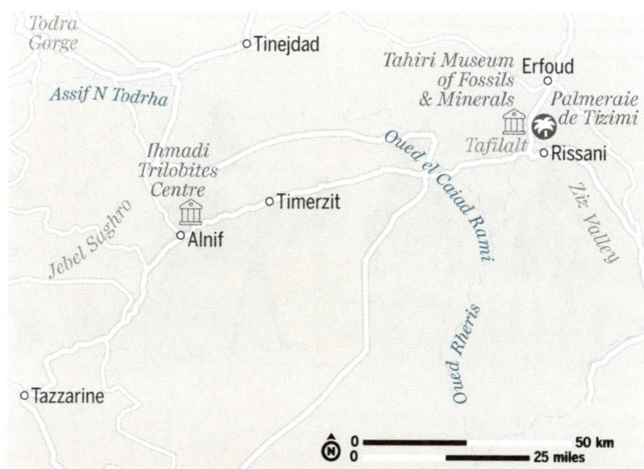

Top left Trilobite, Erfoud region
Bottom left Fossils for sale

Searching for trilobites These marine animals once scuttled along the seabeds in this area. Their exoskeletons and shells have become preserved in the limestone deposits in the area. The Alnif Basin is a particular goldmine for them. Discoveries can be made on a guided hike of the area or in the many shops selling detailed imprints. The **Ihmadi Trilobites Centre** in Alnif is a place to find authentic trilobites, minerals and meteorites – it also has a miniature museum depicting the geology and archaeological discoveries in the area.

Dinosaur bones and footprints Just south of Erfoud, the **Tahiri Museum of Fossils & Minerals** (instagram.com/tahirimuseum, entry Dh25) has a good collection of fossils – including dinosaur bones and footprints dating from 500 million years ago and meteorites from the nearby deserts. There's a completely uncased *Atlasaurus tibia* from the Middle Jurassic period (native to North Africa) plus a mosasaur skeleton – an aquatic squamate reptile that lived between 82 to 66 million years ago – found nearby.

Precious stones and formations Azurite, malachite and aragonite are commonly found in these desert plains, plus sand roses with their intricate petal-like leaves made of sand and gypsum crystals. These remarkable flower-like formations are created by evaporating water from dry lake beds, and leaving behind dissolved minerals, and their shapes are aided by wind and water erosion over thousands of years. They're sold in shops around the area.

Fossil-Hunting Tours

For those wanting to make a unique and thrilling discovery of a millions-of-years-old specimen in the desert, head to the **Tahiri Museum of Fossils & Minerals** or the **Ihmadi Trilobites Centre**, which can arrange half- and full-day fossil-hunting tours (approximately Dh300 for the afternoon). Precious stones, fossils, trilobites, spiral-shaped goniatites and corals, plus sea lilies can still be found in the sand and rocks around Erfoud – if you know where and how to recognise them – as can meteorites which often fall from the sky. Ask about visiting prehistoric burial mounds *(tumuli)* and ancient petroglyphs too.

20 Sleeping Amid SOARING DUNES

DESERT | CULTURE | ISOLATION

Some of the largest sand dunes on the planet can be found in this area of Morocco's Sahara desert. Overnight stays in a desert camp are a chance to fully immerse yourself in the mysterious and otherworldly scenes, and to learn about Bedouin culture.

YONGYUT KUMSRI/SHUTTERSTOCK

How to

Getting here/around Gateways to the Sahara, M'Hamid and Merzouga, can easily be reached by car or CTM bus. Overnight trip with a local tour agency can be booked from Zagora, Ouarzazate and Marrakesh.

When to go Spring and autumn are the best for mild temperatures by day (typically around 21°C to 30°C). Summer days can be hot. Winter days are cold and freezing at night.

Top tip Choose your camp wisely, from basic dwellings with shared showers to huge en suite tents decorated with gorgeous rugs and lamps.

TAGHLAOUIFOTOS/SHUTTERSTOCK

Accessible Dunes

The towering dunes of **Erg Chebbi** soar to 150m in places and it's easy to spend a night in this shapeshifting sea of sand, with camps situated just 15 minutes from the former trading town of Merzouga, once a stopover for caravans on their way to Timbuktu. Some jump aboard a camel to reach their desert dwelling (which takes a couple of hours) and others arrive by 4WD after a short but thrilling 15 minutes bounding over dunes as they go. Camps are personalised experiences with cosy tents varying in Moroccan styles, and they usually include a tajine or couscous dinner, plus some evening musical entertainment. Climb the nearby dunes at sunset to see the mounds change to rose-gold, and the sky erupt into a pallet of orange, pink and purple. Due to the close proximity to Merzouga, and the fact that

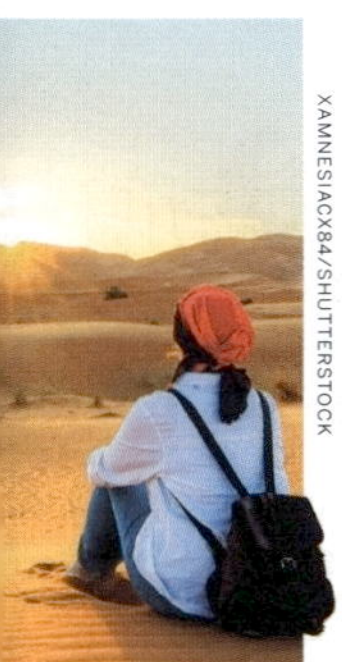
XAMNESIACX84/SHUTTERSTOCK

Art of Riding a Camel

Camels are a daily part of life in this region, and riding is on offer at most camps. For a comfortable experience, wear long trousers to avoid leg-chafing. Lean backwards so you don't fall off when the camel gets up, and sit with a loose back to go with the movement of the animal.

Far left and left Erg Chebbi
Above Desert camp near Merzouga

these are arguably the most impressive dunes in the Sahara, Erg Chebbi is often not the most relaxing experience, sometimes crowded with revving quad-bike engines and the sounds of drumming circles. For a more remote desert experience head to the lesser-visited area of the Sahara known as Erg Chigaga.

Remote Dunes

The dunes of **Erg Chigaga** are located two hours off-road – or three days hiking or aboard a camel – from the dusty town of M'Hamid, 1½ hours south of Zagora. This remarkable stretch of golden sand may not be the tallest, but it's the largest by area in Morocco, spanning some 40km. Desert camps here are quieter than those in Erg Chebbi, with less light pollution and spectacular night skies. **Camp Al Koutban** (campalkoutban.com) is a 90-minute return hike from Erg Chigaga's tallest dunes and has king beds inside big tents. **Erg Chigaga Luxury Desert Camp** (desertcampmorocco.com) has an emphasis on sustainability, with 13 large

4WDs from the Past

Those with a particular interest in desert 4WDing should stop by the **Morocco National Auto Museum** (entry Dh50). Just south of Merzouga off the N13, inside an unassuming building, hides an awesome collection of 69 pristine historic vehicles, ranging from novelty cars like peculiar double-width and half-width 4WDs, a UN vehicle from the 1940s, and classic desert cars including a 1975 CJ5 Jeep, 1972 Chevrolet Blazer and 1977 Iohr Fardier. Note that the building may appear closed but helpful locals nearby will go and find the attendant to open it up for visitors.

Left Morocco National Auto Museum
Below Sandboarding, Erg Chebbi

en-suite tents decorated with plush furnishings. It also offers a more exclusive Private Nomadic Camp experience away from the main camp with just one tent for complete isolation.

Adventurous Pursuits

Hiking, camel riding, sandboarding, quad biking and 4WDing are all possible in these parts. With numerous operators in M'Hamid and Merzouga. **Wild Morocco** (wildmorocco.com) offers nomadic-style multiday treks from the end of September until mid-April, with local guides and camel herders from around M'Hamid. Operators rent sandboards, quad bikes and dune bikes from their shops along the N13 main road through Merzouga. Note that while quad biking and dune biking are popular in Morocco's desert landscapes, there is ongoing discussion of the noise pollution and ecological damage they create. By night, explore the universe beyond – the Sahara is ripe for star and planet spotting, thanks to air with low moisture and a sky typically free of clouds and minimal light pollution. Nomads would travel at night when it was cooler and relied on star navigation for hundreds of years. Upscale camps have their own telescopes, and the **Andromeda Desert Astro Camp** (desertastrocamp.com) offers a programme of astrological events with talks from experts.

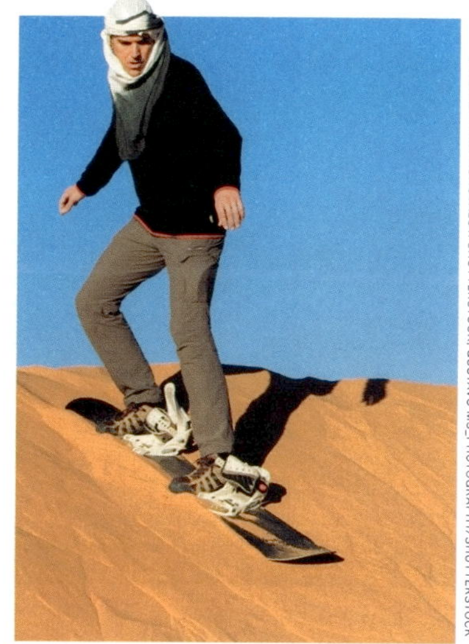

21 Mountain Views & Empty DESERT ROADS

DRIVE | SCENERY | GEOLOGY

Connecting Marrakesh with the southern oases, the 200km Tizi n'Tichka is the highest major mountain pass in North Africa. The thrilling drive through the Atlas Mountains rises to 2260m along twisting switchbacks. Staggering views lie at every turn through high-altitude villages and lush valleys.

ANIA BLAZEJEWSKA/GETTY IMAGES

Dangerous Drive?

Tizi n'Tichka (pictured) became a notorious route due to over 100 hairpin turns, high-altitude, no guardrails and a risk of falling rocks. While treacherous in extreme weather, it's now a well-paved, well-travelled route with plenty of passing spaces, and perfectly fine to drive in a 2WD most of of the time.

Trip Notes

Getting here Self-driving is the best way to experience the route and stop off to explore at will. Less confident drivers can book a driver with a car or go on a Sahara-bound tour from Marrakesh, which will cross the pass.

When to go The road is best explored in the warmer seasons of late spring, early autumn and summer. The road may close during heavy winter snowfalls.

Top tip Take your time and don't drive at night. Most of the road is well-paved and plenty wide enough for two cars to pass, but there's no lighting and sheer drops in places.

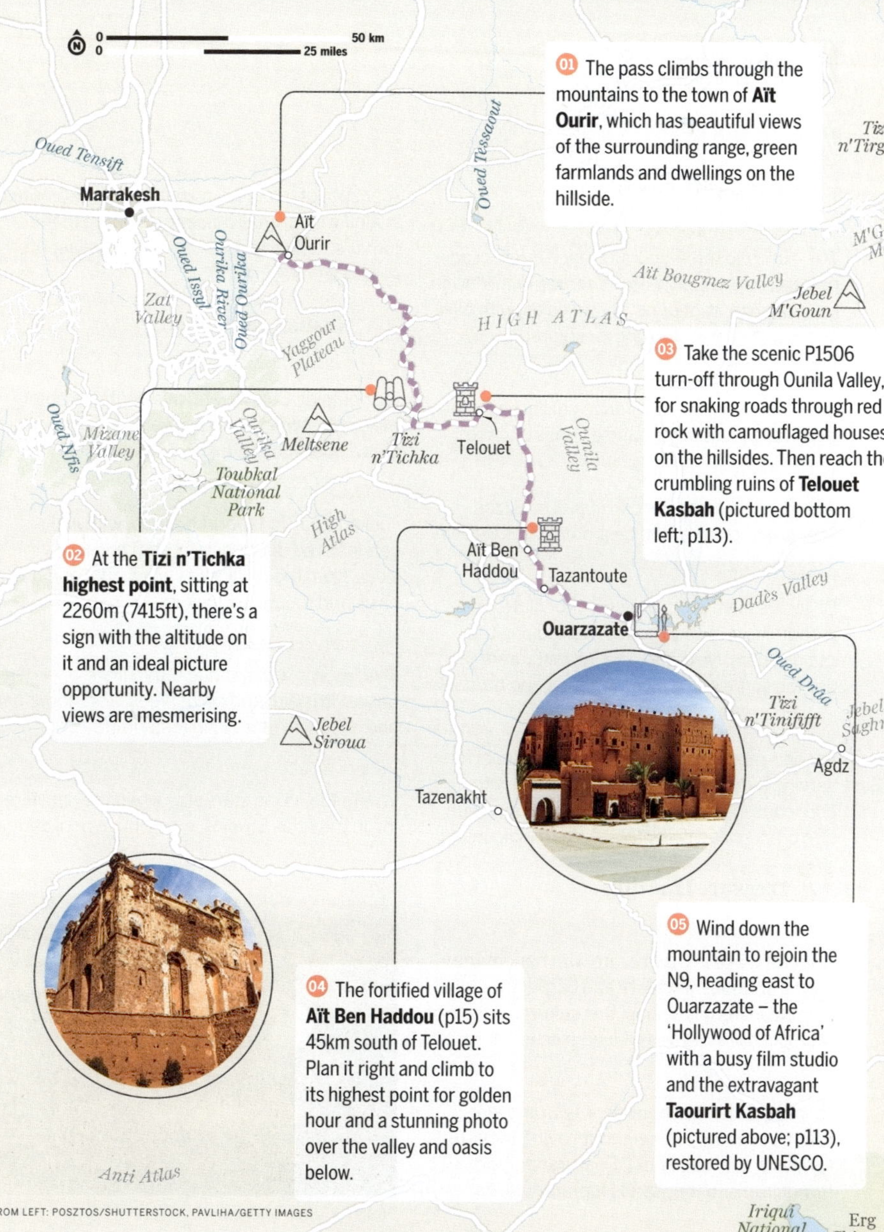

01 The pass climbs through the mountains to the town of **Aït Ourir**, which has beautiful views of the surrounding range, green farmlands and dwellings on the hillside.

02 At the **Tizi n'Tichka highest point**, sitting at 2260m (7415ft), there's a sign with the altitude on it and an ideal picture opportunity. Nearby views are mesmerising.

03 Take the scenic P1506 turn-off through Ounila Valley, for snaking roads through red rock with camouflaged houses on the hillsides. Then reach the crumbling ruins of **Telouet Kasbah** (pictured bottom left; p113).

04 The fortified village of **Aït Ben Haddou** (p15) sits 45km south of Telouet. Plan it right and climb to its highest point for golden hour and a stunning photo over the valley and oasis below.

05 Wind down the mountain to rejoin the N9, heading east to Ouarzazate – the 'Hollywood of Africa' with a busy film studio and the extravagant **Taourirt Kasbah** (pictured above; p113), restored by UNESCO.

FROM LEFT: POSZTOS/SHUTTERSTOCK, PAVLIHA/GETTY IMAGES

Listings

BEST OF THE REST

Ouarzazate Eats

Oz Palace Restaurant €€€

The exquisite three-course French/Moroccan menus change daily. Food is served in the lavish kasbah restaurant or courtyard oasis, with olive and orange trees. Booking is required.

La Kasbah des Sables €€

Dine on Moroccan and French cuisine in seductively lit lounges set around a series of patios.

The Full Sun €€

Friendly cafe for Moroccan classics, pizzas, salads and some of the best breakfasts in town.

Habous €

Delicious pastries, cupcakes, chocolate cakes, smoothies and good coffee overlooking the main square. Next door is a full restaurant under the same name serving wraps and burgers.

Wall of Fame Restaurant €€€

For an American food fix inside the Oscar Hotel, serving burgers, Moroccan-style pokē with couscous instead of rice in a dining room with film posters and collectors' items. Book ahead.

Treasure Hunting

Labyrinthe Du Sud

A secret place in Ouarzazate with handmade crafts, antiques, jewellery and carpets. As much a museum as it is a shop, this cultural archive of Moroccan life has one-of-kind pieces.

Tahiri Museum of Fossils & Minerals

Buy authentic fossils, meteorites, dinosaur teeth and gemstones without having to barter (prices are on each box). Costs range from a few dhirams to thousands for rarer pieces.

Ihmadi Trilobites Centre

A jackpot of trilobites, minerals and meteorites in Alnif with a small museum devoted to the owner's triple passions of geology, palaeontology and archaeology.

Kasbah-Style Digs

Kasbah Tamsna €€€

Just outside Ouarzazate, this boutique hotel mixes Moroccan architecture with Zen decor, plus a pool and top-notch restaurant.

Dar Kamar €€€

Tucked away in Taourirt Kasbah, with African-inspired decor, helpful staff and lovely views from the terrace of Ouarzazate and the oasis and mountains beyond.

OZ Palace Ouarzazate & SPA €€€

Tiled rooms with antique furnishings, a garden oasis with palm and citrus trees, a standout bar and a French/Moroccan restaurant.

Berber Palace €€€

Where the movie stars stay when they are filming in the Atlas Studios, with a huge pool and

TAGHLAOUIFOTOS/SHUTTERSTOCK

Desert camp, near Merzouga

kasbah-style setting, but modern bathrooms, and decorated with film memorabilia.

Relaxing Riads & Guesthouses

Dar Bergui €

This laid-back Ouarzazate city-centre guesthouse has rooms set around a pool, and a terrace with stunning Atlas views, plus home-cooked meals.

Riad Tama €€

Hidden slice of calm in an Ouarzazate residential area, with a tranquil garden centred around a pool, with an upper terrace with oasis and mountain views, plus a games room and tastefully decorated bedrooms.

Dar Farhana €€

Seven beautiful, airy and quiet rooms with tiled floors and window shutters, centred around an inner courtyard with orange trees and a pool, all hidden off a residential street in Ouarzazate.

Oasis Stays

Auberge La Terrasse des Délices €

Simple rooms are set around an interior courtyard and a panoramic terrace overlooking the oasis and offering a gorgeous view of the stars by night. Lovely handmade meals too. Located in Fint Oasis.

Auberge Tissili €

Choose from traditional Amazigh-style en-suite rooms in a building made with earth, clay, sand and wood, or atmospheric Amazigh-style tents in a quieter courtyard at this Fint Oasis retreat.

Gorge Sleeps

Kasbah Petit Nomade €€

This friendly, family-run guesthouse moments from Todra Gorge, comes with oasis views, home-cooked food and plenty of local knowledge on trails in the area.

Auberge Le Festival €€

One of the most creative guesthouses in Todra Gorge. Sleep in an atmospheric cave suite or a rock-walled, solar-powered tower room overlooking the Petit Gorge in a castle-like building with turrets.

Auberge La Vallée €€

At the entrance of Dadès Gorge and surrounded by cliffs, this is a simple but comfortable hotel. Perfect for hikers, there's a Moroccan restaurant on site, and stunning views of the oasis and rocks from many of the rooms.

Desert Camps

Tassili Luxury Desert Camp €€€

Away from the crowds and surrounded by the Erg Chebbi dunes, this is glamping at its finest, including large tents with carpets, fluffy pillows, crisp sheets and a camp lit by lanterns.

Ali & Sara's Desert Palace €€€

A husband-and-wife team created this personalised experience that stays true to Amazigh culture near Erg Chebbi. Tents are dressed with Moroccan furnishings, paintings and lighting.

Dar Tafouyte €€

Merzouga guesthouse running luxury camps with evening entertainment, tajine dinners, and cosy tents with warm showers.

Desert Candles €€€

This friendly Erg Chigaga camp is fun for all ages with super-friendly, multilingual guides.

Camp Al Koutban €€€

Wild Morocco's secluded camp is a 90-minute return hike from Erg Chigaga's tallest dune.

Erg Chigaga Luxury Desert Camp €€€

This eco-friendly deluxe camp has sumptuous tents with comfy beds, soft carpets, and experiences including camel rides, sandboarding, sand-pit baking, music sessions and more.

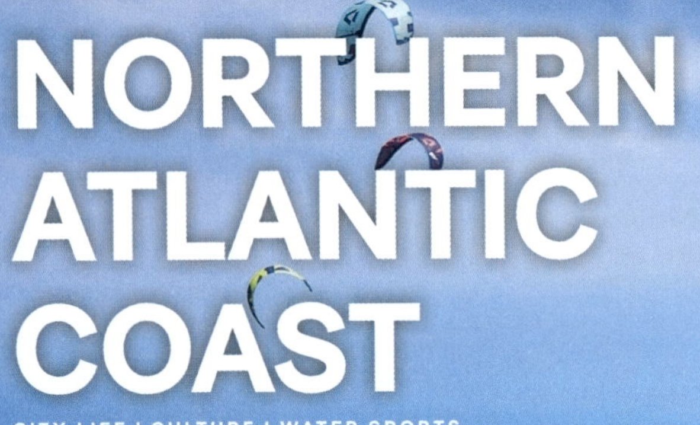

NORTHERN ATLANTIC COAST

CITY LIFE | CULTURE | WATER SPORTS

RESEARCHED BY SARAH GILBERT

NORTHERN ATLANTIC COAST
Trip Builder

This windswept coast is home to Morocco's low-key culture capital, Rabat, and its economic hub, Casablanca. Both have singular historical sights, show-stopping architecture and contemporary museums. Add in wild beaches, wildlife-rich wetlands and easy, breezy Essaouira, a surfing city with small-town vibes.

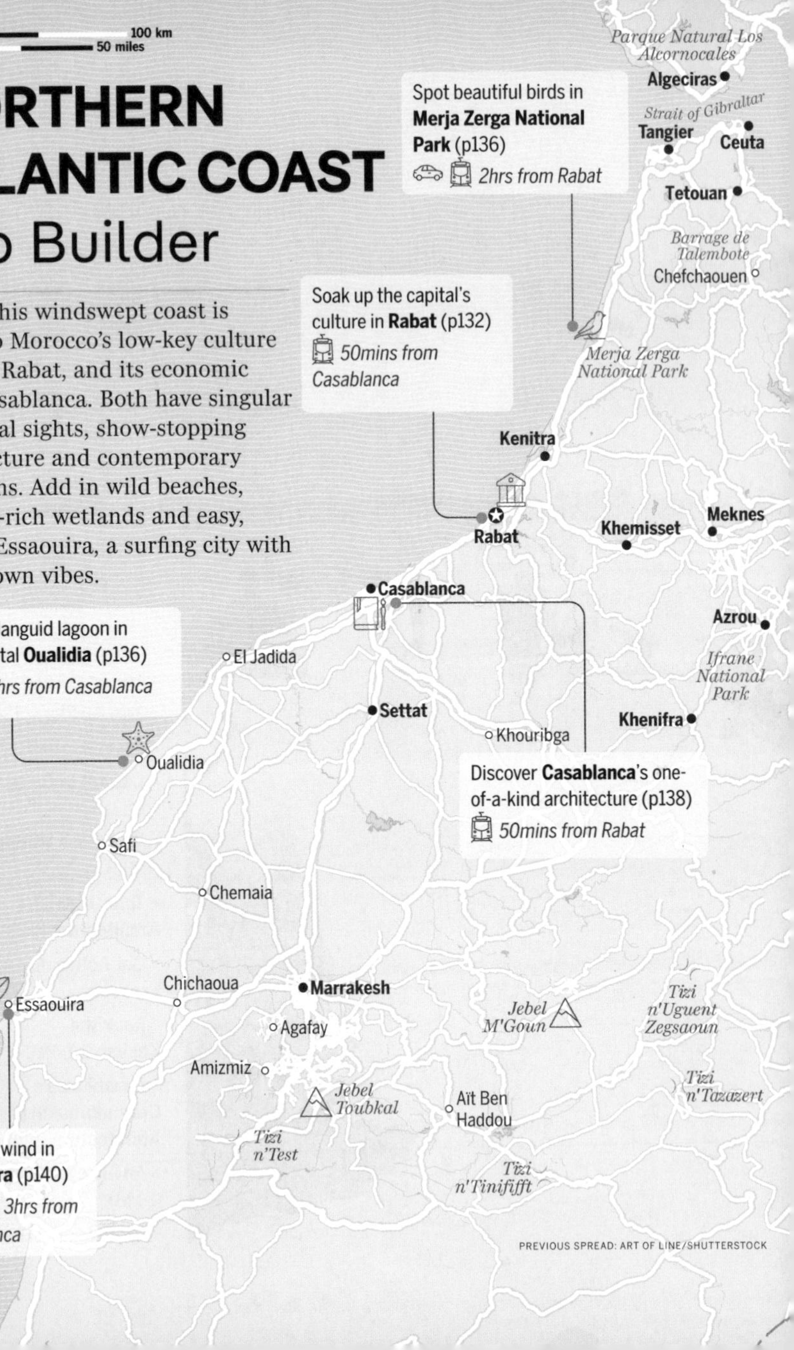
0 100 km
0 50 miles
Parque Natural Los Alcornocales
Algeciras
Strait of Gibraltar
Tangier
Ceuta
Tetouan
Barrage de Talembote
Chefchaouen
Merja Zerga National Park
Kenitra
Rabat
Khemisset
Meknes
Casablanca
Azrou
El Jadida
Ifrane National Park
Settat
Khenifra
Khouribga
Oualidia
Safi
Chemaia
Chichaoua
Marrakesh
Essaouira
Agafay
Jebel M'Goun
Tizi n'Uguent Zegsaoun
Amizmiz
Jebel Toubkal
Aït Ben Haddou
Tizi n'Tazazert
Tizi n'Test
Tizi n'Tinififft

Spot beautiful birds in **Merja Zerga National Park** (p136)
2hrs from Rabat

Soak up the capital's culture in **Rabat** (p132)
50mins from Casablanca

Relax by a languid lagoon in oyster capital **Oualidia** (p136)
2hrs from Casablanca

Discover **Casablanca**'s one-of-a-kind architecture (p138)
50mins from Rabat

Ride the wind in **Essaouira** (p140)
3hrs from Casablanca

PREVIOUS SPREAD: ART OF LINE/SHUTTERSTOCK

Practicalities

ARRIVING

Mohammed V International Airport In Casablanca; direct flights from Europe and the US.

Rabat-Salé Airport/Essaouira-Mogador Airport Budget airlines' hub.

Casa Voyageurs/Rabat Agdal Stations for Al Boraq high-speed trains.

CONNECT

The airports have free wi-fi as do most hotels and restaurants. Buy a Moroccan SIM for the cheapest phone service.

MONEY

A cheap way to cross the Bou Regreg, the river separating Rabat and Salé, is by *flouka* (wooden rowing boat) for Dh2.5.

WHERE TO STAY

Town/ Village	Need to Know
Rabat	High-end hotels are in the upscale suburbs but medina *riads* are within walking distance of the key sights.
Casablanca	Hotels in Morocco's business hub come in all shapes and sizes and can fill up quickly.
Essaouira	Relaxed seaside city with accommodation and dining to suit all budgets and tastes.

GETTING AROUND

Train Efficient train services, including the Al Boraq high-speed train, run between Rabat and Casablanca.

Bus CTM buses travel between Casablanca and Essaouira with stops in several coastal towns.

Car/taxi Take the A1 motorway or the slower but more scenic coastal road.

TOP: CASTLING SHORT/SHUTTERSTOCK
BOTTOM: CHKOUNDA FAHD/SHUTTERSTOCK

EATING & DRINKING

This stretch of the Atlantic coastline puts the focus on just-caught fish and seafood: perhaps simple, but delicious, grilled sardines; fish tajines stuffed with sea bream or octopus; or Oualidia's famous oysters (pictured top left).

Best for Moroccan fine dining The art deco Le Jasmine in Casablanca's Hôtel Le Doge (p150)

Must-try sundowners Le Rooftop at the swanky Royal Mansour Casablanca (p150)

JAN–MAR
Bright sunny days but surprisingly chilly nights

APR–JUN
Temperatures rise and music-festival season kicks-off

JUL–SEP
Beaches are packed as Moroccans escape sizzling inland cities

OCT–DEC
Fewer city visitors, and birds begin migrating to Merja Zerga National Park

22 Capital of CULTURE

HISTORY | CULTURE | ART

A contemporary capital and a historic city, Rabat has spread from its original 12th-century hilltop fortress over a walled medina, the broad boulevards of the Ville Nouvelle and expanses of golden sand. Now sensitively restored UNESCO heritage sites sit next to singular modern architecture.

OLENA TUR/SHUTTERSTOCK

How to

Getting around Rabat and its sister city Salé have their own distinct *petits taxis* but you can navigate between them by tram or *flouka* (wooden rowing boat).

When to go Spring and autumn are the best times to visit, although summer is festival season.

Cultural space The **Fondation Hiba** supports Moroccan art and culture; check out its programme, from dance to theatre and films at the restored art deco **Cinéma Renaissance**.

SCSTOCK/SHUTTERSTOCK

Where History Happened

Built by the Almohads in the 12th century, the clifftop **Kasbah des Oudaias** stands on the original *ribat*, a fortress-monastery that gave the city its name. Perched above the river and the ocean, it served as a deterrent to any would-be attackers. Rabat has since spread well beyond its impenetrable walls but its white-washed streets are ideal for idle wandering; stop off at the serene **Andalusian Gardens** and the **National Museum of Jewelry & Adornment**, before a mint-tea break at **Café des Oudayas**.

The Romans officially founded **Chellah**, a beautiful hilltop site above the fertile river plain, around the 3rd century CE. From 1154, it lay abandoned until the 14th century, when a Merinid sultan built a necropolis on top of the Roman site. An elegant minaret topped by

MOUNIR TAHA/SHUTTERSTOCK

Street Art

Every spring, the **Jidar Street Art Festival** turns Rabat into an open-air art gallery (p146), which brings 12 local and international street artists to the city to make their mark. Do your own self-guided street-art trail, or if you're here for the festival you can watch the artists at work.

Far left Andalusian Gardens
Left National Museum of Jewelry & Adornment
Above Tour Hassan (p134)

a stork's nest is all that remains of a once-impressive mosque and, behind it, the sultan's tomb, with stone carving and mosaic traces.

Royally Informed

The 44m-high **Tour Hassan** was originally part of an ambitious 12th-century Almohad project to build the world's second-largest mosque, but Sultan Yacoub Al Mansour died before it was completed. The mosque was destroyed by an earthquake in 1755, and today just this tower and a photogenic forest of shattered stone pillars stand in testament to his grand plan.

The present king's father and grandfather were laid to rest in the neighbouring marble **Mausoleum of Mohammed V**. Protected by the Moroccan Royal Guard in traditional garb, it is an exquisite example of Moroccan artisanship, decorated with colourful *zellige* (mosaic tilework), intricately carved plaster and a magnificent carved cedarwood ceiling covered in gold leaf.

Sides to the City

Discover Salé's colourful history Visit the **Great Mosque**, **Borj Adoumoue**, **Souq El Kebir**, **Souq El Ghezel** and its twice-weekly public auctions, and **Souq El Merzouk**, Morocco's largest gold jewellery market.

Cycle the city Do a private or group cycling tour with **Vélo Club Rabat**.

Learn from local artisans Join a *zellige* workshop with **Atelier Les Jeunes Artisans** and take home a tile.

Drumming under the bridge Follow the medina wall to Salé's **Bab Lamrissa** arch for drumming under the Rabat bridge, most evenings at sunset.

Jan and Rachid of **The Repose** *riad* and Salé tourist guides share their tips for exploring Rabat and Salé *@thereposeriad*

Left Borj Adoumoue, Salé
Below Mausoleum of Mohammed V, Rabat

Modern Moroccan Art

Vibrant murals decorate the walls of the flagship **Musée Mohammed VI d'Art Moderne et Contemporain**. Inside, temporary exhibitions from renowned international artists are displayed alongside a permanent display of more than 200 modern Moroccan artists, including Ahmed Yacoubi and Hassan Hajjaj. The imposing fortress rising over the Atlantic – once known as Fort Rottembourg or Borg El Kebir – has been reinvented as the **Musée National de la Photographie** and its maze of rooms displays thought-provoking images from contemporary Moroccan photographers, showcasing the country's diverse cultures.

Avant-Garde Architecture

The riverside **Théâtre Royal de Rabat**, designed by Iraqi-British architect Zaha Hadid, is due to open in 2025. The white spaceship-like structure will be one of Africa's largest theatres, with an 1800-seat theatre, a 7000-person amphitheatre and an experimental performance space. Also slated to open in 2025, the skyscraping rocket-shaped **Tour Mohammed VI** soars over the city. At 55 storeys and 250m high, it will be the third-tallest building in Africa, with out-of-this-world views from the observation deck.

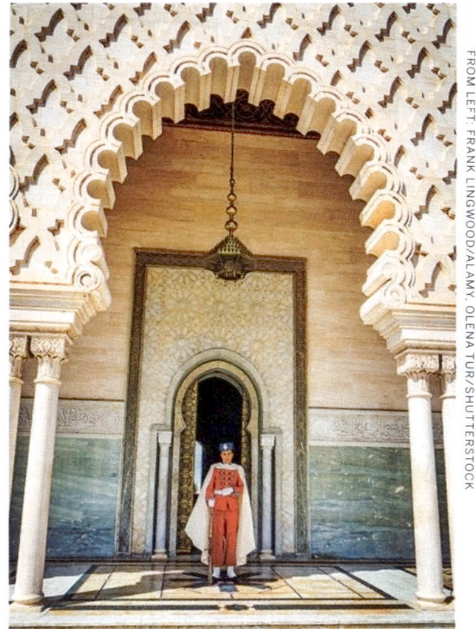

FROM LEFT: FRANK LINGWOOD/ALAMY; OLENA TUR/SHUTTERSTOCK

23 Wondrous WETLANDS

BIRDWATCHING I NATURE I NATIONAL PARK

Morocco's wild and blustery Atlantic coast is prime birdwatching territory. Near the village of Moulay Bousselham, Merja Zerga National Park is Morocco's most important wetland site for migrating birds – it attracts hundreds of species to its lagoons, marshlands and reed beds, offering shelter and sustenance as they break their journey between Europe and Africa.

YOUNES ZAKARIA/SHUTTERSTOCK

How to

Getting here Moulay Bousselham is around a 90-minute drive from Rabat. Or take a train to Kenitra, then a *grand taxi* to Moulay Bousselham.

When to go Birding is good year-round but autumn and winter are best for Merja Zerga, and spring and autumn for Oualidia; summer is peak season.

Spend the night In Moulay Bousselham, **Vila Bea** is a super-stylish beachside bolthole, or splurge at **La Sultana Oualidia**, a luxe, lagoon-side retreat.

RUSLANKPHOTO/SHUTTERSTOCK

Blue Lagoon With its expanse of golden sand and sea-coloured fishing boats bobbing in the harbour, **Moulay Bousselham** makes a perfect stopover between **Tangier** and **Rabat**. It's also the gateway to the **Merja Zerga** (Blue Lagoon), part of the 70-sq-km namesake **Merja Zerga National Park**, of which 4 sq km is water and the rest marshland, with a few villages scattered around its fringes.

More than 100 species of birds visit the lagoon, especially over winter when it can host as many as 30,000 ducks and 100,000 waders. Look out for peregrine falcons, herons, ibises and plovers; winter visitors include greater flamingos and it's the best place in Morocco to spot the marsh owl. Contact experienced birding guide, **Hassan Dalil** (0668434110), for a boat tour.

Oyster catching **Oualidia** is part delightful beach resort, part sleepy fishing village, spread around a languid crescent-shaped lagoon, fringed with golden sands and protected from the wild Atlantic surf by a natural breakwater. Morocco's oyster capital, it's home to farms that produce up to 300 tonnes of oysters annually, and its waterfront restaurants are perfect for slurping some superlative bivalves.

Its coastal wetlands, estuarine waters, salt pans and mudflats are another paradise for birdwatchers, playing host to many bird species, both native and migratory, especially in spring and autumn. You might spot egrets, terns, sandpipers and storks, bubblegum-pink flamingos breaking up their journey from Spain to Senegal, and, of course, oystercatchers.

Top left Flamingos, Oualidia
Bottom left Oysters, Oualidia

Surf & Seafood

The safe, calm waters of Oualidia's lagoon are perfect for swimming, kayaking and paddleboarding, while the wide, sandy beach on either side of the breakwater is good for kitesurfing. And it's an under-the-radar surfing hotspot, with a long-established surf camp and waves to suit both novice and experienced surfers.

In the afternoon, head to the beachfront to buy freshly harvested shellfish from whitewashed wooden shacks. Oysters, razor shells and clams are shucked as fast as you can eat them and served with a squeeze of lemon, all for a few dirhams a shell.

24 Tour Urban ARCHITECTURE

ARCHITECTURE | CULTURE | HISTORY

Anyone who says there's nothing to see in Casablanca apart from the Hassan II Mosque needs to look again. Downtown is a singular fusion of neo-Moroccan and art deco architecture, dating from the early 20th century when the city was the jewel of the French colonies. Take a guided – or self-guided – walking tour to discover this fascinating architectural and cultural heritage.

J.K2507/SHUTTERSTOCK

How to

Getting around Downtown Casablanca can be explored on foot; Quartier Habous and the Hassan II Mosque are around a 30-minute walk away but *petits taxis* are plentiful.

When to go Spring and autumn are the best times to visit, with mild weather and fewer people.

Get a guide Take a guided architecture tour with **Casamémoire** (casamemoire.org; p148) – arrange English-speaking guides well in advance. Tours are free but donations of around Dh200–500 per person are welcome.

FRANTICOO/SHUTTERSTOCK

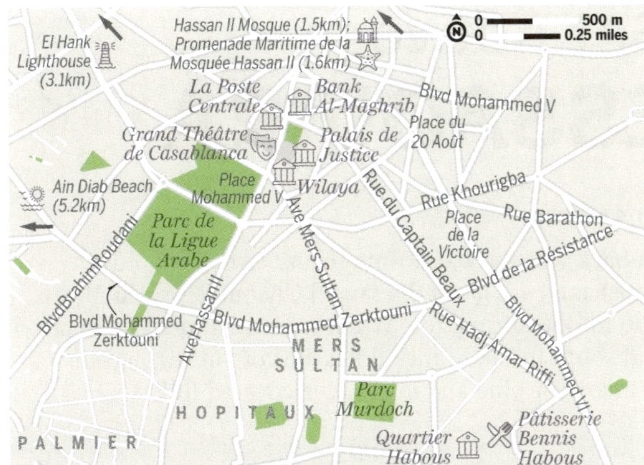

Top left Place Mohammed V
Bottom left Bank Al-Maghrib

Downtown deco Start your architectural odyssey at **Place Mohammed V**. The **Wilaya** dominates the south side, with Gothic and Islamic echoes topped by a modernist clock tower, while the **Palais de Justice** embraces neo-Moorish style. To the north, **La Poste Centrale** is resplendent in art-nouveau-style mosaics, and the **Bank Al-Maghrib** is richly decorated in carved stucco. To the west is the dazzlingly white, ultracontemporary **Grand Théâtre de Casablanca**, designed by a Pritzker Prize–winning architect.

A magnificent mosque The **Hassan II Mosque**'s 210m-tall minaret is a city landmark. Jutting over the ocean, this opulent mosque is one of the world's largest, holding up to 105,000 worshippers. It showcases the finest Moroccan artisanship and took six years to build and around 6000 master craftspeople to carve intricate designs in fragrant cedarwood from the Middle Atlas and pink granite from Agadir. The enormous doors are brass and titanium, and the lotus-shaped ablution fountains are local marble. It's one of two Moroccan mosques open to non-Muslims, with guided tours outside prayer times.

The new medina The **Quartier Habous**, or Nouvelle Medina, was built by French urban planners between 1917 and 1926 to solve a housing crisis. It combines traditional Moroccan architecture and European ideals with wide streets and covered arcades. Stop off for a sweet treat at **Pâtisserie Bennis Habous**, then shop-til-you-drop at the visitor-centric souqs for everything from slippers to shaggy rugs, aromatic spices to olives of every hue.

Casa's Coastline

Morocco's biggest metropolis has a sweet shoreline. The lovely landscaped waterfront **Promenade Maritime de la Mosquée Hassan II** between the Hassan II Mosque and the historic **El Hank Lighthouse** is perfect for an early-morning jog or a seaside stroll. At weekends, it's packed with people taking in the sea views from the oceanfront cafes and restaurants, basking in the beach resorts and promenading up and down the wide pavement. **Ain Diab** beach has a surf school – the waves may not be as impressive as Essaouira's, but they are perfect for beginners. If you are looking for bigger, more consistent swells, try **Dar Bouazza**, 30km to the south.

25 Get Active in ESSAOUIRA

WATER SPORTS I BEACHES I CULTURE

The Wind City's laid-back vibe, arty atmosphere and sweep of golden sand have long attracted musicians – it hosts the famed Gnaoua & World Music Festival – and now it's a hub for kitesurfers too. When you've explored its honey-coloured fortifications, head south to the beautiful beaches of Sidi Kaouki to horse – or camel – ride, or hike over pine and argan tree-covered hills.

CDRIN/SHUTTERSTOCK

How to

Getting around Essaouira is a walkable city and *grands taxis* make regular trips to Sidi Kaouki.

When to go Summer if you want the best kitesurfing conditions, and the rest of the year if you want to surf.

Visit the set You might recognise the ramparts of the 18th-century **Skala de la Ville**. They, along with the hulking Bastion Nord, starred as Astapor in *Game of Thrones*.

RYZHKOV OLEKSANDR/SHUTTERSTOCK

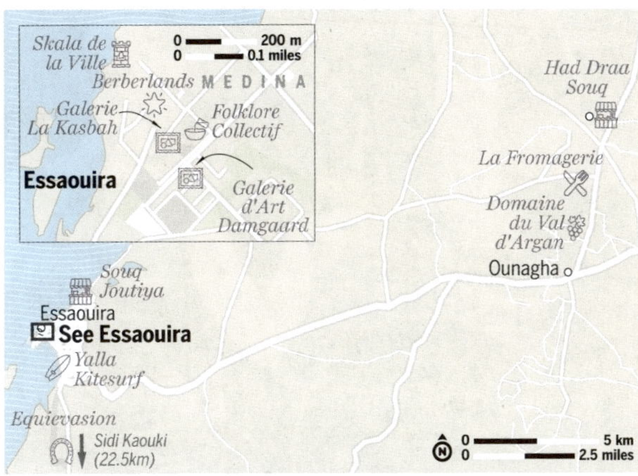

Top left Horse-riding, Essaouira
Bottom left Surfers, Essaouira

Wet and wild Essaouira and Sidi Kaouki are kitesurfing hotspots thanks to the omnipresent gusts of wind, known locally as *alizee*, or *taros* in Amazigh. It's at its breeziest in summer, with reliable winds from March to October. The same goes for wing foiling, also known as wing surfing or just winging. And Essaouira's sheltered bay is a novice surfer's dream. The swells are gentler here than the legendary breaks around Sidi Kaouki, which is ideal for intermediate and advanced wave riders, especially from September to April. **Yalla Kitesurf** has schools in both locations and a team of fun-loving, qualified instructors offering one-to-one and small-group tuition for all levels. It rents the gear too.

Cultural immersion Ride like the wind with **Equievasion**, who offer horse riding for all ages and abilities, from gentle one-hour walks to a full day galloping along the beach in Diabat, and through eucalyptus and argan forests. Experienced riders can enjoy multiday treks, camping under the stars. Encouraging authentic encounters with nature and with people, **Berberlands** leads riverside and forest hikes, with visits to basket weavers, argan-oil cooperatives and to the rural Sunday market **Had Draa Souq**. For local flavours, book a half-day private workshop with **Folklore Collectif**, where budding chefs will learn to rustle up traditional dishes – perhaps couscous, tajine or *bastilla* (a savoury-sweet pie) – while discovering more about its origins. Or try a tasting at **Domaine du Val d'Argan**, Morocco's most southernmost winery, near Ounagha, and a cheese feast at nearby **La Fromagerie**.

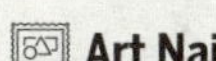

Art Naif

Essaouira has created a unique style of contemporary Moroccan art, dubbed *art naif*. Danish collector Frederic Damgaard was one of the first to bring the work of these Swiri fishermen and farmers to international attention, and serious collectors can still find monumental artworks in his namesake **Galerie d'Art Damgaard**. **Galerie La Kasbah** stocks the work of over 100 local artists with something for all tastes and budgets. And if you want to see some artists in action, head to the former industrial quarter and their makeshift studios, a row of ramshackle fishermen's huts amid the trash and treasure of **Souq Joutiya**.

26 Rock the KASBAH

MUSIC I FESTIVALS I CULTURE

All summer long, music rings out across the magical medinas – and smart suburbs – of Casablanca, Rabat and Essaouira. Expect an exquisitely eclectic line-up, from global superstars to sufi chanters and African-American jazz saxophonists. And many of the concerts are free.

XINHUA/ALAMY

How to

Getting around Essaouira's old town is made for walking, and *petits taxis* are the easiest way to get around outside the medinas of Casablanca and Rabat.

Top tip Many festivals are in peak summer holiday season, so book your accommodation well in advance.

Be a VIP Many concerts are free but to avoid the crush, splash out on a VIP ticket. Be festival-savvy and leave your valuables at home.

ELAMRI BADR/ALAMY

Rhythms of the World

Mawazine (mawazine.ma) – aka Rhythms of the World – transforms **Rabat** into an open-air stage in June, attracting around 2.5 million festival-goers and counting. This nine-day music fest features an eclectic line-up of big names from around the globe (think Elton John), with established and emerging Moroccan, Arab and African artists. It's spread over six venues, including the main stage at the OLM Souissi arena in upscale Agdal, the African stage in riverside B and the Salé beachfront stage focusing on Moroccan music. Its aim is to promote openness and respect for other cultures; inclusivity was a cornerstone of the festival when it was founded in 2001 and most concerts are still free.

Musical Heritage

Diverse cultural influences have created a mix of musical styles. Morocco's oldest musical tradition is Amazigh. Gnaoua arrived with sub-Saharan enslaved people around the 11th century, and Andalusian and Sephardic music with Spanish Muslims and Jews in the 15th century. *Chaabi* is 20th-century folk music sung in Darija.

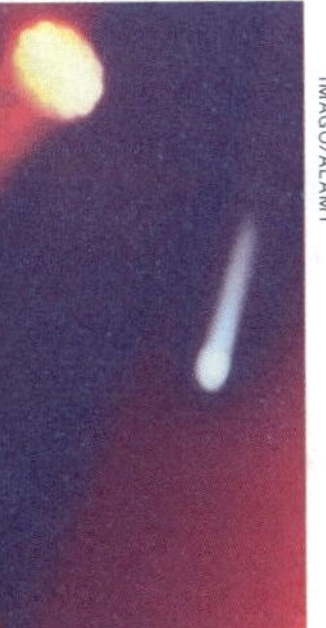

IMAGO/ALAMY

Far left Jazzablanca (p145)
Left Performer at Mawazine
Above Gnaoua music

Master Musicians

One of Morocco's most popular musical events, the feel-good **Gnaoua & World Music Festival** (festival-gnaoua.net) sees up to half-a-million people squeeze into **Essaouira** in June for three days of open-air concerts, featuring more than 400 artists from around the globe. Gnaoua is an ethnic group with a musical and spiritual traditions brought north by sub-Saharan African enslaved people in the 16th century, now on the UNESCO Intangible Cultural Heritage list. Seamlessly blending the secular and the sacred, listen out for the ritualistic chants and hypnotic rhythms on age-old instruments – perhaps *krakebs* (metallic castanets) and the lute-like *sintir* – from gnaoua *maâlems* (masters) such as Hamid El Kasri and Hamid Boussou. The festival kicks off with an energetic parade, and concerts – held around the medina and on the beach – are free.

More Atlantic Coast Music

Visa for Music, Rabat African and Middle Eastern music, with around 400 artists over four days in November.

Jazz au Chellah, Rabat Collaborations between European and Moroccan musicians in the atmospheric surrounds of Chellah.

Été des Oudayas, Rabat In the historic kasbah; everything from rap and *chaabi* to classical orchestras.

L'Boulevard Festival, Casablanca Celebrating Moroccan electronic, rock and underground performers in September.

Printemps Musical des Alizés, Essaouira A must for classical-music fans, with world-class international musicians.

Festival des Andalousies Atlantiques, Essaouira An autumn celebration of Andalusian music and dance, including flamenco.

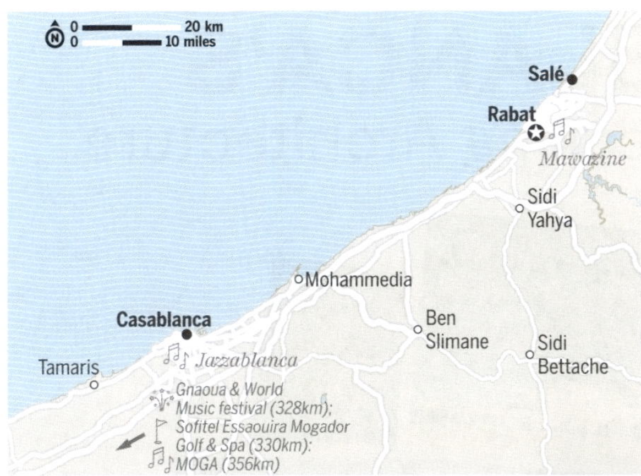

Left Jazz au Chellah, Rabat
Below Gnaoua & World Music Festival, Essaouira

Jazz It Up

In July, the White City plays host to **Jazzablanca** (jazzablanca.com). Anfa Park is home to the two main stages and the more intimate Village and can welcome 8000 festival-goers. The festival is now spread over 10 days; between the two bumper weekends, there are four evenings of two concerts, along with demonstrations of cuisine, design and fashion. It mixes up well-known and up-and-coming artists from Morocco and around the globe, and while jazz is still at the heart of the festival, everything from blues to soul and funk to fusion features on the line-up, alongside top international DJs. Come for the music and stay for the chill-out zones.

It's Electrifying

At Essaouira's boutique electronic music festival, expect five days of electrifying live performances, immersive multimedia experiences and immersion in the windy city's cultural traditions. At **MOGA**, traditional Moroccan musicians join with world-renowned DJs from the likes of Coachella, Burning Man and Tomorrowland, and there is everything from electronic sets atop the medina walls to poolside parties at the luxe **Sofitel Essaouira Mogador Golf & Spa**. **MOGA OFF** curates city-wide cultural and wellness events, from a gnaoua masterclass to DJ workshops and yoga on the beach.

FROM LEFT: ANADOLU/GETTY IMAGES, ABDELMJID RIZKOU/SHUTTERSTOCK

CASABLANCA'S
Groundbreaking Architecture

01 Hassan II Mosque
A city landmark since 1993 and one of the world's largest mosques, it's a masterpiece of Moroccan craftsmanship.

02 La Poste Centrale
Designed by Adrien Laforgue, it's fronted by arches and stone columns and decorated with shimmering art-nouveau-style tilework.

03 L'Eglise du Sacré Coeur
A striking architectural mix of art deco, Moorish and neo-Gothic styles, with twin towers that resemble minarets.

04 Wilaya
This 1930s building designed by Marius Boyer, dominates the south side of Place Mohammed V, topped with a modernist clock tower.

05 Liberty Building
This pioneering 17-storey apartment building was designed by Léonard Morandi in 1949 and was among the tallest buildings in Africa at the time.

06 Bank Al-Maghrib
The carved stucco on the facade and the ornate door with its *mashrabiya* (wooden lattice screen)-like detailing, reference traditional Moroccan architecture.

07 Cinema Rialto
Dating from 1929, one of the country's oldest and most famous cinemas was constructed on classic art deco lines.

08 AXA Assurance
This stunning example of post-independence Brutalist architecture was designed by French-Moroccan architect Jean-François Zevaco in 1977.

09 Tribunal de Premiere Instance
The stucco and tile detailing of Joseph Marrast's Courts of Justice was inspired by an Islamic *iwan* (rectangular vaulted hall).

An Alfresco Museum

SAVING CASABLANCA'S ARCHITECTURE

Downtown Casablanca is an architectural laboratory where cultures were mixed; symmetrical art deco structures rub shoulders with ornate neo-Moorish facades and sleek modernist towers. When the city's 20th-century buildings came under threat, Casamémoire was formed with a mission to save them.

Left L'Eglise du Sacré Coeur
Centre Villa des Arts
Right Immeuble et Passage Glaoui

MITZO/SHUTTERSTOCK

From 1912 to 1956, Morocco was under French rule. The first Resident-General, Hubert Lyautey, chose Casablanca as the base for a strategic port, and tasked French architect and urban planner Henri Prost to create a new city worthy of the colony's economic capital.

French Style

Prost enlisted the help of top international architects who, working alongside local craftsman, were given the freedom to develop a fusion of architectural styles. Their legacy can still be found in the city's show-stopping architecture, an innovative mix of tradition and modernity.

But by the 1990s, much of this colonial-era architecture was under threat. Buildings had fallen into disrepair and were prey to developers who demolished them to make way for uninspiring high-rises. Architectural landmarks began to vanish, including Marius Boyer's Vox Cinema – Africa's largest cinema when it opened in 1935, its bar is thought to have been the inspiration for the celluloid Rick's Café in the iconic film *Casablanca*.

Casamémoire's Creation

It was after the destruction of Boyer's Villa Mokri – a hybrid of art deco and Moroccan craftsmanship – that a group of local architects, including Rachid Andeloussi and the late Jacqueline Alluchon, realised that they had to act, and non-profit Casamémoire was formed in 1995.

Casamémoire took a multipronged approach, including making an architectural inventory of the city, publishing guidebooks, campaigning for buildings to be recognised as part of Morocco's national heritage, and offering their

HEMIS/ALAMY

HEMIS/ALAMY

expertise to would-be developers, with the ultimate goal of making Casablanca's 20th-century architecture recognised by UNESCO. They also wanted to raise awareness of the city's architectural legacy amongst locals; for many, the buildings were a reminder of a painful time in Morocco's history and belonged in the past. So, they set up annual *Journées du Patrimoine* (Heritage Days), a week-long series of events and guided tours around five very different areas of the city, giving locals – and visitors – a chance to see the links to Moroccan culture.

For many, the buildings were a reminder of a painful time in Morocco's history.

Casamémoire believes that the first step is to stop buildings being demolished, the second is to make them useful to the wider community. The art deco **Villa des Arts** was renovated by Andaloussi and reinvented as a contemporary art space championing Moroccan culture and creativity, and the neo-Gothic-meets-art-deco **L'Eglise du Sacré Coeur** is now an events space.

Daring Design

There are more recent flagship architectural projects around the city too, such as **Anfa Place**, a mixed-use oceanfront zone by the award-winning Foster + Partners, and the redesign of **Promenade Maritime de la Mosquée Hassan II**.

And the cutting-edge **CasArts** (Grand Théâtre de Casablanca) now dominates Place Mohammed V. This multiuse arts space – designed by Pritzker Prize–winning French architect Christian de Portzamparc partnered by Andaloussi – is one of the largest theatres in Africa.

A Meander Along Blvd Mohammed V

Dubbed the 'Moroccan Champs-Élysées', start at the art deco **Immeuble et Passage Glaoui**, taking in its beautifully carved plaster-work. A few doors down, the Cinema ABC sign recalls Casablanca's bygone days, as does the **Cinema Rialto**, off to the right. Back on the main drag, the **Maroc-Soir** building on the right demands attention for its neo-Moroccan exterior, complete with sculpted facades and glazed green roof tiles, while up on the left, the art nouveau **Immeuble Martinet** provides a switch up in architectural styles. An imposing facade is all that remains of the original **Hôtel Lincoln**, soon to be reborn, and across the street is French-built **Marché Central**.

Listings

BEST OF THE REST

Dining With a View

La Coupole Essaouira Beach €€

For cool beach vibes, craft cocktails and spectacular sunsets from the rooftop terrace, head to this artsy beachfront restaurant in Essaouira. The tapas are good.

No 17 at The Repose €€

Enjoy Salé views and home-cooked vegetarian dishes made with seasonal ingredients on The Repose's plant-filled roof terrace. There's a cosy salon too; nonguests should reserve ahead.

Le Cabestan €€€

Casablanca's most stylish oceanfront hangout with a Mediterranean-inspired menu and stellar sea views. Opt for just-caught fish paired with a creative cocktail.

Le Rooftop €€€

Dine on Mediterranean fare – or just grab a well-crafted cocktail – on the 23rd floor of the Royal Mansour Casablanca with 360-degree views over the White City.

Cafe Culture

Bondi Coffee Kitchen €€

A contemporary Moroccan-Australian cafe aiming to bring healthy yet delicious eating to Casablanca. Think poke bowls, prawn spaghetti, raw pressed juices and top-notch coffee.

NKOA €€

This super-cool spot in Casablanca takes its inspiration from global flavours, mixing them with Moroccan produce and European culinary techniques in creative dishes, with plenty of vegetarian options.

La Famille €€

This vegetarian Marrakesh cafe has opened an Essaouira outpost, using the same super-fresh ingredients to create dishes bursting with colour and flavour. Don't miss the chocolate cake.

For Foodies

Restaurant Khmissa €€

If the best Moroccan food is served at home, this diminutive family-run restaurant in Essaouira is the next best thing. Cash only.

Le Jasmine €€€

Step into art deco opulence in this fine-dining Moroccan restaurant in Casablanca's Hôtel Le Doge; enjoy shrimp and monkfish tajine and the honeyed Doge *bastilla*.

Taste of Casablanca

Eat like a local on street-food tours, learn to rustle up a tajine at a cooking class, or eat with a local family after a souq trip.

Local Design

Histoire des Filles

Essaouira's first concept store stocks a super-stylish mix of Moroccan and Moroccan-based designers, including Las Chicas caftans, Lalla bags, Luc Baille jewellery and Cote Bougie candles.

Minimal

At this stylish homeware store in Essaouira, pick up a shaggy raffia bag or an equally shaggy *boucharouite* rug, green-glazed pottery from Tamegroute, and contemporary silver jewellery.

Elizir Gallery

Vintage lovers could happily while away a few hours among Abdellatif's treasure trove of fabulous finds in Essaouira; perhaps a Vernor Panton lamp, long-forgotten film poster or antique Amazigh doors.

Galerie Jama

If you don't know your Beni Ourain from your *boucharouite*, visit Mustapha in Essaouira. He specialises in top-quality, vintage rugs from around the country.

Salam Atelier d'Art et d'Artisanat

Shop for iconic prints in Essaouira, such as a teapot, a palm tree or *zellige* designs, or make your own linocut at a workshop.

Le 17 Ocean

Carefully curated selection of homewares and clothing produced by Moroccan designers, from hand-tooled leather bags to raffia shoes; there's a cool on-site cafe too. Located in Rabat.

Heavenly Hammams

Azur Art & Spa

This contemporary spa offers a range of hammam-centric packages, including a gentle scrub for hammam newbies. And, being Essaouira, it combines beauty treatments with a small art gallery.

Spa Le Doge

Head to the traditional hammam of this art deco hotel in Casablanca for a soothing steam, a hearty scrub down, a clay body wrap and an argan-oil massage.

Memorable Museums

Abderrahman Slaoui Foundation Museum

This privately owned house-turned-museum in Casablanca showcases an outstanding collection of Moroccan decorative arts, from Orientalist travel posters to ornate Amazigh jewellery encrusted with semiprecious stones.

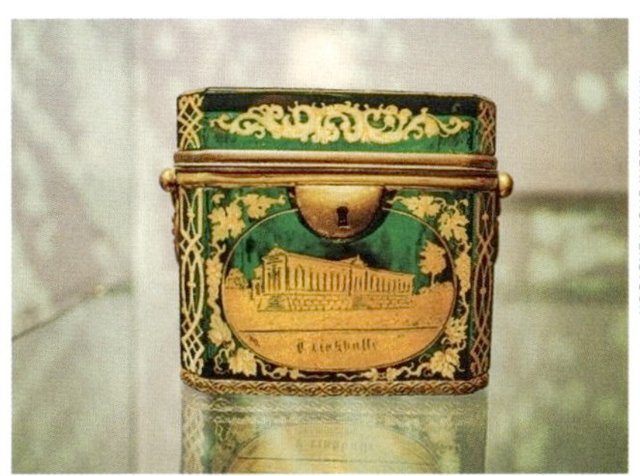

MARK GREEN/SHUTTERSTOCK

Display, Abderrahman Slaoui Foundation Museum

Museum of Moroccan Judaism

Casablanca is home to the only Jewish museum in the Arabic-speaking world. It traces the 2000-year history of Jews in Morocco, with ritual objects, ornate clothing and traditional tools on display.

Casablanca's Museum of Memory

The magnificent Villa Carl Ficke has been restored and now celebrates the White City's urban and social history from the early 20th century to present day in rotating exhibitions.

Villa des Arts

This beautifully restored art deco villa hosts contemporary Moroccan art exhibitions alongside cultural events. The garden cafe is a lovely spot for a sightseeing break.

Surf's Up

Yalla Kitesurf

This professional outfit offers kitesurfing, surfing and wing-foiling lessons and knows Essaouira's waters inside out. It operates in Sidi Kaouki too.

Rabat Surf School

Go for one-to-one tuition or small-group classes at this professional but relaxed surf hangout on Rabat's main beach.

MEDITERRANEAN COAST & THE RIF MOUNTAINS

CULTURE | BEACHES | MOUNTAINS

RESEARCHED BY SARAH GILBERT

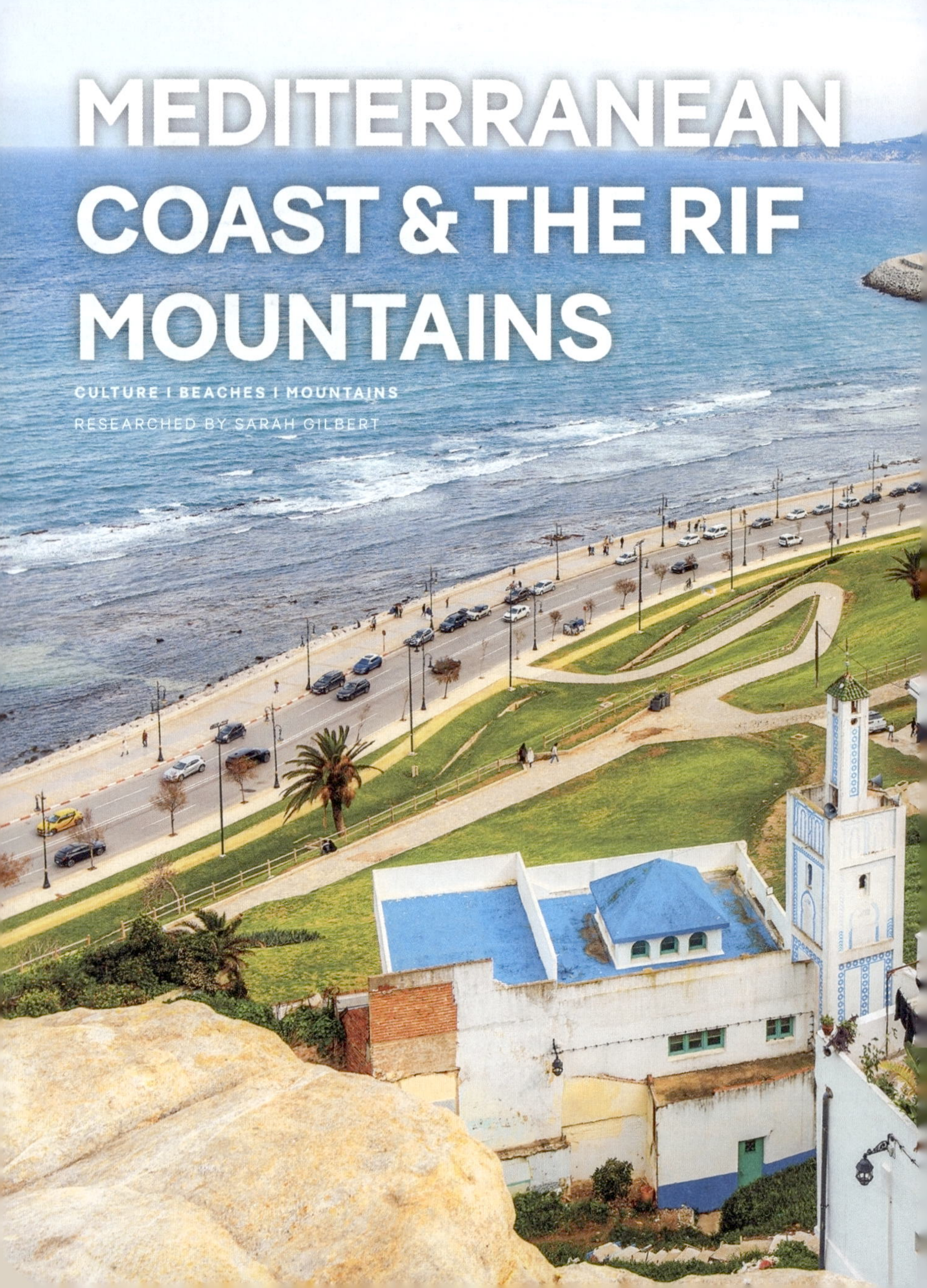

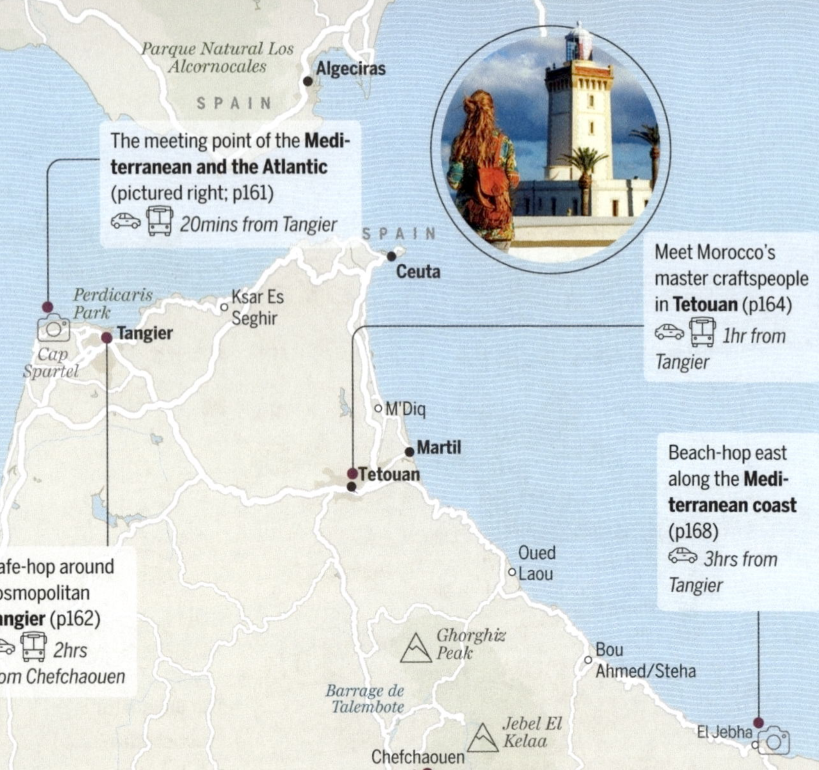

The meeting point of the **Mediterranean and the Atlantic** (pictured right; p161)
20mins from Tangier

Meet Morocco's master craftspeople in **Tetouan** (p164)
1hr from Tangier

Beach-hop east along the **Mediterranean coast** (p168)
3hrs from Tangier

Cafe-hop around cosmopolitan **Tangier** (p162)
2hrs from Chefchaouen

Get snap-happy in the blue pearl of **Chefchaouen** (p166)
1¼hrs from Tetouan

MEDITERRANEAN COAST & THE RIF MOUNTAINS

Trip Builder

Explore Tangier's cultural crossroads, the blue-hued mountain town of Chefchaouen and the crafts capital of Tetouan. All fringed by the Rif's rugged peaks and a coastline dotted with idyllic coves, lapped by the mellow waves of the Mediterranean.

MARGOUILLAT PHOTO/SHUTTERSTOCK
PREVIOUS SPREAD: SERFF79/SHUTTERSTOCK

0 50 km
0 25 miles

Practicalities

ARRIVING

Tangier Ibn Battouta Airport For Tangier and the coast.

Port de Tanger Ville For the fast ferry from Tarifa in Spain.

Tanger Ville For the high-speed train from Casablanca and Rabat.

CONNECT

The airports have free wi-fi as do most hotels and restaurants. Buy a Moroccan SIM for the cheapest phone service.

MONEY

If you're accosted by a faux guide in the medina, be firm about saying no; free tours don't exist.

WHERE TO STAY

Town/Village	Pro/Con
Tangier	Great transport links and everything from large resorts to atmospheric *riads.*
Chefchaouen	This isolated mountain town has plenty of accommodation but the medina can get crowded with day-trippers.
Tetouan	This less touristy city has fewer accommodation options.

GETTING AROUND

Bus Frequent CTM buses travel between Tangier, Tetouan and Chefchaouen.

Taxi Eight-seater *grands taxis* travel between major towns and more remote settlements when they fill up.

Car The best way to explore the Mediterranean and Atlantic coast's secluded bays and out-of-the-way national parks.

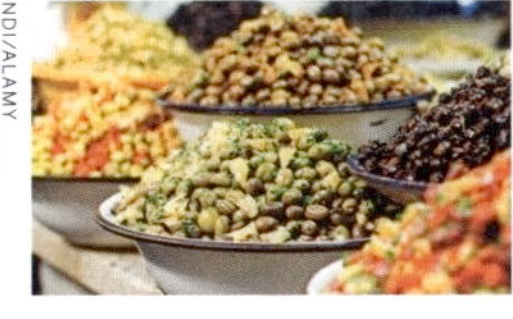

TOP: TUUL AND BRUNO MORANDI/ALAMY
BOTTOM: DP PHOTOGRAPHY/SHUTTERSTOCK

EATING & DRNKING

Invaders have left their culinary mark on the region and there's bountiful produce from Rif farms, including creamy goat's cheese and plump olives and, of course, plentiful supplies of fish. There's everything from hole-in-the-wall joints to contemporary cafes and fine-dining restaurants.

Best cocktail with a view Rooftop bar at the Hotel Nord Pinus Tanger (pictured top left; p172)
Must-try fish restaurant Tangier institution Le Saveur de Poisson (p158)

JAN–MAR
The coolest months, expect rain in January but there's sunshine ahead

APR–JUN
The temperature rises but there's always a sea breeze

JUL–SEP
The busiest period as Moroccan families flock to the coast

OCT–DEC
Mild weather, although December can be crowded and damp

A Cultural CROSSROADS

ART | DESIGN | MUSIC

Tangier is a gateway between Europe and Africa, the Atlantic and Mediterranean, and city living and coastal chilling. With a fascinating past and an exciting future, it celebrates creativity in all its forms, and there's always something new and exciting to discover.

HEMIS/ALAMY

How to

Getting here The Al Boraq high-speed train will whizz you from Casablanca in just over two hours at speeds of up to 320km/h.

When to go June to August is the busiest time with local and Spanish visitors; spring and autumn are perfect.

Houses and gardens Take a peek behind the doors of some of Tangier's mansions and discover their surprising secret gardens on a tour with **Inclusive Morocco** (inclusivemorocco.com).

HEMIS/ALAMY

Gallery-Hopping

Part of the Institute Français, **Galerie Delacroix** hosts free temporary exhibitions that are always worth a look. One of Tangier's most active contemporary spaces, **Gallery Kent** exhibits a new generation of Moroccan artists. **Zawia Tanger** is not a classic gallery but an interactive multi-disciplinary space exhibiting painting, sculpture, photography and video. If you want to get hands-on, artist Mohamed Debdoubi has opened his medina studio, **Atelier 15**, for painting and mixed-media workshops.

JACKIE ELLIS/ALAMY

Local Design

Just outside the Kasbah walls, **Kasbah Collective's** collection of clothes, jewellery and homeware sits alongside local designers. Tangier's original concept store, **Las Chicas**, showcases their own designs and promotes

A Creative City

The dynamic in Tangier is extraordinary, with a new generation of artists, creatives and entrepreneurs. The city has never been more ready to embrace such creativity, and I feel fortunate to be among the stakeholders making this shift possible.

Hicham Bouzid, Artistic Director of Think Tanger. *@thinktanger*

AMINE HOUARI

Far left Kasbah Museum of Mediterranean Cultures (p158) **Left** Ibn Battouta Museum (p158) **Above** Les Fils du Détroit (p159)

contemporary Moroccan creators. **Laure Welfling's** eponymous boutique is filled with colourful, richly embroidered clothes, alongside more affordable accessories. And it's worth checking out the quirky collection of T-shirts at **Rock da Kasbah**. In the same building, the two-room **Donkey Museum** celebrates the role of donkeys in Moroccan society.

Multicultural Museums

The **Tangier American Legation Museum** – a gift to the US from Sultan Moulay Sulayman in 1821 – is filled with interesting artefacts, including a painting by Scotsman James McBey that's been dubbed the 'Moroccan Mona Lisa'. Highlights of the **Kasbah Museum of Mediterranean Cultures** include the mosaic of Venus from Volubilis. And the Kasbah's former prison has been transformed into a contemporary Moroccan art space. In the Kasbah walls, the **Ibn Battouta Museum** is an immersive tribute to the Tangier native, whose 14th-century travels made him the greatest explorer of his

A Fishy Feast

With a historic port, eating in Tangier is all about fish. A long-standing local favourite is **Le Saveur de Poisson**. You'll probably have to queue, the tables are shared and the menu is fixed. First comes fish soup, followed by the catch of the day, olives and just-baked bread, all washed down with a mystery-juice cocktail. Or spend the day with **Blue Door Cuisine**, visit the raucous fish market and learn how to rustle up a seafood tajine. Then work off the gastronomic treats with a stroll along the city's sun-soaked seafront **Corniche** and a cocktail at **Tanja Marina Bay**.

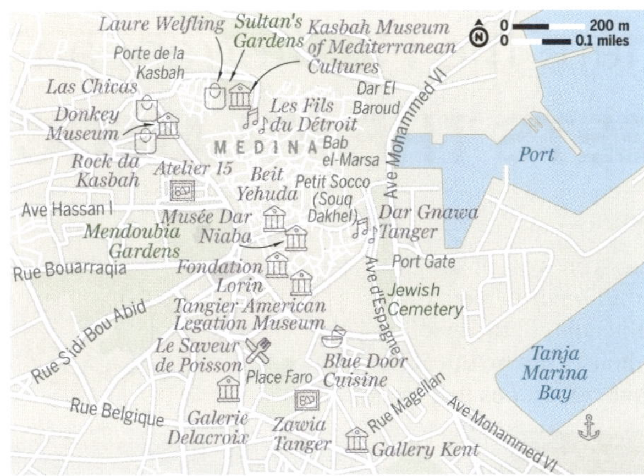

Left Fish market
Below Beit Yehuda

day. In a magnificently restored medina mansion – the office of the Sultan's head of foreign affairs pre-independence – **Musée Dar Niaba** presents a timeline of Tangier's history. Housed in an old synagogue, **Fondation Lorin** traces the history of Tangier through vintage black-and-white photographs. And the long-abandoned Assayag synagogue has been restored to its former glory and become **Beit Yehuda**, a museum preserving the city's Jewish heritage.

Rock the Kasbah

Arab-Andalusian music arrived in northern Morocco with the Muslim and Jewish refugees who fled from Andalusia in the 15th century. **Les Fils du Détroit** is a cupboard-sized venue in the medina that's popular with older musicians; pop in for a mint tea and listen to them strum ouds and beat *darboukas* (goblet drums). Music plays across the city as Tangier celebrates local and international jazz musicians at the annual **Tanjazz** festival in September. With brass bands parading through the medina and electronic after-parties, you don't have to be a jazz buff to enjoy it. And historic **Dar Gnawa Tanger** is the medina home of master musician and Tangier native, Abdellah El Gourd, showcasing the Gnawa tradition and its connection with jazz.

FROM LEFT: BRUNO M PHOTOGRAPHIE/SHUTTERSTOCK, LOIS GOBE/SHUTTERSTOCK

28 Where the Mediterranean MEETS THE ATLANTIC

BEACHES I CULTURE I HISTORY

This scenic drive takes you west of Tangier, weaving together a former billionaire's playground spread over a pine-covered headland, the meeting point of oceans at an iconic lighthouse, the mythical Caves of Hercules, golden beaches and a fabulous fish restaurant.

MEHDI EL KHATTABI/SHUTTERSTOCK

Trip Notes

Getting around Go by car or *grand taxi*. Or the 'Grotte d'Hercule' route of the City Tour Tanger bus can drop you everywhere but the beach.

When to go Beat the summer crowds and go in spring for wildflowers and autumn for mild temperatures.

Pillars of Hercules The ancient name for two promontories flanking the entrance to the Strait of Gibraltar – the Rock of Gibraltar and Ceuta's Monte Hacho.

Arty Asilah

The seaside town of Asilah, 45km south of Tangier, was founded by the Phoenicians around 1500 BCE and has been invaded by the Romans and Portuguese, among others. Now, it is invaded every summer by eclectic artists for the Cultural Moussem, who leave behind vibrant murals on the medina's whitewashed walls.

03 Where the Mediterranean meets the Atlantic, the **Cap Spartel** headland is the most northwesterly point of the African continent; its Hispano-Moorish lighthouse (pictured below) is the oldest in Morocco.

02 **Donabo Gardens** is made up of a series of small, themed botanical gardens, along with pollinators' favourite plants and a fragrant mint maze. The foliage-fringed cafe uses produce plucked on site.

05 For a leisurely lunch or sunset supper, head to the oceanfront deck of **Restaurant L'Ocean** on Plage Sidi Kacem, where seafood is the star of the Mediterranean-inspired menu.

04 The **Grottes d'Hercule** (pictured above) is where mythic hero Hercules took a well-earned rest after creating the Strait of Gibraltar. There are two caves; one has an African-continent-shaped opening for viewing the ocean.

01 The sprawling **Parc Perdicaris** (pictured far left) has sweeping ocean views and well-marked, pine-shaded trails. Visit the former villa of Ion Perdicaris, a Greek-American billionaire kidnapped by a Riffian bandit.

FROM LEFT: GILDAS_29/SHUTTERSTOCK, ALEXEY PEVNEV/SHUTTERSTOCK

29 Cafe CULTURE

CAFES I ARTS I CULTURE

Tangier's cafe culture is unlike anywhere else in Morocco, and it's full of iconic venues once favoured by spies, writers, exiles and rock stars. Moroccan cafes used to be the preserve of men, who could sit for hours nursing a mint tea; today, cafes are far more inclusive, and women won't feel out of place at these visitor-friendly spots.

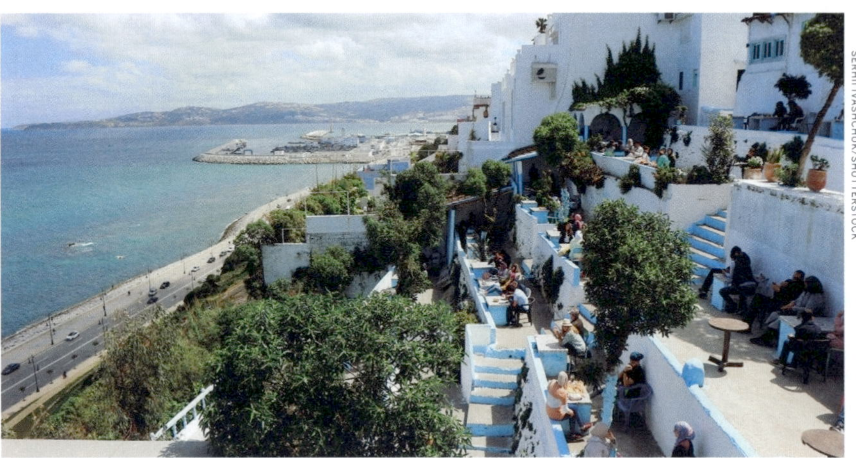

SERHII IVASHCHUK/SHUTTERSTOCK

How to

Getting around Tangier's winding medina streets and the broad avenues of the Ville Nouvelle can be explored on foot; hail a *petit taxi* to go further afield.

Cost A coffee can cost anything from Dh10 to Dh60 for a fancy frappuccino.

Coffee break Take a break from mint tea and try a *nous nous* (half half) – half milk, half espresso and traditionally served in a glass.

BRUNO M PHOTOGRAPHIE/SHUTTERSTOCK

Top left Café Hafa
Bottom left Gran Café Central

The medina Tucked down a narrow alleyway, the hole-in-the-wall **Cafe Baba** is still as smoky as when it was a favourite hangout of the Beat poets and the Rolling Stones. Opened in the 'Interzone' era, it allegedly got its name from the hippies who said 'Thank you, Baba' to the mint-tea server. Or go alfresco at the **Gran Café Central**, opened in 1813. It's prime people-watching territory, with forward-facing tables that overflow into Petit Socco. Some cafe aficionados prefer the neighbouring and equally historic Café Tingis, with its small, wrought-iron balcony.

The Ville Nouvelle Facing the Place de France, the **Gran Café de Paris** was a haunt of spies and secret agents in its heyday, and it's still a popular meeting place for international residents. Inside, the original 1920s section has retained its colonial-era feel with its studded brown leather seating; outside the line of people-watching chairs and tables almost takes over the pavement. A 10-minute walk west of Bab Kasbah, **Café Hafa** is a much-loved cafe with some of the best sea views in the city, especially at sunset. Opened in 1921, it's barely changed since the likes of William Burroughs and Paul Bowles used to lounge here. Its terraced seating still tumbles down a cliffside like a whitewashed amphitheatre, and customers here still sit and gaze over the water to Spain.

Contemporary Cafes

Alma Kitchen & Coffee Great coffee, and healthy and delicious dishes, with lots of vegetarian- and vegan-friendly options.

Las Chicas Take a shopping break in this concept store's lovely balcony cafe, serving tea, coffee and light bites.

Café de la Cinémathèque Set in the 1930s landmark Cinema Rif on the buzzy Grand Socco, this cool cafe is a hub for digital nomads.

Crumby Perfect for brunch and speciality coffee; dine inside or out on slices of cake with a Moroccan twist.

Café à l'Anglaise This cute cafe's decor reflects Tangier's mix of cultures; expect market-fresh dishes and seasonal tajines.

Recommended by **Tim McTighe**, owner of Blue Door Cuisine. *@bluedoorcuisine*

30 Meet Morocco's MASTER ARTISANS

CRAFTS I ARTS I CULTURE

Traditionally passed down from parent to child, some Moroccan crafts could soon die with the *mâalem* (master). But Tetouan's prestigious Royal Artisan School is striving to keep them alive, and on a tour with Green Olive Arts, you can meet the artisans and – with the help of your guide – talk to them in their workshops or get hands-on yourself.

ROBERTHARDING/ALAMY

ROBERTHARDING/ALAMY

How to

Getting here Tetouan is easily reached by bus and *grands taxis* from Tangier and Chefchaouen, both around 90 minutes away.

When to go Half-day Artisans of Tetouan tours (morning or afternoon) run Monday to Friday; book 48 hours ahead.

The cost Tours are Dh550 per person (two-person minimum); contact **Green Olive Arts** (greenolivearts.com) for workshop prices.

Supersized sandwich Ask your guide to recommend their favourite 'Tetouani *bocadillo* (sandwich)' haunt for lunch.

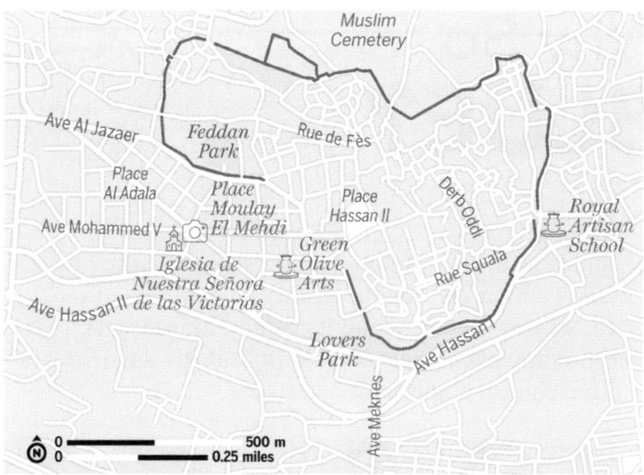

Back to school At the **Royal Artisan School** (Dar Sanaa), time-honoured Moroccan crafts, including woodcarving, ironwork, brass etching, embroidery and *zellige* tile making, have been passed down from masters to apprentices since 1919. The building itself is a work of art, its soaring courtyard a riot of painted and carved wood, ornate stucco and mosaic tiles, and filled with exquisite examples of the school's work.

You might meet Mohammed, a third-generation metal worker, or Mariam, who will show you the differences between Tetouani and Fassi (from Fez) *zellige*; or the women who teach embroidery – the only all-female class – who can explain the different techniques from Tetouan, Fez and Rabat.

Get hands-on Or you can try it yourself in a workshop at Green Olive Arts' light and airy studio. Perhaps Moroccan geometric design, known as *tastir*, which is the basis of many Moroccan crafts – including *zellige*-making – where the artisan will show you how to create intricate patterns the traditional way with just a compass, ruler and pencil.

Have fun embossing designs on leather with an array of age-old iron tools or cutting geometric and organic forms into cedarwood. You can try Arabic calligraphy, wood carving and brass engraving too. But if you want to try *s'duf* – the ancient art of inlaying wood with luminous shell and metal – you'll need to join the artisan in his workshop just outside the medina.

Top left Sculpture workshop, Royal Artisan School
Bottom left Wood painting workshop, Royal Artisan School

Spanish Style

Tetouan was the capital of the Spanish protectorate in Morocco from 1912 until 1956, and it has preserved much of its colonial-era architecture. **Place Moulay El Mehdi** (aka Plaza Primo) is a large circular plaza ringed with cafes and the unusual sight of a Catholic church, **Iglesia de Nuestra Señora de las Victorias**. Leading off the plaza, the pedestrianised Av Mohammed V is a popular place to *dar un paseo* (take a stroll) in the evenings, passing imposing buildings such as Dar Tair at its eastern end; look up to see a majestic bronze statue of a man sitting atop an eagle.

31 Why So BLUE?

CULTURE I NATURE I HIKING

Tucked into the green folds of the Rif Mountains, the beauty of the blue-washed medina of Chefchaouen – or simply Chaouen – has made it one of the most-visited cities in Morocco. As you wander along its cobblestone streets, there are Instagrammable scenes aplenty, so set off early to beat the day-trippers striking a pose down every aqua-coloured alleyway.

ECSTK22/SHUTTERSTOCK

How to

Getting here There are regular CTM buses from Tetouan (one hour) and Tangier (2½hrs), and further afield from Fez (around four hours), and Rabat and Casablanca (around seven hours).

When to go Spring and autumn are the best times to visit; try to go during the week to avoid the weekend crush.

Top tip Don't be a day-tripper. Beat the crowds by staying overnight; take a hike and relax at a hammam.

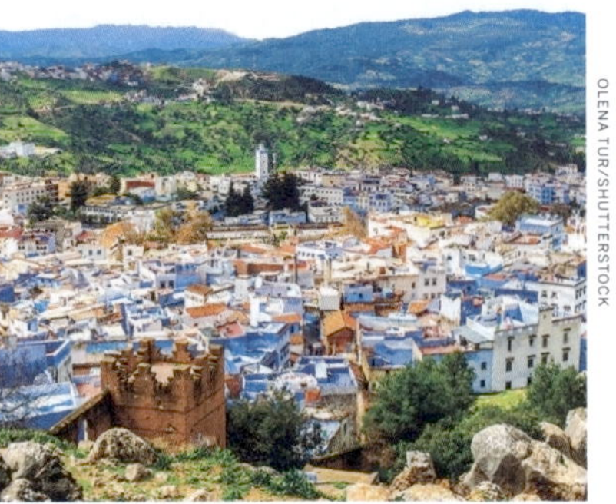

OLENA TUR/SHUTTERSTOCK

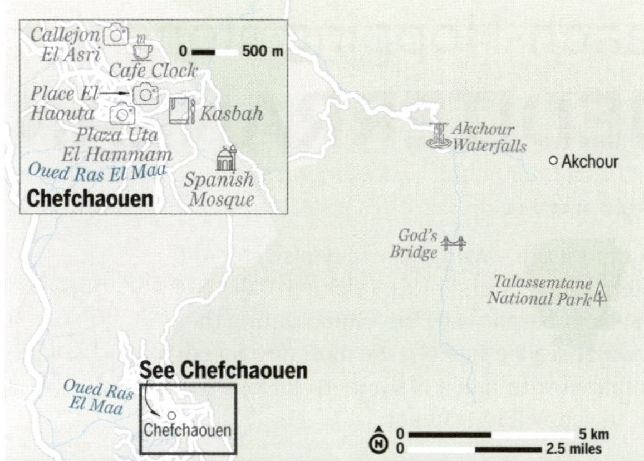

Top left Street, Chefchaouen
Bottom left View of Chefchaouen from the Spanish Mosque

Take a shot With a blue-hued staircase lined with colourful plant pots, **Callejon El Asri** is probably Chaouen's most photographed street. And picture-perfect **Place El Haouta** is a small square with a very ornate fountain and a row of cafes under Andalusian-style arches. Dubbed the **Paid Set**, an enterprising local has set up his patio ready for passing photographers. He's decorated it with hanging plants and vintage artefacts – step through the door, pay your Dh5 and take your uninterrupted shot. The **Little Blue Street** is just that: narrow blue steps flanked by blue walls leading to a blue doorway. Remember that locals live behind those doorways, so always ask permission before taking their photo; plenty of photogenic felines are willing to pose.

Take a view East of the medina, cross the bridge over the **Ras El Maa** to start the 20-minute uphill walk to the **Spanish Mosque**. The views are spectacular, but be warned, it gets crowded with sunset snappers. The 15th-century **Kasbah** looms over the buzzy **Plaza Uta El Hammam**. Climb its Portuguese Tower for sweeping views over the medina; its dusky terracotta walls are particularly photogenic at sundown. The view from **Cafe Clock**'s roof terrace is something to savour. Order from the menu or join the chef on a cooking workshop. Go souq shopping before getting hands-on in the kitchen, then sit down to enjoy the fruits of your labour.

Wild Nature

The wild and wonderful **Talassemtane National Park** is on the city's doorstep. The shimmering **Akchour Waterfalls** and the natural stone arch of **God's Bridge** are Chaouen's most popular hikes but keen hikers should stay long enough to explore more of the **Rif Mountains** with a local guide. The park's higher reaches are home to the rare and endangered Moroccan fir, as well as lush green fields of cannabis. Wildlife can be shy, including foxes and wild boars, but you might have better luck spotting the birdlife, with raptors wheeling on thermals, including golden eagles and black-shouldered kites.

32 Beach-Hopping along the MEDITERRANEAN

BEACHES I FISH FEASTS I WILD NATURE

For a truly Moroccan experience – with a short Spanish stop-off – beach-hop along the Mediterranean. From Fnideq (pictured), the N16 hugs the shoreline, curving around beaches and circumnavigating the Rif's rocky crags, with spectacular sea views. Even the most developed resorts are undiscovered compared with much of southern Europe but don't expect to have any of it to yourself in summer.

MOROCKO/SHUTTERSTOCK

Slices of Spain

Set on a peninsula jutting into the Mediterranean, thanks to historical conquest and colonial legacy, **Ceuta** has been in Spain's possession since 1668. Along with **Melilla**, 380km to the east – which became Spanish in 1497 – it's the only European territory on mainland Africa, and Morocco has been demanding its return since 1956.

Trip Notes

Getting around Car is the easiest way to explore the coast but *grands taxis* hop between towns.

When to go Try to avoid July and August, when Moroccan families descend in their droves; May and June, and September and October are less hectic.

Riffian rebel A cave near El Jebha is said to have been the hideout of Abd el-Krim, leader of a revolt against the Spanish in the 1920s.

FROM LEFT: CURIOSO.PHOTOGRAPHY/SHUTTERSTOCK, YOUNESS EL ALAMI/SHUTTERSTOCK

01 Stop off in **Ceuta** (pictured left) for a compact chunk of Spain; stately Hispanic architecture, imposing forts and historic museums, not to mention beaches, tapas bars, beer and vino.

02 Head to **Tamuda Bay** for some glitz and glam. The stretch of coastline between Fnideq and M'diq is lined with increasingly luxe resorts, but the beaches are still free.

03 Sleepy most of the year, **Oued Laou** explodes with Moroccan sun-seekers in July and August. The closest beach to Chefchaouen, its namesake river flows here from the Rif Mountains.

04 In the pocket-sized port of **El Jebha**, white cubist buildings are sheltered by mountains that tumble into the sea. Take a boat from the harbour to reach its postcard-perfect beaches.

05 If you can't decide between beach and mountains, try **Al Hoceima National Park** (pictured left). Hike and bike your way around, and take a short cruise with Rif Croisiéres for some great seabird-spotting.

Tangier's Literary Legacy

FOLLOW IN LITERARY FOOTSTEPS AROUND TANGIER

From 1924 to 1956, Tangier was an International Zone and a unique melting pot of cultures. It became a hotbed of intrigue, fabled for its hedonistic excesses, attracting intellectuals, spies and rock stars. The list of writers who sought inspiration in the city is long, including the Beat Generation.

Left Café Colon
Centre Tangier American Legation Museum (p158)
Right St Andrew's Church

GLEN BERLIN/SHUTTERSTOCK

The international spotlight first turned on Morocco's literary scene when charismatic American author Paul Bowles settled here in 1947 – soon followed by his wife Jane – where he remained until he died in 1999.

He produced four novels, more than 60 short stories and numerous musical scores. He also translated the work of several Moroccan storytellers, including Mohamed Choukri *(For Bread Alone)*, Mohammed Mrabet *(Love With a Few Hairs)* and Larbi Layachi (*A Life Full of Holes*, under the pseudonym Driss Ben Hamed Charhadi). Like much of Bowles' work, their novels are packed with sex, drugs and surprising poetry.

Bowles' first and most celebrated novel *The Sheltering Sky* (1949) was turned into a film by Bernardo Bertolucci more than 40 years later. In a cameo, he sits at a table inside the classic **Café Colon** on Rue de la Kasbah; the art deco **Cine Alcázar** opposite got a much-needed facelift for its starring role. Another of his favourite hangouts was **Gran Café Central** in the Petit Socco, the hub of the medina and the place to see and be seen.

His second novel, *Let it Come Down* (1952), tells the bleak tale of a bank clerk who gives up his humdrum job in New York and moves to Tangier during the last days of the International Zone before Moroccan independence. His new life unravels when he becomes entangled in the city's corrupt underbelly, gradually descending into a spiral of drug use, immorality and violence.

In the **Tangier American Legation Museum** (p158) – the first American public property outside the United States – the Paul Bowles Wing is filled with memorabilia,

IMAGEIMAGE/ALAMY

SAIKO3P/SHUTTERSTOCK

including first editions of his books, his musical compositions and battered leather suitcases, along with copies of the Moroccan folk music he recorded for the Library of Congress in Washington DC.

Bowles' presence in Tangier – plus its low living costs and relaxed morals – drew the attention of the Beat Generation, a post-WWII American literary counterculture movement combining engagement in worldly experiences with a quest for deeper understanding. Bowles describes many of his encounters with the Beats in his autobiography *Without Stopping*.

> The international spotlight first turned on Morocco's literary scene when charismatic American author Paul Bowles settled here in 1947.

A Beat Generation pioneer, William Burroughs, moved to Tangier in 1954. He penned his most famous novel *Naked Lunch* while holed up at the Hotel El Muniria. When poet Allen Ginsberg and author Jack Kerouac visited, they allegedly found pages of the novel scattered around his room, which they helped him organise amid a haze of hashish.

If the **Gran Café de Paris** is more famous for Jason Bourne these days, during the International Zone years – or, as Burroughs called it, the Interzone – it was a hangout for playwright Tennessee Williams and Ian Fleming, the creator of James Bond, among others. They went to Dean's Bar when they craved something stronger than mint tea. Sadly, this icon of Tangier nightlife has closed its doors; the sign has been stolen too.

A Curious Church

Consecrated in 1905, **St Andrew's Church** is one of Tangier's most charming oddities. The bell tower of this Anglican church resembles a minaret, while the interior has the Lord's Prayer in Arabic over the altar. It was painted by Matisse from his window at the **Grand Hôtel Villa de France**, and Times correspondent, Moroccan explorer and Tanjaoui socialite Walter Harris is among the international residents buried here. Legend has it that only three Christians ever visited **Chefchaouen** before 1920; one was poisoned, one stayed for an hour pretending to be a rabbi, and the other was Harris, the author of *Morocco That Was*.

Listings

BEST OF THE REST

Local Flavours

Le Salon Bleu €€

Overlooking Tangier's Kasbah and the ocean, sip on a fresh juice and choose from a menu of made-for-sharing *kemias* (Moroccan mezze), little dishes of deliciousness.

Nono Sea Taste €€€

Chef-owner Nora Larini's menu mixes up Moroccan, Mediterranean and Asian flavours to great effect, in dishes such as seafood paella and sushi. Plus, views over the Bay of Tangier.

El Morocco Club €€€

There are three venues in one in Tangier's Kasbah: a sophisticated restaurant serving Moroccan-meets-Mediterranean fare, a seductively lit piano bar, and a pretty terrace cafe.

Hotel Nord Pinus Tanger €€€

At the highest point of the Kasbah, a rooftop bar for creative cocktails and sea views paired with nibbles such as smoked almonds.

El Cielo €€

Moroccan-meets-Middle Eastern at this creative garden restaurant in Chefchouen's medina. From tajines to shish, and couscous every Friday. Reservations recommended.

Sofia €

Behind Chefchaouen's main square, this female-owned restaurant serves fresh, traditional dishes at open-air tables; don't miss the tangy *harira* soup, fluffy couscous and *pastela* rolls.

Fornaccio Coffee & Kitchen €

Escape the medina hubbub in Chefchaouen for a top-notch coffee break at this stylish cafe. And stay for breakfast or tapas with a Moroccan twist.

La Perle d'Assilah €€

A French-meets-Asian menu and daily specials showcasing the catch of the day. The two- and three-course set menus are good value.

Dar Al Maghrebia €

This small, wallet-friendly Asilah restaurant serves up tasty dishes in atmospheric surrounds, with a selection of *bastillas* , kebabs, *briouats* (stuffed pastries) and tajines.

El Reducto €€

Enjoy Moroccan and Spanish fare in this palatial restored Tetaouni *riad.* Head to the rooftop terrace for vino, tapas and stunning views.

Memorable Museums

Villa Harris Museum

The Moorish Revival–style villa of Walter Harris in Tangier houses paintings by major European artists from the early 20th century who visited Morocco, alongside modern Moroccan artists.

Dar El Oddi

This beautifully tiled *riad* has been restored and opened to the public as a cultural centre celebrating Tetouan, with vibrant artworks, vintage tourism posters, postcards and stamps.

Centro de Arte Moderno de Tetouan

This small but perfectly formed museum is set in Tetouan's striking former railway station. It displays contemporary artists, including Mohammed Drissi and Mohamed Hamri.

For Bookworms

Les Insolites

This curated bilingual bookstore and art gallery hosts interesting events. Staff are happy to offer recommendations and discuss Tanjaoui life.

Librairie des Colonnes

Opened in 1949, this Tangier institution was once the haunt of Paul Bowles, Samuel Becket and William Burroughs. There are frequent book readings and events, including author appearances.

Kiosk

The home of cultural collective Think Tanger, dedicated to promoting art and creativity in the city and beyond, with books, magazines, contemporary art prints and more.

Shop 'til You Drop

DARNA

The yellow building opposite Tangier's Grand Socco houses a craft shop and an inexpensive restaurant in a sunny courtyard, both run by Association DARNA, which helps women in need.

Madini Parfumeur

This Tangier perfume shop has been bottling scents for over a century. Rainbow-coloured jars line the walls filled with vanilla, musk, orange blossom and rose water.

Boutique Majid

Listen to Majid's tales of the Rolling Stones and other visitors to Tangier, while he shows you his wonderful collection of jewellery, antique textiles, artefacts and vintage rugs.

Topolina

French designer Isabelle Topolina's beautifully tailored, one-of-a-kind pieces are crafted from recycled and upcycled vintage finds and fabrics from sub-Saharan Africa. The store is located in Tangier.

La Botica de la Abuela Aladdin

This sweet-smelling Chefchaouen store is a riot of colour. The owner makes soaps, lotions and solid perfumes by hand from vegan-friendly, all-natural ingredients.

SERFF79/SHUTTERSTOCK

Centro de Arte Moderno de Tetouan

Heavenly Hammams

La Tangerina

This Kasbah *riad* boasts a beautiful traditional hammam, with vaulted arches and mosaic-tiled walls. Open to nonguests.

Hotel Riad Cherifa

Have the pretty blue-tiled hammam at this Chefchaouen *riad* to yourself as you're steamed, exfoliated and massaged with essential oils. Couples can book a DIY session too.

Art House

Galerie Conil

This long-established gallery has three locations in the medina – one in the Kasbah and two close to the Petit Socco – exhibiting the work of contemporary painters and sculptors.

Fondation Pour la Photographie

It's worth taking a taxi to this small photography museum, set in a beautiful villa in an upscale Tangier neighbourhood. Interesting exhibitions, a small shop and helpful staff.

FEZ

LABYRINTHINE STREETS | SOUQS | ANCIENT ATMOSPHERE

RESEARCHED BY TARA STEVENS

FEZ
Trip Builder

Lose yourself in a labyrinth of alleys where artisans hammer copper, dyers soak wool and weavers' shuttles clatter behind half-open doors. Spices scent the air as the call to prayer drifts from multiple minarets, and *riad* (traditional house built around a garden) courtyards beckon with mint tea and stillness.

Feast on traditional **medina** foods and savour the flavours of Fez (p178)
2hrs from Bab Bou Jeloud

Marvel at the intricate Islamic artistry of **Medersa El Attarine** (p192)
10mins from Bab R'Cif

Roam the medieval lanes of the **medina** (pictured above; Fez El Bali) in search of artisanal treasures (p182)
1hr from Bab Bou Jeloud

Wander the **Mellah**'s (pictured right) historic streets and uncover Fez's Jewish heritage (p190)
1hr from Bab Semmarine

Sink into the steam of a hammam, or soak in a natural hot spring at **Sidi Harazem** (p185)
30mins from Fez El Bali

Practicalities

ARRIVING

Fès–Saïss Airport The airport is 17km south of the city centre; *grands taxis* to the medina (30 minutes) cost Dh150–200, or take Bus 16 to Gare de Fès (40 minutes; Dh5).

CONNECT

Wi-fi is widely available in hotels, cafes and *riads*. SIM cards from Orange, Maroc Telecom or Inwi are cheap and reliable.

MONEY

Carry small notes for taxis, tips and medina purchases. Cards are accepted in most hotels and many restaurants, but cash remains king.

WHERE TO STAY

Neighbourhood	Pro/Con
Fez El Bali	Grand *riads* and hidden courtyards in the heart of the medina maze.
Batha	Near the medina, with mid-range hotels and traditional guesthouses.
Fez El Jdid	Limited places to stay, but a more undiscovered feel.
Ville Nouvelle	Modern hotels on wide, leafy boulevards with a thriving cafe culture.

GETTING AROUND

Walk the medina The only way to explore the medina (Fez El Bali) is on foot – vehicles can't enter its web of alleys. Bring sturdy shoes and expect to get lost; that's part of the experience.

Petits taxis Red petits taxis serve areas around the medina. Insist on the meter (fares start at Dh10), as some drivers try to overcharge tourists.

TOP: GLEN BERLIN/SHUTTERSTOCK
BOTTOM: EKATERINA POKROVSKY/SHUTTERSTOCK

EATING & DRINKING

Fez is Morocco's culinary heart, where age-old recipes thrive in bustling family-run canteens, as well as palatial *riad* restaurants. Try breakfast *bissara* (pictured top left; fava-bean and garlic soup) and street food in the souqs. Climb steep stairs to rooftop terraces for tea. Snag a round of *khobz* (fresh bread) and fresh cheese in the produce market at R'Cif for an impromptu picnic.

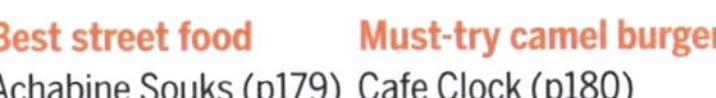

Best street food
Achabine Souks (p179)

Must-try camel burger
Cafe Clock (p180)

MAR–MAY
Warm, breezy days – perfect for medina mooching and mountain rambles

JUN–AUG
Searing heat (40°C+) empties the streets; evenings are balmy and festive

SEP–NOV
Cooler, with golden light – lovely for sightseeing

DEC–FEB
Crisp mornings, occasional rain – quieter and great for cosy *riad* relaxing

33 Fez on A PLATE

STREET FOOD I LOCAL LIFE I FEAST

Fez is a city that you taste as much as you see. Among its rambunctious souqs you'll find sizzling grills, steaming cauldrons and hole-in-the-wall fry shops that reveal the soul of Morocco one bite at a time. Come hungry, leave inspired.

JOSE HERNANDEZ CAMERA 51/SHUTTERSTOCK

How to

Getting here/around Fez's street-food stalls come to life around noon. Walking is ideal for the medina, but taxis are perfect for zipping back and forth to the Ville Nouvelle.

Food tour A Traditional Foods of the Fez medina tour (@fezguidedtours, from Dh400 per person) reveals lip-smacking local delicacies.

Taste the Ville Nouvelle Combine cold beers with street treats like **Cyrnos'** legendary *maakouda* (crispy fried potato cakes).

JANNICK TESSIER/GETTY IMAGES

Savouring Street Food

The **Achabine Souks** hum with the clang of metal ladles against steaming pots, the hiss of meat hitting hot grills, and the rhythmic slap of a giant wooden paddle in a cauldron of hot *bissara*. Spices perfume the air – cumin, cinnamon, paprika – mingling with the unmistakable scent of smoke from wood-fired ovens. In the produce market near Place R'Cif, a stallholder slices open a freshly grilled, stuffed camel spleen, before stuffing it into hot *khobz* (bread) – rich, smoky and adored by locals. Elsewhere, skewers of lamb and liver brochettes char over glowing coals, their juices dripping onto the flames. Then there are the sweet things: flaky *m'hanncha* (marzipan stuffed coils), sticky *chebakia* (sesame knots dripping in honey) and crisp *faqas,* the Moroccan answer to biscotti,

M REEL/SHUTTERSTOCK

Fez's Flower Waters

Every spring, as orange blossoms and rose petals fill the markets, copper stills begin their journey through Fez's neighbourhoods. Rented by home cooks, they spend a day or two in each house, distilling fragrant flower waters drop by drop – a centuries-old ritual that infuses traditional cakes and pastries with the scent of spring.

Far left Spices for sale in a souq
Left *Khobz* (bread)
Above *Chebakia* (sesame knots dripping in honey)

made to be dipped into tiny glasses of fiercely strong coffee and syrupy mint tea.

Digging in at Moroccan Canteens

Within the riotous symphony of smells and movement, unmarked doorways – often with a grill or stack of tajines outside – lead to simple, bustling canteens where Fez's workers fuel up on home-style cooking. Inside, the air is warm with the scent of slow-cooked beans, stewed lentils, smoky fried aubergine and peppers, or chips, on cheap china plates, always with plentiful rounds of crusty *khobz*. A bubbling tajine of beef and prunes arrives at the table, the meat soft enough to cut with a spoon, its sauce thick with caramelised onions and fragrant with cinnamon. Next to it, golden fried sardines, marinated in a rich chermoula sauce, are tossed onto a plate, crunchy and hot from the oil. The pace is fast, the chatter constant, the food as reassuring as coming home.

Cooking Fez: Four Ways to Learn

Courtyard Kitchen Fez A fresh take on Moroccan cuisine, with a focus on vibrant, vegetarian-friendly dishes.

Cafe Clock Explore Moroccan baking and patisserie, from honey-soaked pastries to fluffy *msemen* pancakes. A hands-on class with a sweet reward.

Riad Anata An intimate, traditional cooking experience where you'll learn classic recipes in a cosy *riad* setting. Ideal for home cooks seeking authenticity.

Palais Amani A lively, social class for those who love to cook and share. Join a group, learn Moroccan classics and feast together in a grand setting.

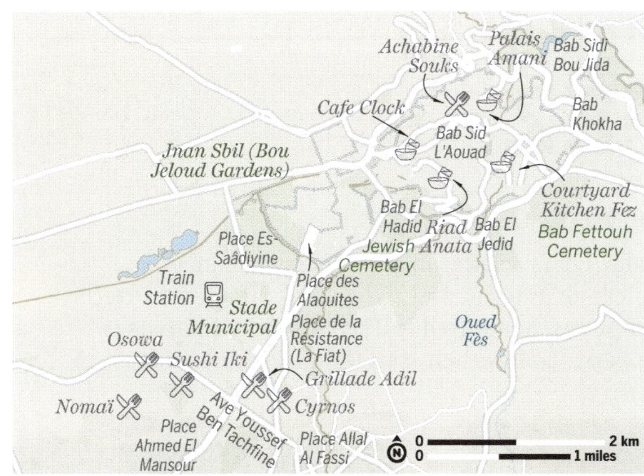

Chic Dining in the Ville Nouvelle

The medina may be all spice and smoke, but the Ville Nouvelle tells another story. Here, lamb kebabs, like those at **Grillade Adil**, are served on leafy pavement terraces, juxtaposed by a burgeoning international scene that stretches far beyond Morocco. In the Champs de Course neighbourhood, minimalist **Sushi Iki** chefs press slabs of pink tuna onto perfect pillows of rice and craft *chawanmushi* (Japanese egg custard) from black sesame seeds. Nearby, **Osowa** dishes up Korean fried chicken, lacquered in a variety of sticky glazes and served with pots of fiery kimchi, and **Nomaï** serves crunchy panko prawns and the best pizza in town. This is the Fez that hip young Moroccans escape to when they want a break from tradition; where a cold beer can be claimed from any number of bars hidden behind blacked-out windows around Boulevard Mohammed V, and a steak-frites dinner feels as natural as a tajine. It's not the Morocco of postcards and cliches, but a critical part of the city's evolving palate – a reflection of Fez as it is now, as much as it has ever been.

Left *Msemen*
Below Making the most of seasonal produce at the Courtyard Kitchen Fez

FROM LEFT: BARTOSZ LUCZAK/SHUTTERSTOCK, CAMILLA LINDQVIST/THE COURTYARD KITCHEN

34 Makers of FEZ

WEAVING | ARTISANSHIP | HERITAGE

Fez is a city of artisans. Looms clatter in tiny workshops, metal is hammered into exquisite pierced lanterns, and *zellige* tiles are pieced together like intricate puzzles. In the souqs, hand-dyed leather is stitched into bags and *babouches* (leather slippers). Follow their trail for a tactile connection to Moroccan heritage and artistry.

JOE DORDO BRNOBIC/SHUTTERSTOCK

How to

Getting around Exploring Fez's artisan workshops means walking.

When to go Spring and autumn offer the best weather for exploring Fez's workshops. Early mornings or late afternoons help avoid the busiest medina crowds.

Hidden gem Seek out Fez's last traditional brocade maker, where shimmering silk and gold-threaded fabrics are still woven by hand.

Scavenger Hunt A playful, insightful, self-guided tour to uncover Fez's artisanship (p193).

BZ TRAVEL/SHUTTERSTOCK

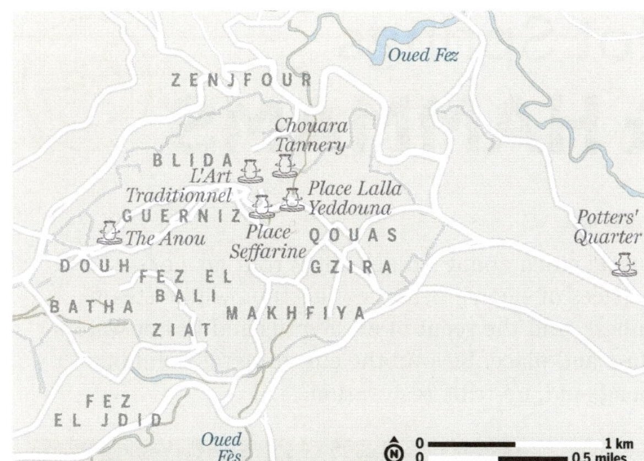

Top left Chouara Tannery
Bottom left Place Seffarine

Threads of Fez In quiet workshops across the medina, looms clatter as wool and cotton twist into carpets, blankets and hammam towels. At **The Anou**, women artisans pass down techniques that have shaped Moroccan textiles for centuries, artfully connecting past and present, craft and creativity.

Beating metal into light In the glow of workshop doorways **Place Seffarine** skilled workers chisel delicate patterns into brass and copper lanterns and cookware, their hands guiding each cut with practised precision. Visit the workshop where the finest mosque doors and palace lanterns are made through **L'Art Traditionnel**.

Shaping earth into art Beyond the medina walls, in the **potters' quarter** of Ain Noqbi, artisans form the *zellige* tiles and pottery that define Moroccan interior design. Clay is pressed, carved and fired, each tile cut by hand before being arranged into elaborate geometric mosaics. Watching the process is hypnotic, as clay slowly transforms into objects of beauty.

Handcrafting leather Beyond the dye pits of the **Chouara Tannery**, where skins are soaked in vats of saffron and pomegranate bark, leather artisans work in tucked-away workshops, turning butter-soft hides into belts, bags and *babouches* as craftspeople stitch, emboss and cut, shaping pieces that carry the spirit of Fez far beyond its walls.

The Last Brocade Master of Fez

On the edge of the **Place Lalla Yeddouna** artisans complex (worth a wander architecturally, though largely empty of artisans), the last of Fez's brocade makers, Abdelkader Ouazzani, sits at his loom, hands moving with practised precision as he creates textiles once prized by sultans – each metre of his brocade takes days to complete. The technique relies on a complex system of foot pedals and wooden punch cards, guiding each shimmering thread into place. Once central to Fez's textile heritage, this fading art offers a rare glimpse into a past where royal robes and palace drapes were crafted by hand.

35 Hot Springs & HAMMAMS

BATHING | ARCHITECTURE | RITUAL

Bathing in Morocco is as much about ritual, as it is routine. Fez's hammams have long been spaces of cleansing and connection, where steam curls through vaulted chambers, and the scent of eucalyptus and flower waters transport you to another time and place. Beyond the city, mineral-rich hot springs draw locals seeking age-old, no-frills restoration.

RIAD DAR BENSOUDA

How to

Getting here/around *Riad* hammams in the medina are easily walkable. A *petit taxi* can drop you in the Ville Nouvelle. A *grand taxi* is needed for the hot springs at **Sidi Harazem**.

When to go Mornings and weekdays are quietest at the hot springs.

What it costs Expect to pay upwards of Dh350 for a *riad* hammam, Dh150 for a middle-class public hammam, and Dh50 at the hot springs.

MOUNIR TAHA/SHUTTERSTOCK

The ritual A traditional Moroccan hammam experience unfolds in stages, each designed to soften, cleanse and revive. It begins in a steam-filled chamber, where the heat loosens muscles and opens pores. A generous lathering of black soap – an olive-based paste rich in vitamin E – follows, preparing the skin for the next step.

The scrub Enter the *kessa*, a coarse glove wielded by the *kessala* (attendant) to slough away layers of dead skin. Bring your own *kessa* for exfoliation – local shops sell them cheaply. The *gommage* (scrub) is vigorous, revealing baby-soft skin beneath. At higher-end hammams, the treatment may continue with a mineral-rich *ghassoul* (clay mask) to draw out impurities. Some add a final touch – rose- or orange-blossom-infused water, poured over the hair in slow, perfumed cascades.

The destinations For a private hammam in a *riad* setting, **Riad Laaroussa**, **Dar Bensouda** and **Karawan Riad** offer indulgent experiences steeped in history. In the Ville Nouvelle, **Nausikaa** is a marble-clad communal hammam, and **Narcisse** (women only) is popular with well-heeled Moroccans who prefer a little privacy. Beyond Fez, the magnesium-rich waters of **Sidi Harazem** were once bottled and sold across Morocco. Facilities are basic, but it offers an unvarnished, communal experience in a setting that feels unchanged by time.

The extras Massages, ranging from deep tissue to Argan-oil-infused relaxation, are available at many hammams.

Top left Dar Bensouda *riad*
Bottom left Sidi Harazem

Sidi Harazem: A Brutalist Bathing Legacy

The mineral-rich hot springs at **Sidi Harazem** bubble up beyond a striking 1960s brutalist complex designed by French-Moroccan architect Jean-François Zevaco. Built as part of a Moroccan Railways (ONCF) workers' holiday resort, complete with a small souq and a handful of simple restaurants (all still operational), its concrete arches and geometric forms now stand weathered by time. Locals gather here to soak in the magnesium-rich waters, believed to ease joint pain and aid digestion. The hotel remains open, and though its grounds and circular pool have pretty much abandoned to nature, it's a fascinating dose of architectural nostalgia nevertheless.

36 Hiking Mt ZALAGH

ANCIENT TRAILS | VIEWS | ECOTOURISM

A 20-minute drive north from Fez, Mt Zalagh's rocky slopes, olive groves and shepherd trails offer a peaceful escape. Stony paths wind through sleepy hamlets where panoramic views stretch from the Middle Atlas to the Rif – a welcome breath of fresh air from the rather more chaotic medina, and a glimpse of the rural rhythms beyond the city walls.

DRISS FILA/SHUTTERSTOCK

How to

Getting here/around You can get to the trailhead at Cafe Coursica by *petit taxi*, but it's best to go with a guide for navigating the trails. Day trips further afield to Moulay Yacoub and Immouzer require a *grand taxi*.

When to go Spring and autumn offer mild temperatures and clear views. Cooler air in winter sharpens the horizon, making for dramatic panoramas.

What it costs Full-day €100 (Dh1052), half day €60 (Dh631). Prices include transport and guiding.

JULIAN SCHALDACH/SHUTTERSTOCK

A Hike into Old Morocco

Certified mountain guide Soufiane Hamani is the founder of **The Green Caravan**, an ecotourism cooperative that explores Morocco's natural landscapes with a special focus on the Fez prefecture. You can ascend Mt Zalagh with a guided hike with Hamani.

Mt Zalagh rises to 832m above the old city, its slopes a patchwork of olive groves, thorny acacia, dry-stone terraces and pockets of wild *doum* palms, their fronds harvested for weaving baskets, hats and brooms. Here, life slows to a snail's pace, where shepherds herd their flocks along dirt tracks and subsistence farming still shapes daily life and feeds the city's markets.

Caravan roads and vantage points From the ridge, the landscape opens in all directions. The Middle Atlas spreads south, while on clear days, the Rif Mountains rise faintly to the north. From here the entire Fez region unfolds, with tarmacked roads following the faint scars of old caravan routes that once linked Fez to the great trade hubs of the Sahara and beyond. Traders arrived here with silks, spices and gold, pausing before continuing to the Atlantic and Mediterranean coasts.

Space, silence and the wind at your back A steep, rocky climb leads to the summit, where birds of prey circle on the thermals. Far from the medina's frenetic energy, it's ideal for stringing a hammock and brewing a pot of hot tea, before ambling back downhill.

Top left Mt Zalagh
Bottom left Barbary macaque, Ifrane National Park

Best One-Day Hikes from Fez

Ifrane National Park A scenic hike through ancient cedar forests, home to Barbary macaques and rare birdlife. Trails wind past Lake Iffer and the Ramsar-protected Lake Afennourir. Altitudes from 1500m to 2200m.

Skoura M'Daz A flexible hike (8km to 20km) through green fields, waterfalls and Amazigh villages. Includes lunch in a traditional Amazigh home.

Tichoukt Massif A challenging climb to Tichoukt Summit (2790m) – the highest in the region – that rewards with sensational, desert-like mountain views. Starting from Oum Gniba, it's perfect for seasoned hikers.

Recommended by Soufiane Hamani, *founder of The Green Caravan @hmn.coufiane, @the.green.caravan*

Traditional
FEZ CRAFTS

01

02

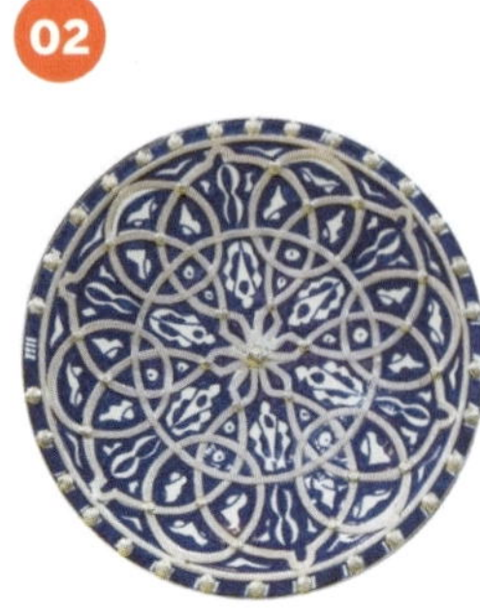

03

04

05

01 Amazigh Rugs
Handwoven on wooden looms, these brightly coloured rugs blend bold Amazigh motifs with centuries-old weaving traditions.

02 Pottery
Fez's signature blue-and-white ceramics, crafted from local clay, are hand-painted with delicate arabesques and geometric patterns.

03 Leather
Tanned using ancient techniques, Fez's supple leather bags and jackets blend durability with the city's long-standing artisanal tradition

04 Zellige
Precision-cut glazed tiles form intricate geometric mosaics, a hallmark of Fassi (from Fez) artisanship seen in mosques, fountains and courtyards.

05 Hammam Buckets
Hewn from cedar, these traditional buckets hold scented water for the ritual of purification in Moroccan hammams.

06 Babouche
Soft leather slippers, traditionally dyed yellow, crafted in Fez's

tanneries and worn across Morocco for generations.

07 Copper Tajines
Beaten into shape by hand, these gleaming tajines retain heat, perfect for slow-cooked Moroccan stews.

08 Wood Carving
Cedarwood panels, doors and furniture featuring intricate geometric and floral designs.

09 Stucco Plasterwork
Ornate, hand-carved plaster designs decorating *riads,* mosques and *medersas* (Quranic schools).

10 Bone Accessories
Inlay work on serving spoons, decorative hair combs, and brooches using camel bone and horn.

01 ANDREA CHIOZZI/SHUTTERSTOCK, **02** TWABIAN/SHUTTERSTOCK, **03** GEORGIOS TSICHLIS/ SHUTTERSTOCK, **04** THE-FANCY-DESIGN-STOCK/SHUTTERSTOCK, **05** LORA LIU / SHUTTERSTOCK, **06** STEVEPHOTOS/SHUTTERSTOCK, **07** ROSA FREI/SHUTTERSTOCK, **08** ANGELA N PERRYMAN/SHUTTERSTOCK, **09** SVETLANASF/ SHUTTERSTOCK, **10** HEMIS/ALAMY, **ENVELOPE** MADDYZ/SHUTTERSTOCK, **POSTCARD** JOINTSTAR/SHUTTERSTOCK

Jewish Morocco

TRACING A CENTURIES-OLD JEWISH LEGACY

For centuries, Fez was home to one of Morocco's most influential Jewish communities. Its Mellah (Jewish quarter) still holds echoes of this once-thriving world, from grand synagogues to crumbling balconies overlooking the neighbourhood's main thoroughfare. Exploring Fez's Jewish heritage offers a deeper understanding of Morocco's layered and complex past.

Left Gate, the Mellah
Centre Jewish cemetery
Right Aben Danan Synagogue

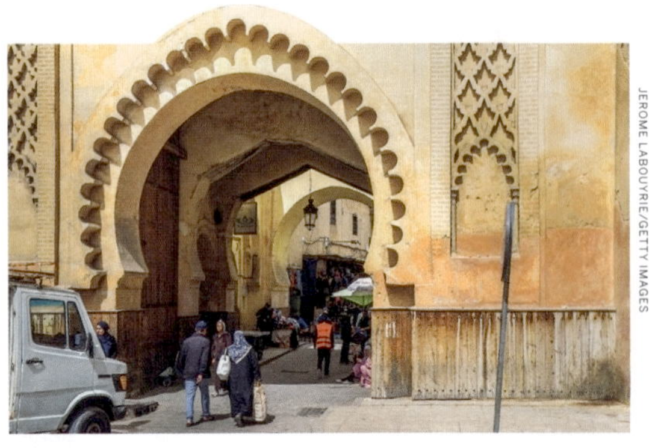

JEROME LABOUYRIE/GETTY IMAGES

A City Within a City

The **Mellah**, established in 1438, was the first designated Jewish quarter in Morocco. Located near the royal palace in Fez el-Jdid, it provided protection while separating the Jewish community from the Muslim population. Unlike the tightly packed lanes of the medina, the Mellah comprised wider streets and houses with open balconies – a rarity in Moroccan architecture. These wooden balconies, once lined with merchants watching the market below, now stand weathered by time, remnants of a once-bustling quarter. By the 19th century, Fez had one of the largest Jewish populations in North Africa, with synagogues, schools and community centres woven into daily life. The **Jewish cemetery**, its whitewashed tombs sloping down a hillside, is one of the most atmospheric places in the district, home to the grave of Sol Hachuel, a young Jewish martyr whose story is still told today.

A Legacy of Learning & Trade

Fez's Jewish population played a crucial role in the city's economy, particularly in crafts and trade. Many were skilled goldsmiths and silversmiths, a tradition that continues in Moroccan jewellery. Others were involved in textile production, leatherwork and commerce, often acting as intermediaries between local traders and European markets. The Jewish influence extended beyond business – scholars and rabbis from Fez contributed to religious and intellectual life, shaping Moroccan Judaism in ways that endured even after most of the population emigrated.

RNDMS/SHUTTERSTOCK

ANIBAL TREJO/SHUTTERSTOCK

The Decline & Dispersal

The mid-20th century saw a dramatic shift. As Morocco gained independence in 1956, waves of Jewish families emigrated to Israel, France and Canada, drawn by economic opportunities and political change. Today, only a handful of Jewish families remain in Fez, and the Mellah is a shadow of its former self. Yet traces of Jewish life remain – not just in architecture and historical sites, but in the enduring relationship between Jewish and Muslim Moroccans, who share a deep cultural connection despite their separate faiths.

Though much of the community has moved on, the legacy of Jewish Fez remains woven into the city's identity, a moving testament to Morocco's multicultural past.

Preserving the Past

Efforts to restore and protect Jewish heritage in Morocco have gained momentum in recent years. The 17th-century **Aben Danan Synagogue**, one of the oldest in North Africa, has been carefully restored, its painted wooden ark standing as a testament to centuries of worship. The **Museum of Moroccan Judaism** (p151) in Casablanca and restoration projects across the country, including in Fez, highlight Morocco's commitment to preserving this shared history. Walking through the Mellah today, the faded Star of David still appears above some doorways, and old traders' signs can be spotted in the souqs. Though much of the community has moved on, the legacy of Jewish Fez remains woven into the city's identity, a moving testament to Morocco's multicultural past.

Aben Danan Synagogue – A Doorway into the Past

Tucked away in the Mellah, the **Aben Danan Synagogue** is the most striking of two surviving synagogues in Fez. Built in the 1600s, it features a beautifully restored wooden ark, blue-and-white tiling and a *mikvah* (ritual bath) hidden beneath the floor. Once a centre of Jewish life, it's now a quiet but powerful reminder of Fez's rich religious heritage. Visitors can explore the space, often with little more than a caretaker to unlock the doors and share its story. It's a must-visit for anyone tracing Morocco's Jewish history.

Listings

BEST OF THE REST

Medersas, Mosques & Museums

Dar Batha Museum

Once a royal palace, this museum showcases centuries of Moroccan craftsmanship – embroidered caftans, Fassi ceramics, and painted wood – framed by orange-blossom gardens and Andalusian arches.

Medersa El Attarine

A masterpiece of Merinid artisanship, the Attarine Medersa is a study in precision – *zellige* mosaics in hypnotic symmetry, cedarwood carved like lace and Kufic inscriptions winding through snowy stucco.

Bou Inania Medersa

The Bou Inania Medersa still functions as a Quranic school, its marble floors worn smooth by generations of students. Opposite, La Magana – a 14th-century water clock – once signalled prayer times with remarkable precision.

Zawiya of Moulay Idriss II

The final resting place of Fez's founder, this sacred shrine is one of Morocco's holiest. Non-Muslims can't enter, but the surrounding stalls – laden with candles and incense – create a hushed, almost hypnotic atmosphere.

Kairaouine Mosque and University

Home to the world's oldest continually operating university, this vast complex includes a mosque for 20,000 worshippers and a library safeguarding rare manuscripts, accessible only by special permission.

Nejjarine Museum of Wooden Arts & Crafts

Housed in a restored *funduq* (inn), this museum celebrates Morocco's woodworking traditions with an extensive and fascinating collection of carved cedar doors and ancient farm tools, beauty products and Quran boards.

Crafts & Treasures

Henna Souq

Built on the site of a medieval hospital, this peaceful cobbled square is lined with pottery, hammam essentials and curiosity shops, its past as a place of care still quietly lingering.

Place Seffarine

The clang of hammers fills this square, where Jewish coppersmiths introduced metal beating in the Middle Ages. Great for top-quality cookware and vast pots hired for wedding feasts.

The Anou

Supporting Amazigh artisans, this cooperative connects weavers to buyers, preserving traditional techniques and ensuring fair pay. Dyeing and weaving workshops are offered on site.

L'Art Traditionnel

L'Art Traditionnel specialises in intricately filigreed bronze lanterns, exhibiting centuries-old techniques. Visits to the workshop showcase the artistry behind these handcrafted pieces.

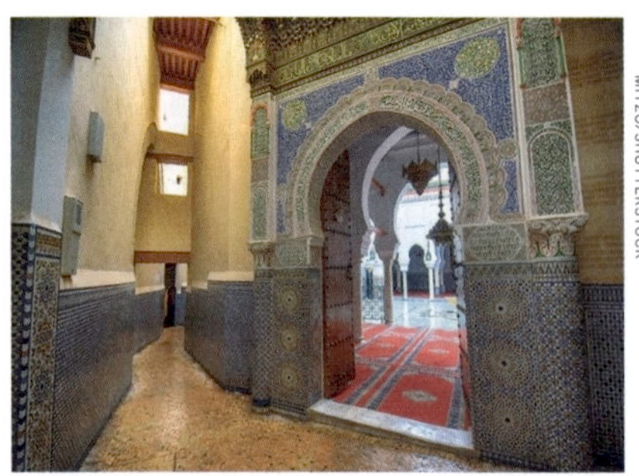

Kairaouine Mosque and University

La Maison d'Art Berbère

Youssef Salih's expertise guides buyers through an exceptional collection of vintage Moroccan rugs, sourced by a team who scour the country for the finest, most authentic pieces.

Médin Art

Covetable gifts from chunky jewellery and kids' toys to locally designed fashion, prints, scented candles and artisanal deli products.

Rooftop, Courtyard & Garden Dining

Cafe Clock €

The rooftop views of Bou Inania's minaret are so close you could touch it. Live music, cultural events and the legendary camel burger have made this a true Fez institution.

Ruined Garden €

A rambunctious garden with plenty of hidden corners. The menu riffs on street food, while order-ahead lamb *mechoui* is worth planning for. By evening, a fire pit is lit for cosy gatherings.

Darori €

Standout Moroccan home cooking, served with a smile, in a cosy courtyard. Menus follow the seasons – think lamb, artichoke and pea tajine.

Almandar €

A simple rooftop spot with excellent home cooking. The chicken, preserved lemon and olive tajine is rich and deeply flavoured. Pizza and burger options are useful if travelling with kids.

Bistrot Laaroussa €€

A French-inspired menu served on a rooftop with sweeping medina views. Bistro classics, seasonal salads and a Moroccan daily special.

Fez Café €€

To dine under a giant olive tree is a magical setting for sumptuous dishes like goat's cheese tarts, or steak and mash with mushroom sauce.

Dar Roumana €€

A romantic courtyard and intimate dining room set the scene for date nights. Start with cocktails in front of the fire, followed by market-fresh, Franco-Moroccan fusion dishes.

Fondouk Bazaar €€

A splash of Marrakesh style in Fez, with colourful decor and a spacious roof terrace. Fresh, composed salads and sharing plates make it a standout for vegetarian travellers.

Palais Fez Dar Tazi €€€

Rambling roof terraces and a fire-lit dining room set the scene for emblematic Moroccan dishes. The salad spread is superb, as is the spicy chicken *mhammar*. Service can be slow.

Ishq €€€

A breath of fresh air in hyper-traditional Fez, this contemporary space serves a modern Moroccan menu designed for the curious palate. Portions run small.

MB €€€

Fez's finest French restaurant. Offers expertly crafted dishes – like scallop and prawn with potato foam – in a sleek, industrial space.

Walking with Insiders

Fez Guided Tours

This women-run tour company offers highly personalised explorations of the medina and the Mellah, with day and half-day options. Specialty food tours provide an insider's take on Fez's vibrant culinary scene.

Culture Vultures

The immersive Fez Artisan Visit excursions head into hidden workshops, where artisans practise age-old crafts. Self-guided Scavenger Hunts provide a hands-on way to uncover the city's rich artisanal heritage.

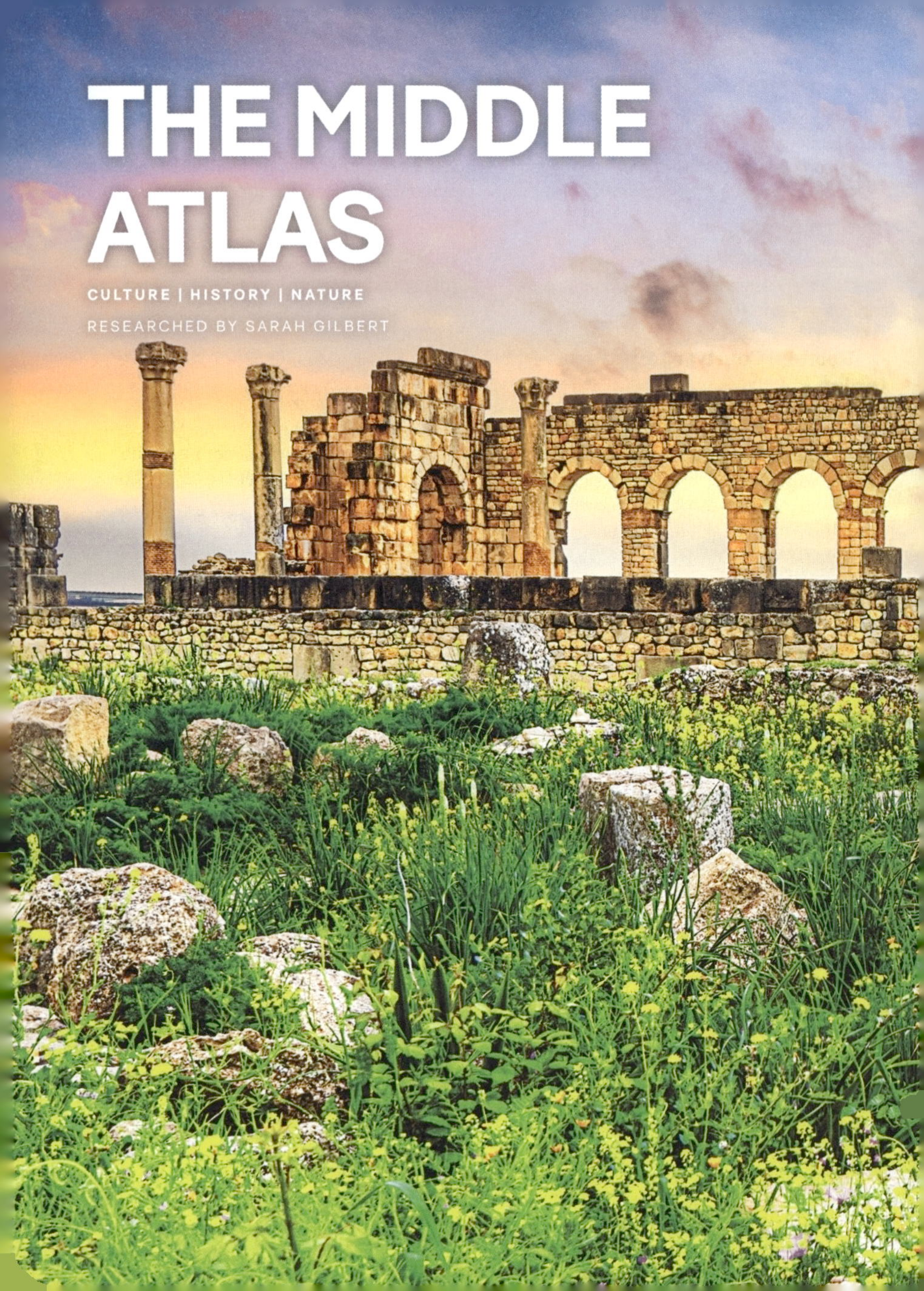

THE MIDDLE ATLAS

CULTURE | HISTORY | NATURE

RESEARCHED BY SARAH GILBERT

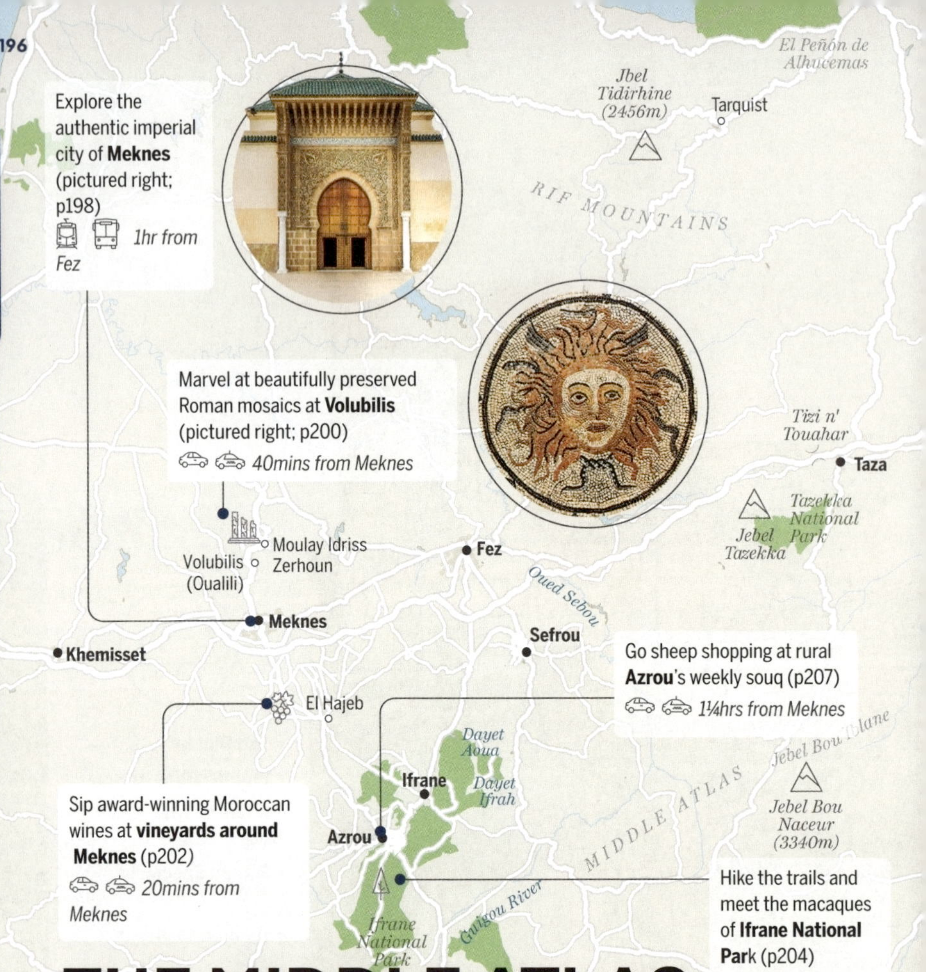
El Peñón de Alhucemas
Jbel Tidirhine (2456m)
Tarquist
RIF MOUNTAINS
Tizi n' Touahar
Taza
Tazekka National Park
Jebel Tazekka
Moulay Idriss Zerhoun
Volubilis (Oualili)
Fez
Oued Sebou
Meknes
Sefrou
Khemisset
El Hajeb
Dayet Aoua
Ifrane
Dayet Ifrah
Jebel Bou Iblane
Jebel Bou Naceur (3340m)
MIDDLE ATLAS
Azrou
Guigou River
Ifrane National Park
0 40 km
0 20 miles

Explore the authentic imperial city of **Meknes** (pictured right; p198)
1hr from Fez

Marvel at beautifully preserved Roman mosaics at **Volubilis** (pictured right; p200)
40mins from Meknes

Go sheep shopping at rural **Azrou**'s weekly souq (p207)
1¼hrs from Meknes

Sip award-winning Moroccan wines at **vineyards around Meknes** (p202)
20mins from Meknes

Hike the trails and meet the macaques of **Ifrane National Park** (p204)
50mins from Meknes

THE MIDDLE ATLAS
Trip Builder

Discover the less-visited imperial city of Meknes, admire a far-flung Roman ruin, hike through fragrant forests of cedar with mischievous macaques, go sheep shopping at the weekly souq of an age-old Amazigh town and watch women weave their history in wool.

FROM LEFT: JEROME LABOUYRIE/SHUTTERSTOCK, NICSCURRY/SHUTTERSTOCK
PREVIOUS SPREAD: DAVID IONUT/SHUTTERSTOCK

Practicalities

ARRIVING

Fès–Saïss Airport The region's primary airport for both international and domestic flights, one hour east of Meknes.

Meknes Al Amir The station for trains to/from Fez.

CONNECT

The airport and most hotels and restaurants have free wi-fi but the signal is patchy in more remote areas.

MONEY

Cash is king at rural souqs, small stores and restaurants, so stock up when you see an ATM.

WHERE TO STAY

Town/ Village	Need to Know
Meknes	Good transport links plus characterful – and wallet-friendly – *riads*.
Moulay Idriss	This picturesque town has some lovely mid-range *riads* within touching distance of Volubilis.
Azrou	A transport hub with budget accommodation in town; you'll need a car for more atmospheric rural lodgings.

GETTING AROUND

Bus CTM and Supratours buses travel between Meknes and Azrou.

Taxi Eight-seater *grands taxis* travel between smaller towns and remote villages when they fill up.

Car With your own wheels, you'll be able to explore the Middle Atlas at your own pace.

EATING & DRINKING

Local produce is plentiful and fresh. Expect to eat a lot of tajines (stews), brochettes and couscous; Meknes has a fabulous food souq, Moulay Idriss is famed for its *kefta* (pictured bottom right; meatballs) and many excellent wines hail from this region.

Must-try artisan cheese Domaine de la Pommeraie (p210)

Lunch with a sublime view Scorpion House (p200)

TOP: MATYAS REHAK/SHUTTERSTOCK
BOTTOM: SRI WIDYOWATI/SHUTTERSTOCK

JAN–MAR
Ski the slopes of Morocco's Aspen at the Michlifen resort

APR–JUN
Hike Ifrane's trails and celebrate Sefrou's Cherry Festival

JUL–SEP
Crowds of pilgrims arrive in Moulay Idriss for the August *Moussem* (Festival)

OCT–DEC
The tail end of hiking season, with cooler weather

37 A Tale of TWO CITIES

HISTORY | CULTURE | CITY LIFE

Moulay Ismail's imposing imperial city is separated from Meknes medina by impregnable ramparts and bastions. When he died in 1727, he had completed a 45km city wall, with 20 gates surrounding more than 50 palaces. Following an extensive restoration, it still gives you a sense of the sultan's grand design, while the medina is a relaxed slice of authentic Moroccan life.

JEROME LABOUYRIE/SHUTTERSTOCK

How to

Getting here There are regular trains from Fez to Meknes Al Amir (around 30 minutes).

When to go Spring and autumn are the best times to visit.

One-of-a-kind craft You won't find the delicate and disappearing art of Damascene anywhere else in Morocco.

Tasting Meknes Take a foodie tour with professional English-speaking guide, Bouchra Jamai (0661815237), including the spectacular covered market, piled high with aromatic spices and pyramids of olives.

THOMAS WYNESS/SHUTTERSTOCK

The imperial city **Mausoleum of Moulay Ismail** boasts a grandeur befitting a sultan, with a succession of courtyards decorated with dazzling *zellige* (colourful geometric mosaic tilework), intricate stucco work and ornate cedarwood doors. Non-Muslims can look through the doorway to his tomb. Below **Koubbat As Sufara**, Moulay Ismail's reception hall, lies a subterranean network of rooms known as Habs Qara (Qara Prison). Now thought to have been a food store, some guides will still tell you that it was a dungeon for Christian enslaved people. Moulay Ismail considered the **Heri Es Souani** royal granary and stables one of his finest architectural projects. The cavernous, thick-walled, barrel-vaulted storerooms were filled with provisions for siege or drought and cooled by underfloor water channels.

The medina The grandest of all imperial gateways, **Bab El Mansour** is adorned with sparkling *zellige* and engraved Quranic panels. An inscription boasts 'I am the most beautiful gate in Morocco', and the two marble columns are thought to have been stolen from **Volubilis** (p200). The beating heart of the medina, **Place El Hedim** is particularly lively in the evening when families like to stroll, eat at the square's cafes, and listen to storytellers and musicians. The palatial residence of **Dar Jamai** is a masterclass of Moroccan architecture, now home to the National Museum of Music. Not as lavish as its Fassi (from Fez) namesake, **Medersa Bou Inania** does have stunning *zellige*, delicate stucco and carved cedarwood.

Top left Mausoleum of Moulay Ismail
Bottom left Heri Es Souani

Who Was Moulay Ismail?

Born in 1645 to a descendant of the Prophet Muhammad and an unknown black enslaved person, Sultan Moulay Ismail ruled Morocco for 55 years. Dubbed 'The Bloodthirsty', in 1672 he celebrated inheriting the throne by murdering all who refused to submit to his rule.

A string of military campaigns brought most of Morocco under his control, subduing the Amazigh tribes, liberating Tangier from the British and relieving the Spanish of most of their Moroccan territory. He was a lover as well as a fighter; with more than 500 women in his harem, he allegedly fathered over 800 offspring, a Guinness world record.

38 Roman SPECTACLE

RUINS | HISTORY | CULTURE

The sight of a triumphal arch rising out of the fertile plain is spectacular. But the most incredible thing about **Volubilis** is the many beautiful mosaics preserved in situ that tell of a way of life in one of the furthest reaches of the Roman Empire: Morocco's grandest and best-preserved Roman ruin – and UNESCO World Heritage Site – dates from 3 BCE.

SAIKO3P/SHUTTERSTOCK

How to

Getting here Volubilis is 40 minutes by car or *grand taxi* from Meknes and 10 minutes from Moulay Idriss.

When to go It's surrounded by wildflowers in spring; the sun can be fierce in summer and there's very little shade. The light is best in the early morning and late afternoon.

Cost Adult/child Dh100/50

Stay for lunch Indulging in a leisurely lunch at **Scorpion House** *(scorpionhouse.com)* in Moulay Idriss is something to savour.

CORTYN/SHUTTERSTOCK

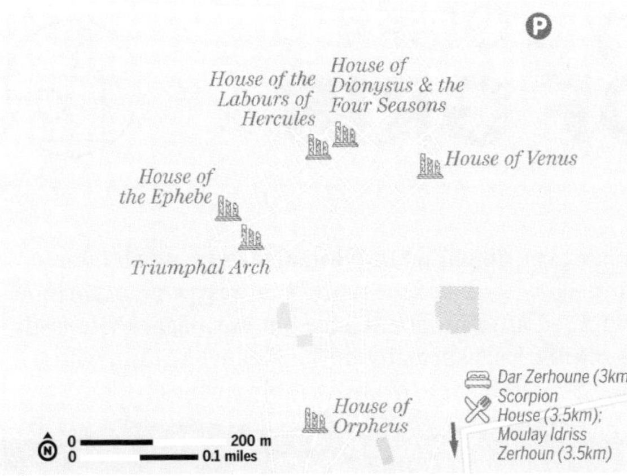

Top left Volubilis ruins
Bottom left Dionysus and Ariadne mosaic, House of Dionysus and the Four Seasons, Volubilis

Historic Highlights

The Triumphal Arch This marble archway honouring Emperor Caracalla and his mother was built in 217 CE. Originally topped with a bronze chariot, it was destroyed in 1755, restored in 1932 and the mistakes rectified in the 1960s.

House of the Ephebe Just west of the Triumphal Arch, the house is named for the nude bronze sculpture discovered here, now on display in Rabat. The banquet hall has a colourful mosaic of Bacchus, the Roman god of wine and pleasure, in a chariot drawn by panthers.

House of Dionysus and the Four Seasons About halfway down the Decumanus Maximus – the main street – the mosaic depicting Dionysus discovering a sleeping Ariadne is one of the site's finest.

House of the Labours of Hercules Mosaics depict Hercules' 12 labours. Several of these heroic feats allegedly occurred in Morocco, making him a popular figure at the time.

House of Orpheus The grandest house in the residential quarter has three stunning mosaics depicting Orpheus charming animals with his lyre, and a dolphin mosaic in the dining room, symbolising good luck.

House of Venus The home of King Juba II has two fine mosaics; one shows Hercules' lover, Hylas, being seduced by two nymphs. The other is of a bathing Diana, the virgin goddess, being spied on by the hunter Acteon – she turned him into a stag as punishment.

A Sacred Town

Perched prettily across two hills, **Moulay Idriss Zerhoun** is swamped every August by pilgrims venerating Moulay Idriss I at the country's largest *moussem*. Morocco's first Islamic leader was the great-grandson of the Prophet Muhammad.

He fled Mecca in 786 CE and settled near Volubilis, converting local Amazigh tribes and establishing the Idrissid dynasty. The town was off-limits to non-Muslims until 1912 and still feels unspoilt and unexplored. Beat the day-trippers to Volubilis and spend the night at the women-run **Dar Zerhoune**. From there, you can saddle-up a donkey and ride to the ruins, then explore with Hajiba for an insight into local daily life.

39 Try a Glass OF GRIS

WINE | HISTORY | CULTURE

Begun by the Phoenicians, continued by the Romans and – much later – developed by the French, Morocco was one of the world's largest wine exporters in the 1950s. The industry slumped after independence but has been revitalised, with ever-increasing boutique wineries, especially in the Meknes region, where oenologists and the terroir have created some award-winning wines.

STEVE ESTVANIK/SHUTTERSTOCK

How to

Getting here The wineries are around 20km south of Meknes; there's no public transport so you will have to hire a car or private driver.

Cost Tours of Villa Volubilia start at Dh240 and are Dh450 at Les Celliers de Meknes; both need to be reserved in advance.

A glass of gris? Moroccan speciality gris is a very pale rosé, made by gently pressing red grapes with very little skin contact.

HEMIS/ALAMY

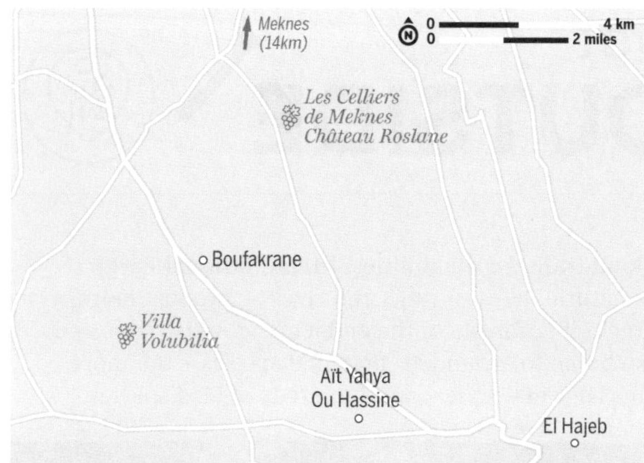

Top left Barrels, Les Celliers de Meknes Château Roslane
Bottom left Wine, Les Celliers de Meknes Château Roslane

Villa Volubilia Founded by the French in the early 20th century and reborn in the early Noughties; today you can tour the winery before tasting award-winning wines from its Volubilia and premium Fleur de Volubilia ranges. You'll learn about the history of Moroccan wine and the now almost-organic vineyard, and visit the cellars where wine is stored in French oak barrels and, more recently, gigantic clay amphora, to give the wine more minerality.

If you don't have time for a leisurely lunch, opt for the **Exploration and Taste Tour** (villa-volubilia.com), including a tasting of four wines – two reds, a rosé and a gris – paired with flavoursome goat's cheese, dried fruit and the estate's (also award-winning) olive oil.

Les Celliers de Meknes Château Roslane The oldest and largest wine producer in Morocco, this is North Africa's first winery to be listed as a *château viticole* (wine estate). They offer a tour of the cellars and a tasting of four premium wines – a red and white AOC (Appellation d'Origine Contrôlée), Morocco's only sparkling wine and a dessert wine.

It's attached to an elegant boutique hotel (roslaneboutiquehotel.com), set among luxuriant gardens, decorated with modern Moroccan rugs and textiles, with balconies overlooking the vineyards. After the tasting, you could indulge in lunch or dinner at L'Oliveraie, with dishes showcasing local produce. Spa treatments also feature wine; treat yourself to a suite for the chance to bathe in a wine barrel.

Four Award-Winning Wines from Villa Volubilia

Fleur de Volubilia Rouge A blend of 50% Cabernet Sauvignon and 50% Syrah aged for 18 months in stone amphorae, this elegant red pairs with meats, cheeses and gently spiced tajines.

Fleur de Volubilia Gris This Moroccan speciality is made with 100% Grenache grapes. Dry, crisp and refreshing, it's perfect with seafood and sweet-and-savoury dishes.

Fleur de Volubilia Fruity with hints of orange blossom, this dry white blends 70% Viognier and 30% Rolle. An easy-drinking aperitif, it's ideal with seafood and goat's cheese.

Volubila Kosher This complex red blends 65% Shiraz and 35% Tempranillo, and its dark fruit flavours are best enjoyed with red meats and zesty tajines.

40 Get OUTSIDE

WILDLIFE | HIKING | SKIING

Crisscrossed with hiking trails for all abilities, Ifrane National Park's diverse ecosystems – fed by natural lakes, springs and rivers – support more than 1000 species of flora, including forests of the emblematic Atlas cedar and evergreen holm oak. It's also home to around 40 mammal species – the most famous is the endangered Barbary macaque – and hundreds of bird species.

MARKETA1982/SHUTTERSTOCK

How to

Getting here You can reach Ifrane and Azrou by bus but you'll need your own transport to get around.

When to go Spring and early summer are perfect for hiking, or winter if you want to ski.

Get a guide English-speaking professional guide, Saleh Boudaoud (0643031867), offers hiking, biking and macaque-tracking tours.

Brrrrrr Alpine Ifrane – dubbed 'Little Switzerland' – holds the record for Africa's lowest ever recorded temperature, -23.9°C in 1935.

ALLISON H. SMITH/SHUTTERSTOCK

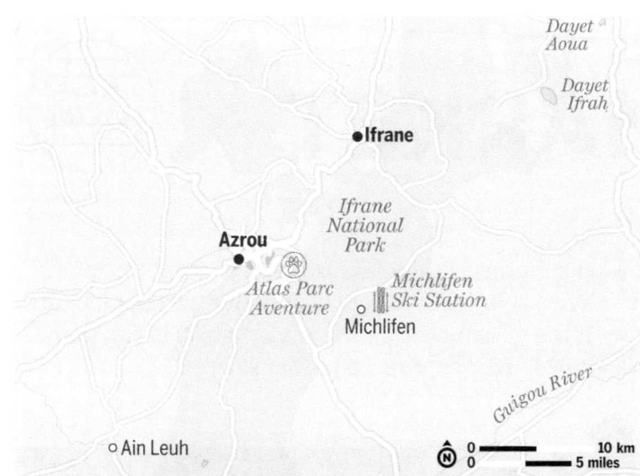

Top left Cedar trees, Ifrane National Park region
Bottom left Monkey, Ifrane National Park

Take a hike The **3M Squared Loop Trail** – aka the Monkey Trail – gives you a good chance of spotting mischievous macaques, and it's great for trail runners and mountain bikers too, shaded by lofty oak and cedar trees. Enlisting a guide will not only keep you on the right path but give you an insight into the park's flora and fauna.

Run among cedars The park is a favourite with Moroccan athletes for high-altitude training, and trail running is becoming increasingly popular. The Trail des Cèdres (traildescedresifrane.com) weaves through the forest in May, covering 58km or 100km in stages. You'll cross rock-strewn plateaus watched over by rugged goats, and scramble up hills that macaques take in their stride.

A macaque's-eye view Whizz over the forest on a zip wire at family-friendly **Atlas Parc Aventure**; there are rope courses, swing bridges and vertical tree climbing too. Troops of macaques often stop by – and not just for the best pizza in the Middle Atlas; they love to tackle the climbing frames before chilling in a hammock.

The Moroccan Aspen The diminutive **Michlifen Ski Station** is around 20km south of Ifrane. Don't expect the Alps or Aspen, but it is fun when the snow gods are kind, with two lifts and skiing, snowboarding, snowshoeing, cross-country skiing and sledging on offer. The snowiest months are from mid-January to mid-March.

Don't Feed the Animals

Once widespread across Europe and North Africa, the Barbary macaque is a one-of-a-kind primate. Currently classed as endangered, the largest remaining population is in **Ifrane National Park**. The hardy macaques can tolerate the freezing winters and scorching summers, and live in large matriarchal groups of around 12 to 60.

Their biggest challenges are human-made: logging and climate change are threatening their habitat, and although poaching has decreased thanks to the work of conservation groups, many young macaques get trafficked as illegal pets. Troops closer to towns are regularly fed by visitors, making them more susceptible to obesity, stress and disease.

41 To MARKET

SOUQS | CULTURE | VILLAGES

Life moves at a mellow pace in the Middle Atlas except, that is, on souq day. Villagers – usually men – descend in their droves to shop for sheep, pick up fresh produce and catch up with the gossip over a mint tea or two. There's even a chance to get a haircut or a close shave at a pop-up barber's shop.

MALCOLM P CHAPMAN/SHUTTERSTOCK

How to

Getting here Azrou is a transport hub for buses and *grands taxis*; Guigou is best reached on a tour from Sefrou or Bhalil.

When to go Spring and autumn are the best times to visit the region; towns and larger villages have their set souq days.

Rug know-how If you don't know your *Beni Ourain* from your *boucherouite*, Culture Vultures (culturevultures.ma) in Sefrou runs tours to weaving cooperatives around Guigou.

STUDIOANGHIFOTO/SHUTTERSTOCK

Azrou Souq Every Tuesday morning, hundreds of people descend on the peaceful mountain town of **Azrou** on mules, motorbikes and bicycles. Before first light, pickups roll into town with their baaing and bleating cargo, along with mountains of potatoes from Meknes, and piles of pungent onions and fragrant herbs from the fertile valleys around the Middle Atlas.

Watch as shepherds clad in thick *djellabas* (hooded cloaks) check out a potential sheep purchase, examining teeth and prodding haunches before an intense to-and-fro over the price. Figure agreed, they sling a single sheep over their shoulders or skilfully herd a flock to the car park.

Guigou Souq For a more remote slice of rural Amazigh life, head to this Sunday souq around 60km south of **Bhalil**. Surrounded by fertile farmland, the region is famed for onions and garlic. On the way, discover how the onions are planted, harvested and stored and how much the workers get paid.

You will hear a symphony of baas of every timbre as men drive their sheep and goats to the livestock souq, on foot or in trucks; get there early to watch them test-driving a donkey or picking out the most virile ram. Women make good use of the wool, creating flat-weave and shaggy rugs in bold colours, covered in ancient Amazigh symbols.

Top left Azrou Souq
Bottom left Bhalil

Live Like a Troglodyte

There's more to the picturesque Amazigh village of Bhalil – 5.5km from Sefrou – than meets the eye. Cave dwellings formed by the Atlantic dating back to the 4th century punctuate the hillsides; they have served as shepherd's huts for centuries, but some of the town's modern-day troglodytes have turned them into spacious stone-walled salons that keep out the scorching summer heat.

The best person to reveal Bhalil's secrets – including the women who sew djellaba buttons and the rural souq at nearby Guigou – is community-minded Kamal Chaoui, whose eponymous guesthouse (kamalchaoui.com) is decorated with local arts and crafts, where dinners are both communal and convivial.

42 Made in the MIDDLE ATLAS

CRAFTS | CULTURE | VILLAGES

Throughout Morocco, you can watch brass being beaten, leather being tooled, a potter at the wheel, and a weaver at the loom. Textiles are deeply rooted in Amazigh culture and every home begins with a weaving – there is always wool available to make a warm blanket or a shaggy rug. Getting to meet the makers is an extra-special experience.

LAURA MCADAMS/FLICKR.COM

How to

Getting here *Grands taxis* – or car – are the best way to get around this region; Ain Leuh is around 30 minutes from Azrou.

Top tip Go with a guide – or in the case of Anou, book a translator – to learn more about the artisans' lives.

Hit the trails Some fine hikes start in Ain Leuh, ranging from four hours to three days, taking in spectacular scenery, isolated Amazigh villages and superb birding at Ramsar wetlands.

LAURA MCADAMS/FLICKR.COM

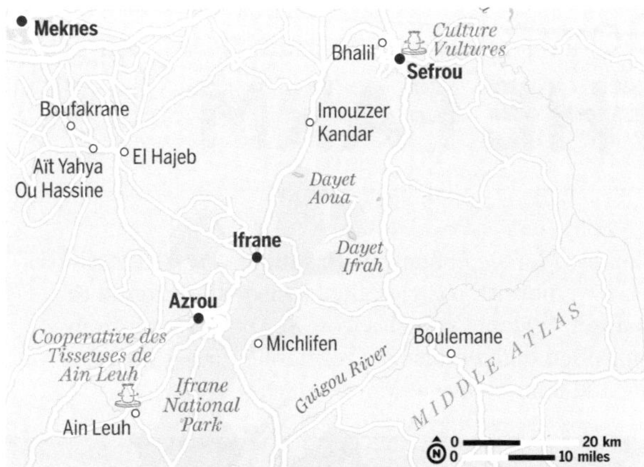

Top and bottom left Weaving, Cooperative des Tisseuses de Ain Leuh

Trendsetting Tisseuses The women weavers of the **Cooperative des Tisseuses de Ain Leuh** have always been trailblazers. When the cooperative was founded in 1977, it was one of the first to be officially recognised, helping the women to become financially independent, as well as showcasing their unique and beautiful designs. Now their *hanbel* (flat-weave) rugs are considered some of the finest in the country. After the sheep are sheared, the wool is combed and carded before being spun into a thick yarn and coloured with natural dyes. And their designs aren't on paper; like their weaving skills, they are passed down through the generations and inspired by the world around them.

Meet the makers On **Culture Vultures**' (culturevultures.ma) Sefrou Artisan Quest, you'll get to meet and – with the aid of your guide – talk to artisans in their workshops, tucked along the medieval medina's twisting alleyways. The guides from this arts organisation, based in a restored *funduq* (inn), prefer to see themselves as facilitators, helping you to connect with the artisans, with the conversation led by you. The tour is organic; you'll drop in on artisans – weavers, ironmongers, embroiderers – watch them work and chat about their work and their lives. Perhaps Hassan, a tailor facing stiff competition from machine-made caftans; Abdel, who makes decorative tassels; or Mohammed, who chisels and carves the region's traditional wooden ploughs.

The Anou Cooperative

This award-winning co-operative (theanou.com) is fair-trade shopping at its finest. Owned and managed by more than 600 artisans from around Morocco, it cuts out the middleman and gives 100% of the price tag back to the makers – buy in the souqs, and they only receive 4% on average.

Book a visit through their website and order a home-cooked tajine if you want to stop and chat. If you can't get to a cooperative or Anou's shop in Fez, you can buy online or design a ravishing rug in any size and colour. Safe in the knowledge that your dirhams go directly to the makers.

43 Down on THE FARM

FOOD | NATURE | CULTURE

If Fassi cuisine is arguably Morocco's finest, with sublime *bastilla* (savoury-sweet pigeon or chicken pie) and moreish pastries, the fertile plains around the Middle Atlas are its bread basket. Seek out cherries from Sefrou, olive oil from Moulay Idriss, fluffy couscous piled high with seven vegetables, native brown trout, healing organic honey and a new wave of Moroccan cheesemakers.

DOMAINE DE LA POMMERAIE.

How to

Getting here It's a one-hour drive from Meknes and 30 minutes from Sefrou.

When to go March to May and September to November are the best months to visit.

Sweet as honey The Middle Atlas is famed for its health-giving honey, such as thyme and fig.

Lake tour The lakes of Dayet Aoua, Ifrah and Hachlaf, 22km to the south, make a scenic drive when water levels are high.

DOMAINE DE LA POMMERAIE.

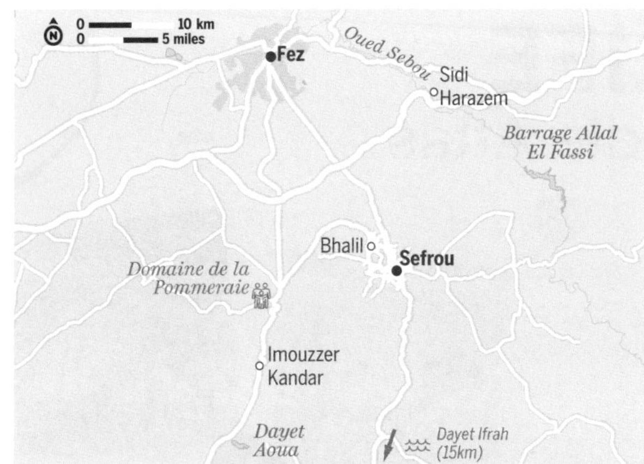

A feast of fromage At the idyllic small farm, **Domaine de la Pommeraie**, Tarik Lechkar produces world-class *fromage* using age-old Amazigh techniques. Book in for a tasting and you'll tour the aromatic garden, meet the goats – you can milk them too – and sample some seasonal organic cheeses. Like wine, it's all about the terroir; the goats feast on fragrant herbs, alfalfa, wheat, beans and lentils, and those flavours transfer to the cheese.

There's creamy Jben, matured for only 48 hours, or 21-day-matured Berbere Cedre, or Le Vert d'Atlas, similar to Roquefort but with a mould that turns green rather than blue. All perfectly paired with the farm's hand-pressed olive oil, just-baked bread from the wood-fired oven and plump olives.

Stay the night Book into one of the three rustic rooms, and you'll wake to a five-star breakfast with homemade jams, perhaps bitter orange or tangy lemon, honey from Tarik's bees (they live near Azrou) and a black-truffle omelette in season – he grows the fragrant fungi on a neighbour's farm.

Barbecued trout and goat's-cheese tajine appear on the dinner menu, with vegetables from the organic garden. Go hiking – or biking – through the hills to hidden caves used for cold storage, and learn some Amazigh lore en route. There's saffron-picking during the November harvest – you can sample it in tea or the chicken and saffron tajine.

Top and bottom left Farm produce, Domaine de la Pommeraie

Couscous Wars

Couscous is the national dish of Morocco; a symbol of ritual, hospitality and celebration, it is traditionally served on Fridays (the Muslim holy day) at home. Its origins are unclear, but some food historians believe it dates back to 12th-century Imazighen.

Morocco and Algeria regularly engage in so-called 'couscous wars' over its invention. However, they put aside their differences to join with Tunisia and Mauritania and had it inscribed on UNESCO's Intangible Cultural Heritage list in 2020. Hand-rolling couscous is a time-consuming, laborious process and a dying art. To get hands-on, visit a farm outside Sefrou with Inclusive Morocco (inclusivemorocco.com).

WILDLIFE
of the Middle Atlas

02

04

05

01 Barbary Macaque
The only macaques outside Asia. Watch them enjoying stress-busting grooming sessions and youngsters using the forest like a jungle gym.

02 Barbary Stag
Africa's only native deer was extinct in Morocco before being reintroduced into **Tazekka National Park**.

03 North African Boar
With poor eyesight but a great sense of smell, it's happiest rootling around oak forests between dusk and dawn.

04 Barbary Sheep
Native to North Africa's rocky mountains, with thick curled horns, they're genetically closer to wild goats than sheep.

05 North African Hedgehog
Paler than their European cousins, with longer snouts and legs, larger ears and a spine-free patch on their heads.

06 African Golden Wolves

These secretive, monogamous mammals are often confused for golden jackals but are more closely related to grey wolves.

07 Levaillant's Woodpecker

Listen out for a rhythmic tap, tap, tap and the laughter-like call of this woodpecker, with green plumage and a crimson crown.

08 North African Crested Porcupine

One of the world's biggest rodents, this prickly, nocturnal species has been known to take on lions and leopards.

09 Eurasian Otter

Found in lakes, rivers and marshes, this elusive otter is territorial and solitary, and near threatened thanks to hunting and water pollution.

10 Barbary Lion

Extinct in the wild, there's a global breeding programme underway to save these genetically different felines, including at Rabat Zoo.

Listings

BEST OF THE REST

Local Flavours

Ryad Bahia €€

Located in Meknes, this pretty *riad's* restaurant has candlelit tables around its courtyard. There's a short set menu of traditional Moroccan dishes, including tajines, *kefta* (meatballs) and couscous, cooked to order and beautifully presented.

Restaurant Dar Baraka €€

The cosy, ground-floor salon of a family *riad* in Meknes has become a restaurant. The menu is filled with Moroccan favourites; expect large portions of traditional home cooking.

Aisha €€

Head to this tiny, family-run restaurant in Meknes for generous portions of home-cooked food, perhaps just-baked bread and *harira* soup, grilled brochettes or fluffy couscous.

Coffe Shop Meknes €

If you're craving a good cup of coffee, head to this quirky cupboard-sized cafe in the medina.

Dar Zerhoune €€

This lovely Moulay Idriss *riad* serves home-cooked dishes, such as *kefta* and tajine, or lighter soups, salads and pizza. Dine on the roof terrace with sweeping views to Volubilis or in an air-conditioned salon.

Grillade Albanna €

One of Moulay Idriss's most popular *kefta* joints; meatballs are served with salad and fresh bread.

Roman City €€

A two-minute drive from Volubilis, serving Amazigh, Arab, Andalusian and Mediterranean-influenced dishes. The terrace has panoramic views over the ruins and there's a lovely garden.

Le Palais des Cerisiers €€€

The set menu at this Azrou hotel's restaurant specialises in fresh local produce, such as goat's cheese and trout, as well as tajines and pasta dishes.

Foodie €

If you're tired of tajines, head to this popular restaurant in central Ifrane for its US-diner-style menu: think bumper burgers, popcorn chicken nuggets and hand-cut fries.

Café Restaurant La Paix €

Popular with both locals and visitors to Ifrane for its range of international dishes and moreish selection of patisserie.

Restaurant Al Farah €

Simple tables under a shady tree, opposite the knife-grinders and blacksmith in Sefrou's medina. There's no menu: go for the feast of spit-roast chicken with *harissa* (hot chilli paste), chips, beans, bread and salad.

Cultural Spaces

Centre Culturel d'Azrou

Opposite Azrou's iconic rock, the Middle Atlas Heritage Interpretation Centre has displays on the region's geology, ecology and ethnology, with examples of traditional costumes and crafts, medicinal plants, fossils and more.

Sefrou Museum of Multiculturalism

In an old carpenter's *funduq* (inn), this micro museum with a big message tells the story of Sefrou in an inventive way, exploring the contributions made by its mix of cultures.

Monastery of Tioumliline

Founded in 1952 by French Benedictine monks who set up a school, dispensary and home for orphaned children. It closed in 1968 and was left to decay but there's a rebuilding project underway.

 Craft Shopping

Coin des Artisans

In this diminutive damascene (metal inlaid with intricate silver wire) workshop in Meknes medina, Abdellah demonstrates the labour-intensive and collaborative effort needed to make everything from bowls to bracelets.

Ensemble Artisanal de Azrou

There's an impressive selection of crafts on display here, from carved wood, ceramics and wrought-iron work to gorgeous rugs, hand-woven before your eyes. And all cheaper than in the cities.

 Festival Frenzy

International Volubilis Festival of Traditional World Music

In Meknes and among the ruins of Volubilis, this September festival brings together diverse cultures and musical genres, showcasing artists from Morocco, to Spain and Senegal.

Sefrou Cherry Festival

Recognised by UNESCO, this annual four-day festival celebrates the cherry harvest in June. There's plenty of folk music, along with displays by local artists, parades and the crowning of the Cherry Queen.

Festival National d'Ahidous

Amazigh tribes from across the Atlas descend on Ain Leuh for a three-day competition between troupes of *ahidous* performers, a complex form of dance, music, poetry and song.

MOROCCAN NATURE DESERT/SHUTTERSTOCK

Oum Er Rbia Springs

 Take a Hike

Afenourir Lake

A four-hour hike from Ain Leuh, via the volcanic lake and Ramsar site, with spectacular scenery and excellent birdwatching.

Zaouia Ifrane

A strenuous six-hour trek into Ifrane National Park, from Ain Leuh to the tiny village of Zaouia Ifrane, surrounded by mountains and waterfalls, passing through several Amazigh villages.

Oum Er Rbia Springs

A three-day hike from Ain Leuh via Zaouia Ifrane and the Ramsar site Ouiouane Lake, staying in mountain *gîtes* (huts) or wild camping.

Tazekka National Park

This small park offers off-the-radar caving and hiking; although the Gouffre de Friouato cave system was closed at the time of writing, there are other caves to explore, ideally with a qualified guide.

SOUTHERN MOROCCO

ADVENTURE | BEACHES | MOUNTAINS

RESEARCHED BY JADE BREMNER

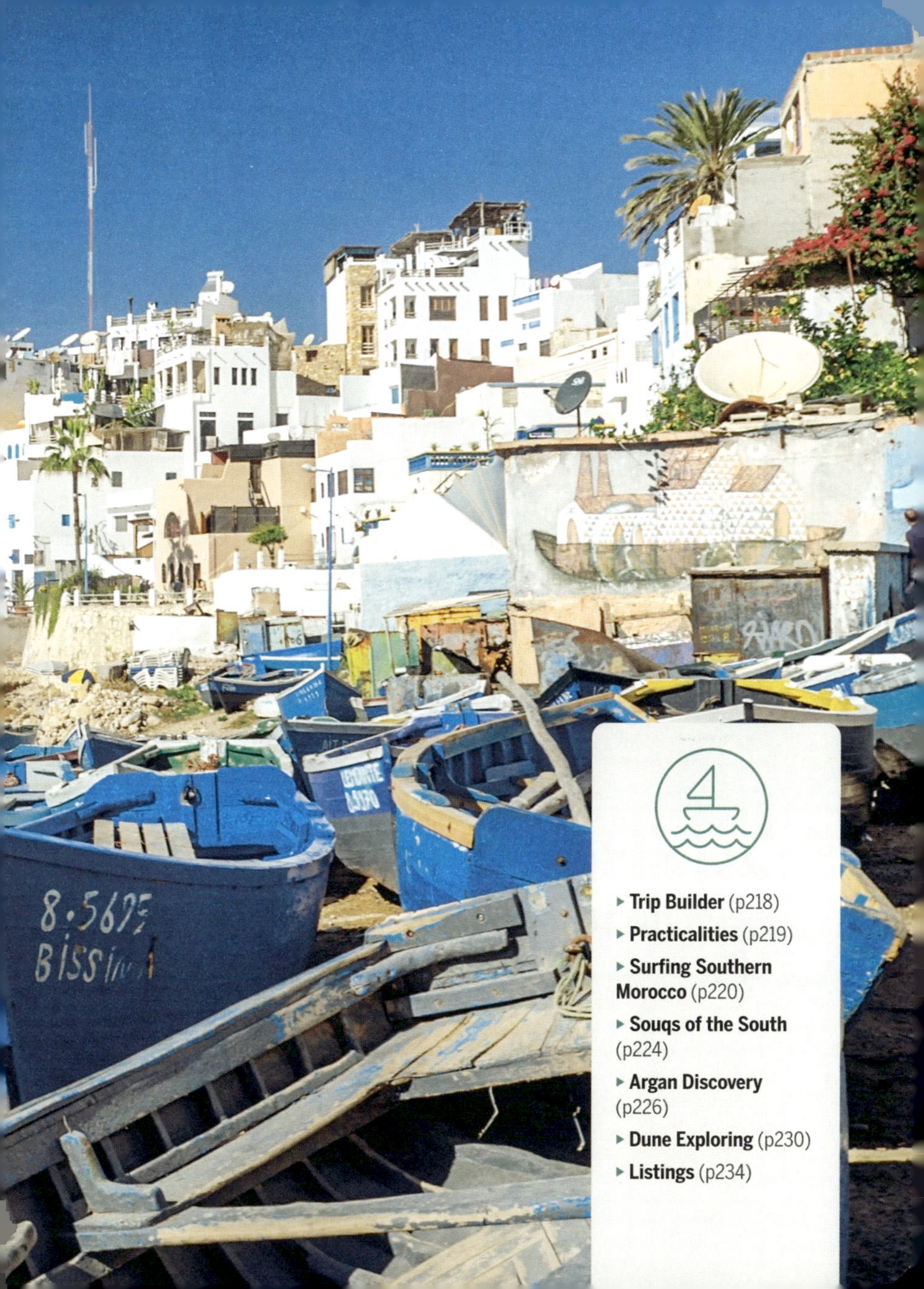

0 20 km
0 10 miles

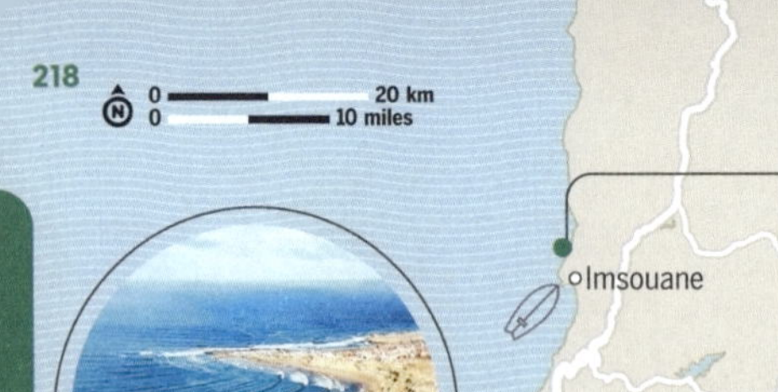

Surf the longest wave in Africa at the Magic Bay in **Imsouane** (pictured; p222)
2hrs from Agadir

Stretch at Surf Berbere's rooftop yoga classes by the coast in **Taghazout** (p221)
30mins from Agadir

Try *amlou* paste at the **Musée de l'Argan** (p226)
30mins from Agadir

Haggle for crafts at **Souq Al Had** in Agadir (p225)
40mins from Taghazout

Spy free-roaming oryx, gazelle and ostriches in **Souss-Massa National Park** (p231)
40mins from Agadir

Imsouane
Assif N Aït Moussa
Argana
Tamri
Tassademt
Aghroud
Taghazout
Tamraght
Aourir
Taroudant
Agadir
Oulad Teima
Oued Sous
Khenafif
Aït Melloul
Al Massira International Airport
Souss-Massa National Park
Biougra
Sidi R'bat
Belfaa
Aït Baha
THE SOUSS
Jebel Lkest (2359m)
Idaougnidif
Tafraoute
Tizi Mlil Adrar Mqorn

SOUTHERN MOROCCO
Trip Builder

Wild Atlantic coastline meets the fertile valleys of the Anti-Atlas Mountains in Southern Morocco, where the chaos of big-city life slows down in laid-back coastal surf towns and sleepy mountain villages. Further south, the Western Sahara region is vast and empty until Dakhla, a traditional fishing town on a 40km peninsula, and Morocco's kiteboarding epicentre with a vast lagoon that's home to pink flamingos.

Camp overnight in the wild Western Sahara region with **Dakhla Rovers** (p233)
14hrs from Agadir

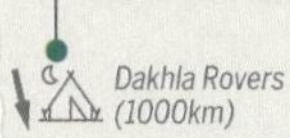

Practicalities

ARRIVING

Agadir Airport The primary gateway, with direct flights from major European cities.
Dakhla Airport Direct flights to Paris, Madrid, Lanzarote and Gran Canaria, plus internal flights to Agadir, Casablanca and Rabat.

CONNECT

Stay connected with a local SIM card (data-only; at the airport). Top up in most convenience stores.

MONEY

Carry cash as virtually no businesses take cards, aside from resorts, hotels and upmarket restaurants. ATMs at major towns only.

WHERE TO STAY

Town/ Village	Pro/Con
Agadir	Low- and high-end stays, a beach and a nice marina. Not as laid-back as other spots.
Taghazout	Luxury boutiques to dorm rooms. Not much to do except surf.
Dakhla	Well-decorated guesthouses and sprawling kitesurfing retreats. Far from anywhere else.

GETTING AROUND

Bus **CTM** (ctm.ma) and **Supratours** (supratours.ma) offer routes between major Moroccan cities to Agadir.

Taxis Reasonably priced for short journeys.

Car rental A good option for off-the-beaten-track discoveries with reasonably priced rental cars. 4WD required for desert driving.

TOP: ESSAYFY ABDELKRIM/SHUTTERSTOCK
BOTTOM: PICTURE PARTNERS/SHUTTERSTOCK

EATING & DRINKING

From laid-back surf cafes to local restaurants serving steaming tajines – standards are generally high. Smart attire is never required. Regional specialities include *amlou* paste (pictured bottom left), made using almond, honey and argan oil from the region.

Best for seafood
My Octopus (p235)

Must-try super bowls
Let's Be Healing Food (p222)

JAN–MAR
Pleasant temperatures around 21°C; consistent waves

APR–JUN
Argan trees in bloom and temperatures around 24°C

JUL–SEP
Temperatures around 27°C; Dakhla's windy kiteboarding season

OCT–DEC
Average highs of around 25°C; surf season begins

44 Surfing Southern MOROCCO

BEACHES | WAVES | OUTDOORS

Facing the Atlantic, with year-round warm weather and thousands of kilometres of surf-able coastline, Southern Morocco is the place to find the waves of your life. There are dozens of legendary spots, plus secret beaches and completely uncrowded waves to discover.

POLAKPHOTO/SHUTTERSTOCK

How to

Getting here/around For ultimate freedom, rent a car and go in pursuit of the best waves. Alternatively, surf guides can take care of the logistics of getting to remote beaches.

When to go Winter, specifically between September to March, is surfing season when the swells are biggest and most consistent in the Atlantic Ocean.

Souk to surf Those bringing surfboards to Morocco via Agadir and Marrakesh can use the Souk to Surf service (souktosurf.com) for transfers between the big cities and surf towns, plus take surfboards on the buses.

SALVADOR AZNAR/SHUTTERSTOCK

Atlantic Swells

Storms out in the vast Atlantic Ocean have ravished Morocco's beaches for hundreds of years, but it wasn't until the 1950s and '60s that American and European surfers discovered perfect surfing waves here. Over the years more and more spots have shot to fame. This land of right-hand rides includes the most famous of them all: **Anchor Point** (known as Almadraba locally), a fierce point break considered the best wave in Morocco by many. It works with a northwest swell and is rideable from 1m to 4m, and suitable for intermediate and advanced surfers. **Killer Point** is another notable wave with fast sections, bowls and barrels for more experienced surfers, and **Banana Beach** is a long right-hand wave on a mostly sandy beach.

SWUERFEL/SHUTTERSTOCK

Surf Yoga

Pre- and post-surf yoga is incredibly popular. Try **Kaladanda** (kalananda-yoga.com) and **Ocean Tribe** (instagram.com/weareoceantribe) in Tamraght; the former has a charming garden alongside ayurvedic consultations, and the latter has a beach-facing terrace. **Surf Berbere** (surfberbere.com) in Taghazout offers rooftop yoga with an ocean soundtrack.

Far left Surfer, Anchor Point
Left Banana Beach
Above Taghazout (p222)

Surf Towns

Fishing towns have morphed into surf towns along the coast north and south of Agadir, with the epicentre being **Taghazout**. This once laid-back fishing village now has dozens of surf guesthouses and stays, and is overrun with visitors carrying surfboards under their arms. The sleepy and quieter **Tamraght** to the south has been pegged as the next Taghazout. It has a long sandy beach with waves for all abilities, and point breaks, including **Devil's Rock**, surrounded by surf-rental shacks, and **Banana Point** with gentle peeling waves in smaller swells and punchy rides in bigger swells – plus an awesome sunset spot on the clifftop above. **Sidi Ifni**, 175km south of Agadir, is even sleepier with plenty of room, an empty surf break, an exposed beach break and oodles of charm – with painted blue-and-white buildings. To the north of Taghazout is **Imsouane**, which has three surfing spots for different conditions, including an insanely long right-hand wave

Top Eats in Taghazout & Tamaraht

Teapot Cafe €

Small punchy Taghazout cafe, with tacos, smoothies and pokē bowls, homemade kombucha and tofu.

Cafe Surf Berbere €

Killer coastline Taghazout spot with sunsets and grilled seafood dishes.

Let's Be Healing Food €

Healthy smoothies and salad bowls, plus a tempting dessert counter, in Tamraght

Seaside Boutique Hotel & Kitchen €€€

Smart poolside restaurant on the Atlantic with live music, fish plates, hearty burgers and tajines.

Manouche €€

Cosy spot with a colourful patio and delicious Lebanese eats, from falafel to baba ganoush.

Moncef Sedki, co-owner of Mint Surf. *@mintsurf*

Left Tajines, Taghazout street café
Below Devil's Rock

peeling off the pier of a working fisherman's village on 'Magic Bay'. The town has mushroomed into a vibey surf hangout with cafes, hostels, restaurants and board-rental shops.

Surf Stays

For communal surfing experiences, stay at one of the many guesthouses running surf lessons and guiding. British-owned **Surf Maroc** (surfmaroc.com) set the benchmark with boutique accommodation at their design-orientated Amouage guesthouse, and a pool overlooking the ocean. On their trips, local surfers take groups to the best spot along the coastline for their ability. Breakfast, lunch and dinner is included. Moroccan-American–owned **Mint Surf** (mintsurfmorocco.co.uk) in Tamraght is a super-welcoming (and more affordable) surf package including meals, with gorgeous rooms in a traditional *riad,* and an open-roof courtyard and pool at its centre. In Sidi Ifni, **Ifni Surf** (ifnisurf.com) has a simple and great-value surf house with smart, shared dorm rooms, plus four private rooms, and a communal balcony with sea views. Surf spots are walkable in Imsouane, and rental and food can easily be added on at **Olas Surf House** (olassurfmorocco.com) – a terrific stay in beautifully designed rooms with natural tones, and a superb restaurant/cafe overlooking the surf on Imsouane Bay.

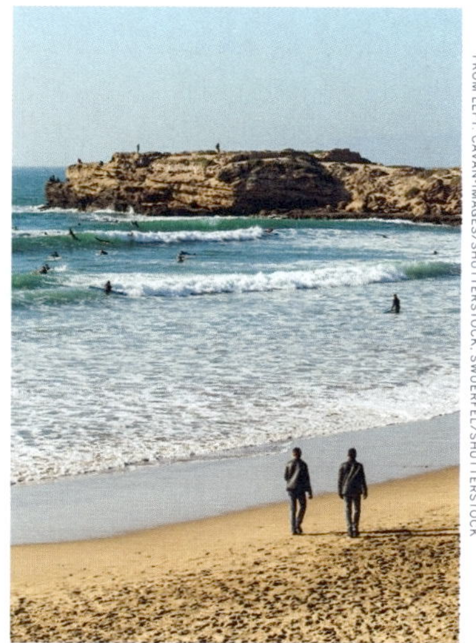

45 Souqs of THE SOUTH

SHOPPING | LOCAL LIFE | ARTS AND CRAFTS

Wandering narrow lanes, getting lost in souqs and walled medinas, plus breathing in the spices and smells of fresh breads in municipal markets are some of the most evocative experiences to be had in Morocco. Interact with local life, find Amazigh artisans and local produce, then test your haggling skills.

GRANT ROONEY/ALAMY

How to

Getting here/around CTM buses connect the main cities, but for smaller towns a car is better. There's usually street parking near souqs, but the busier ones may require parking further away and walking.

When to go Souqs are open all year round, although some are only open at the weekend. Hours are long, usually from 9am to 9pm in most places.

Bring cash It's very unlikely vendors will accept cards. Bring cash for purchases; bigger souqs will likely have an ATM in the area.

ARGANAHF/SHUTTERSTOCK

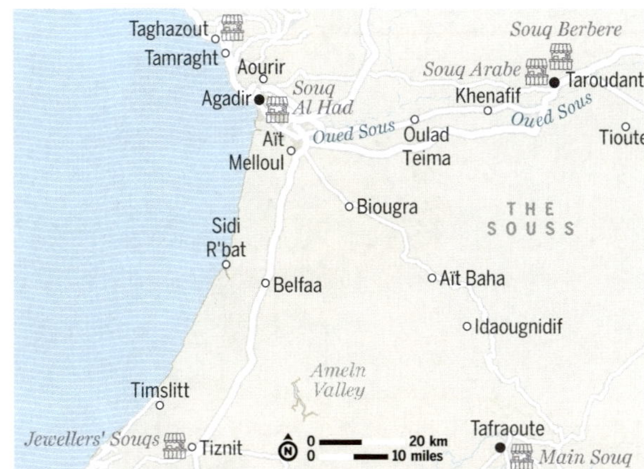

Souq Al Had Agadir's humongous walled Souq Al Had is the largest in the region, with a labyrinth of 6000 traders touting everyday goods, from spices and Moroccan furniture to pottery and vegetables. This is a superb place to get argan oil or *amlou* (argan-nut butter) – watch it being ground in front of you.

Lanes of Taghazout The quaint fishing village turned surfers hangout of Taghazout has a warren of small shops from the main road leading through the old town to the beach. Vendors sell locally made gifts and homeware. Pick up Amazigh rugs, leather sandals, handcrafted pottery, locally designed surf T-shirts and colourful beach throws.

Tafraoute's main souq Morocco's 'Amazigh heartland' has a chilled main souq, with dozens of stalls touting leather goods, pottery, textiles, slippers and jewellery to visitors. It's a lot more laid-back than the bigger cities, with the chance to haggle for a bargain, thanks to its lower footfall.

Taroudant's souqs Dubbed 'Little Marrakesh', this small village punches above its weight when it comes to souqs. The **Souq Arabe** offers crafts, and bold statement pieces like wrought iron and rugs, while the **Souq Berbère** is a mismatch of everyday items, from clothing stores to pharmacies.

Jewellers' souqs Inside the Tiznit City Walls are more than a hundred silver jewellery traders, and some of southern Morocco's best silversmiths (some local craftspeople and some work by southern Saharan tribes). Picturesque blue-doored shops have windows full of earrings, bracelets and daggers.

Top left Souq, Taroudant
Bottom left Souq, Tafraoute

Amazigh Jewellery

Jewellery is an important part of Amazigh culture. The ethnic group from North Africa crafts designs that are rich with geometric shapes and unique symbols, such as Fatima's Hand – a symbol of protection against negative energy and evil. Often pieces include precious stones set in silver for decorative purposes as well as practical reasons – horned bracelets, for example, were used by women to defend themselves. Amazigh jewellery designs can be found at most souqs in southern Morocco – if you're looking to purchase an expensive piece made with precious metals and gems, go to a reputable vendor.

46 Argan DISCOVERY

NATURAL WORLD | MASSAGE | COOKING

Frizzy argan trees producing argan oil are endemic to this area. These valuable crops can be found in the 2.5-million-hectare Arganeraie Biosphere ecosystem established by UNESCO in 1998, running from Essaouira to Gueluim. Indulge in the healing benefits of argan oil, eating it or being massaged with it.

TOLOBALAGUER.COM/SHUTTERSTOCK

How to

Getting here Get out of the cities by car or on a tour to see argan trees scattered on the roadsides. The Musée de l'Argan is a five-minute taxi drive from Taghazout or a 30-minute drive from Agadir.

When to go The argan harvest takes place between June and August, when fruits are handpicked by farmers before being dried. However, argan can be tried all year round in southern Morocco.

Eat it Argan oil is slathered on everything from salads and crêpes to tajines and couscous in southern Morocco, and it's never a bad idea.

PAWEL MICHALOWSKI/SHUTTERSTOCK

Desert Gold

The world's first argan museum, **Musée de l'Argan** (lemuseedelargan.com, guided entry from Dh40), is a terrific stop to get acquainted with this hardy, thorny and slow-growing tree, which has been fundamental to the local community for centuries. Here visitors can learn, through interactive displays, why this is the only place where argan trees grow and why they are vital to biodiversity – offering leaves to goats, flowers to bees, oil for cooking and therapy for skin. The argan tree takes 10 years to bear fruit, but can live hundreds of years. Local women are vital to the production of argan oil, and visitors can see the laborious process of making it, and have a go at removing the kernels by hand themselves with a stone, as local women do. The oil for beauty products is natural and the edible

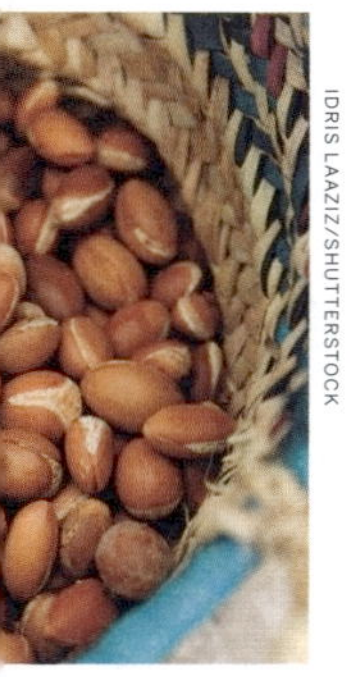

IDRIS LAAZIZ/SHUTTERSTOCK

The Last Curtain

Many efforts have gone into preserving the argan tree, which is the last curtain in front of the desert. The trees are vital to protecting the local environment, helping to prevent desertification by providing soil stabilisation and absorbing water. The government hopes to plant another 200,000 trees by 2025.

Far left Argan tree
Left Argan fruit
Above Cooking with argan oil

oil is processed before it's eaten. Tastings include the chance to try *amlou,* a nut butter made with almonds, argan honey and pure argan oil. The centre also runs hikes nearby to discover the trees in their natural habitat. The museum shop is a terrific place to take home argan produce, and even make your own in an argan-oil workshop.

Cooking with Argan

Most restaurants in the region cook with argan oil – it's commonly listed on the menu and appears in almost all breakfasts, along with the thick brown *amlou* paste, which is rich with vitamins, minerals, proteins and fibre. **Souq Al Had** in Agadir is a great place to not only buy a fresh jar of the gloopy nutty butter, but watch the process of it being ground right in front of you. Argan oil has numerous reported health benefits, including being full of vitamins, nutrients and antioxidants with cancer-fighting properties, plus heart-boosting properties, as well as being

Tree-Climbing Goats

Free-roaming goats, usually in a herd, eat the fruits and leaves of the argan trees, plus the shells shedded by those collecting the kernels. These nimble mammals can be seen up in the branches of the trees, leaving passers-by in awe of how they've reached such lofty heights. Tree-climbing goats are regularly spotted on the N1 and P1000 between Taghazout and Imsouane, and there's often a handful of goats in the same tree. Herders are nearby – they are happy to let people take pictures for a few dirhams; make sure the goats are free to roam before you do.

Left Goat feeding in an argan tree
Below Bottled argan oil

good for digestion. It can be bought at every convenience store in the area. Cooking classes at the Musée de l'Argan are a good way to learn how to use it when making tajines, couscous and salads.

Argan-Oil Massages

From preventing stretch marks to treating acne and skin infections, slathering argan oil on your body has numerous reported benefits. Hairdressers in the area also swear by its moisturising properties, which supposedly give life to dry locks. Almost all hammams and massage treatments in these parts use argan oil, including the **Tamraght Spa House** (tamraghtspahouse.com), which offers wild rich Moroccan spa rituals for both men and women, and **Beautiful Massage Ait Bihi** (facebook.com/BeautifulMassageTaghazout), which uses the therapeutic oil in its hammam treatments and massages. **Tagahazout Golden Spa** (taghazoutgoldenspa.com) uses natural organic products for all of its treatments, including the argan-oil massage and argan-infused black-soap scrub. Try their Amazigh massage – designed to revive weary limbs after a long journey (or heavy surf session).

FROM LEFT: JENS OTTE/SHUTTERSTOCK, PAOLO AIRENTI/SHUTTERSTOCK

Dune EXPLORING

DESERTSCAPES | WILDLIFE | OUTDOORS

Southern Morocco is home to a fascinating number of desert creatures, and projects here have made efforts to breed four threatened North African ungulates – scimitar oryx, addax, dama gazelle and the dorcas gazelle – plus protect other endangered species. These can be sighted in certain areas.

JULIAN SCHALDACH/SHUTTERSTOCK

How to

Getting here/around Car, preferably a 4WD, is the best way to get to remote parks and sand dunes. For those without wheels, day tours to dunes leave from the hubs of Agadir, Taghazout and Dakhla.

When to go Sand dunes and desert nature reserves are pleasant to visit in the cooler winter months. Alternatively visit early in the morning at sunrise or later in the day at sunset for the most active wildlife.

Gear Bring a pair of binoculars for examining wildlife at better range.

KRASNOVA EKATERINA/SHUTTERSTOCK

Desert Safari

The 33,800-hectare **Souss-Massa National Park** (entry Dh150) is one of Morocco's most significant wildlife reserves, set 20km south of Agadir on the Atlantic coast amid sand dunes, fertile valleys and coastal steppes. It is a refuge for several gazelle species, red-necked ostriches, the scimitar-horned oryx and North African ostrich. Jackals, red foxes, wild cats, genets and Eurasian wild boars can also be found here, plus rare birds and animal species, including the northern bald ibis. There are two ways to discover it: one via 30km of dirt roads (where visitors self-drive with a refuge guide), and the other is with a prearranged 3km hiking tour with a guide, both arranged via the **Rokein Information Center** at the park entrance, near the village of Takate. Don't miss the small but informative display about the wildlife you're

DAMIAN LUGOWSKI/SHUTTERSTOCK

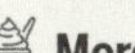

Moroccan Gelato

Nico and Martina, creators of Morocco-inspired ice-cream brand **Gelato & More** (instagram.com/gelatoandmoredakhla), fuse Italian techniques with Moroccan ingredients – try chocolate and vanilla, or the date, saffron and cumin varieties. Find it around Dakhla at **Ocean Vagabond Lassargand**, **Tour d'Eole** (p235) and **MIA Resort Dakhla**.

Far left Souss-Massa National Park
Left Gazelle, Souss-Massa National Park
Above Northern bald ibis, Souss-Massa National Park

about to see in the information centre, with real ostrich egg shells you can hold and information boards on the 300 species of flora in the park, including 13 endemic to southwest Morocco.

Mini Sahara Thrills

Scale Morocco's dunes on a camel, quad or sandboarding tour, which leave from Agadir and go 1½ hours south of the city to the **Dunes of Rasmouka**. Home to a banana oasis, this area is dubbed the 'small Sahara' and offers the chance to walk and play in sandy dunes and visit a traditional Amazigh village. North of Taghazout, quads and sandboards can be rented from the roadside vendors at the entrance of the **Timlalin Dunes**, sitting opposite the coastline and offering sweeping Atlantic Ocean views. By night, locals have bonfires and play music here – it's also a great place for stargazing.

White Dune in Dakhla is more of a remote experience. This striking lump of pale sand is surrounded by piercing blue ocean at high tide

African Crocodiles

Extinct West African crocodiles used to live in Morocco less than a century ago. However, it's possible to see 300 Nile crocodiles just outside Agadir in a botanical garden setting at the **Crocoparc** (crocoparc.com), which opened in 2015 to preserve and spread awareness of the reptiles. See the carnivorous reptiles, up to 7m long and weighing up to a tonne, from a raised boardwalk that snakes around a lagoon. Don't miss the cave with freshly hatched baby crocodiles (a few inches big!), and the Monster's Tunnel, where you can come face to face with a croc with only perspex glass between you.

Left Crocoparc
Below Saharan fennec fox

and is only reachable by 4WD or quad bike. Park your vehicle at the base and climb the dunes by foot and admire the pink flamingos often visible in the distance. Those with eagle eyes may spot dolphins and killer whales (orcas) out to sea. Note that while quad biking is popular in Morocco's desert landscapes, there is ongoing discussion of the noise pollution and ecological damage it creates.

Natural Diversity

To get away from the crowds and see nature in its purest form, head 1000km south of Agadir, to the area of **Dakhla** in the Western Sahara region, just north of the Tropic of Cancer, sitting on a sandy peninsula that stretches 40km on the Atlantic coastline. Local outfit **Dakhla Rovers** (dakhla-rovers.com) is run by a pair of marine biologists who offer captivatingly wild-desert tours from one to seven days with some serious off-roading to explore the area's natural diversity through fossil-finding, bird spotting and mammal encounters – looking for species such as the big-eared Saharan fennec fox. Captivating geographic features in the area include the sabkha of Imlili, a vast desert depression with salted bottom and natural pools of salt water filled with fish. The guides can also take you to lesser-visited white, sandy, wind-ravaged but breathtaking beaches such as **Plage Porto Rico**.

Listings

BEST OF THE REST

Best Places for Coffee

Espresso Lab €€

One of the best cups of coffee in Agadir, this marina spot has a terrace opposite the boats and a minimalist indoor space.

Cafe Caramel €€

Where stylish Agadir locals meet for a coffee before work, or for brunch on the weekend. Finish with a salivatingly good cake.

Friends Eatery & Coffee House €

A cosy, comfortable and friendly cafe, with a range of coffee blends and brewing techniques.

Cafe Terassa €

Always a friendly vibe at this sunny Dakhla cafe, facing the bay. Tasty breakfast and crepes too.

Vasano €

Delicious coffee, juices and breakfast with style in Dakhla. Fast wi-fi and friendly owners, plus a B&B as well.

Teapot Cafe €€

Right in the centre of Taghazout – serving fine coffee, teas and kombucha, plus a whole host of healthy eating options – from pokē bowls to tacos.

Hey Yallah €

Uber chic setting with a smart gift shop attached and delicious brews in the little surf town of Tamraght.

Bihi Imessouane €

On the N1 road before the turnoff to Magic Bay, this outdoor cafe is run by Bihi, who makes delicious coffee and tea out of a vintage Renault.

Agadir Riad Sleeps

Riad Villa Blanche €€€

Gorgeous Agadir luxury boutique hotel with elegant rooms around an internal courtyard, plus a spa, fine dining and a pool.

Riad les Chtis d'Agadir €

City location and eclectic mix of colourful rooms, and a nice terrace, this *riad* is a characterful stand-out with good-priced stays.

Riad l'étoile d'Agadir €€

Light-filled *riad* with clean walls and pops of colour. Great location in Talborjt, and has a rooftop pool. No kids under 12 years.

Surf & Kite Stays

Logis La Marine €€

Art deco–inspired guesthouse on the oceanfront in Sidi Ifni. Some rooms have fabulous ocean views. Friendly staff. Nice chill areas inside and outside – round the corner from board-rental shops.

Kitesurfing, Dakhla (p233)

Ifni Surf €

Smart hostel-style accommodation in Sidi Infi with shared rooms and a clean, friendly vibe. Specialising in surf packages and Sahara surf tours.

Nid d'Aigle €€

On the cliff edge in Mirleft, where paragliders launch. Guesthouse with incredible views, clean colourful rooms, in-house dining and a stunning infinity pool.

Greenwave Ecolodge €€

With a beachfront location in Mirleft, close to the dunes, this place has a remote eco-chalet vibe and a year-round pool.

Taghazout Villa €€

Surf Maroc–run space with a real community vibe, with communal dinners by night, and surf guiding and coaching packages by day along the coastline for groups of various abilities.

Tour d'Eole €€€

Fanciest kitesurfing base in the Dakhla area, with desert-edged bungalows, rooms, suites, and villas with a private pool and sun terrace. Plus there's a superb restaurant.

MIA Resort Dakhla €€

Small, tastefully decorated cabins with en-suites facing the Atlantic Ocean in Dakhla. Gorgeous pool area, plus yoga studio and co-working space.

Olo Surf Nature €€

Laid-back surf vibe overlooking Imsouane's bay, with relaxing rooms decorated with wicker furnishings and crisp white linens. Awesome cafe too.

Imi Bay Surf House €€

Located up the cliff overlooking the bay in Imsouane, this stunning option has apartments (sleeping up to six) and rooms decorated with airy, neutral tones, some with terraces facing the ocean.

Mint Surf €€

Combine a surf retreat with a classic *riad* at this excellent stay. Ideal for solo travellers or groups, communal meals – included in surf packages – are enjoyed around a shimmering, central outdoor pool.

Best Moroccan Eats

Agadir Medina Coco Polizzi €€

Family-friendly place inside the medina with top tajines. Enjoy them on the terrace dining alfresco, overlooking a well-maintained kids' playground.

Suerte Loca €€

Reasonably priced Moroccan-Spanish menu served in a warm ambience with colourful interiors. Great location in Sidi Ifni. There's often live music.

Nomad €€

Delicious fish options in Sidi Ifni, including a seafood-heavy paella and tempting dessert menu offered in an atmospheric Moorish decor.

TalhaMar €

Local favourite fish restaurant on Dakhla lagoon with tables overlooking the oyster nets. Rustic decor, and a simple menu of fresh oysters, seafood tajines and whole roasted fish.

My Octopus €

Small Dakhla fish restaurant that's heavy on octopus-based dishes; paella, calamari and whole octopus, plus other fresh seafood dishes.

Restaurant Pescador €€

Beautiful sunset spot next to the Oum Lbouer (or Westpoint) surf spot in Dakhla, selling alcoholic drinks and lots of fish dishes depending on what's been caught that day.

Practicalities

Right Suite, La Mamounia (p77)

EASY STEPS FROM THE AIRPORT TO THE CITY CENTRE

Most visitors arrive by plane into Marrakesh, Agadir, Fez (pictured) or Tangier from Europe, and Casablanca from the US. Ryanair and EasyJet are the main budget airlines, though you can frequently find similar prices on Air Arabia. Royal Air Maroc serves the US. Marrakesh and Casablanca have good shopping and eating options. Elsewhere, it's fairly basic so prepare accordingly.

AT THE AIRPORT

SIM CARDS/ ESIMS

You'll find someone selling SIM cards immediately after security. All the main mobile phone suppliers – Orange, Inwi and Maroc Telecom – sell SIM cards and have multiple offices in bigger towns and cities. eSIMs work well in Morocco with a wide range of plans.

CURRENCY EXCHANGE

Offices are found near baggage reclaim at all airports. Rates are better at banks in the city.

HAMZA MAKHCHOUNE/SHUTTERSTOCK

WI-FI Free and fast at main airports. Coverage does not generally extend outside the arrivals hall.

ATMS Found in the arrivals hall of all airports. Visa and Mastercard are widely accepted. American Express is not.

CHARGING STATIONS These are becoming more commonplace in departure lounges. They are free. Plugs are Type C and Type E, both 220V/50Hz.

ENTRY/EXIT FORMALITIES

Visas Generally you do not need a visa for stays under 90 days. You will require a valid passport with at least six months remaining. Landing cards are no longer required.

Duty-free allowances 1L of spirits and 1L of wine. Cameras and video cameras are OK. Drones are not allowed and will be confiscated.

GETTING TO THE CITY CENTRE

GRANDS TAXIS These are regulated and prices are clearly displayed on signs outside the arrivals hall of all airports. Marrakesh now has a ticket counter where you prepay for your taxi (next to the exit at arrivals). Fares depend on your destination.

TRAIN A shuttle train connects Casablanca Airport with the city centre (30 minutes, Dh70).

RIDESHARING Uber has yet to hit Morocco, though there are a handful of local alternatives such as inDrive. They are not regulated.

PRIVATE TRANSFER Many *riads* (traditional houses built around gardens) and guesthouses offer transfer from the airport in vehicles ranging from luxury Mercedes to smart people carriers. This can be the most comfortable way to arrive into a new city. Prices can be anywhere from Dh200 to Dh1000. Check with your hotel to avoid unpleasant surprises.

BUS Airport buses are a budget-friendly way to reach the centre of town, though they can be unreliable and overcrowded. Bus 19 (Dh30) runs from Marrakesh Airport, Bus 16 (Dh4) from Fès–Saïss Airport, and Bus AE (Dh25/50) from Rabat and Agadir airports. Tangier has its own airport bus (Dh40), which goes straight to the city centre.

OTHER POINTS OF ENTRY

Morocco is accessible by ferry, overland routes and even helicopter.

Ferries from Spain are the most popular option. The Algeciras–Tangier Med (about 40 minutes from Tangier town centre) route operates multiple daily crossings (1½ to two hours, from €29). The Tarifa–Tangier Ville ferry is faster (one hour, from €39). Longer routes, such as Barcelona–Tangier Med, take 30+ hours, starting at €80. Delays are common in peak seasons. Always check ferry schedules and land-crossing updates before travelling.

Overland routes The towns of Ceuta and Melilla are Spanish enclaves with Moroccan land borders. Both crossings involve strict security, long queues and occasional closures. While customs operations function normally, sporadic border tensions exist. In 2024, Moroccan authorities blocked over 11,300 attempted crossings into Ceuta and 3300 into Melilla.

Helicopter One, rather fun alternative is Helity (helity.es), which operates helicopter transfers between Málaga and Ceuta (25 minutes, one way from €195). Weather disruptions are possible.

Train services from Spain to Morocco do not exist, but a high-speed rail link between Tangier, Rabat and Casablanca makes onward travel easy. Buses run from European cities to Morocco via Algeciras, where you'll need to catch a ferry.

TRANSPORT TIPS TO HELP YOU GET AROUND

Morocco's trains are the fastest and more comfortable way to travel between major cities, while buses cover more remote areas. Grands taxis are very affordable, but can be cramped – it's worth buying two seats. Hiring a car offers most flexibility for exploring beyond the beaten path and is always cheaper than private transfers.

DRIVING
Morocco's highways are excellent – remember you need cash for tolls. Mountain and coastal roads can be rough, so drive carefully. Avoid off-roading or desert driving. Speed limits are strictly enforced – police issue fines swiftly, even for minor infractions.

PRIVATE TRANSFERS
Private transfers are hassle-free and ideal for direct, comfortable travel, especially for longer distances. They're costly compared with hiring a car and limit flexibility for detours or unplanned stops, but it's a solid option if you're travelling as a group.

Car rental from Dh300–600 per day

Tangier to Casablanca high-speed Al Boraq train from Dh150

Grand taxi from Dh50–200

LEFT LUGGAGE Left-luggage options in Morocco vary by city. Major train stations, including Casa Voyageurs and Marrakesh, offer secure lockers (from Dh20 day). Some bus stations provide storage, though security varies. Many hotels and *riads* hold luggage for guests free of charge. In Marrakech, City Lock Ma in Gueliz (citylockma.com) operates 24/7, offering storage at €6 (Dh63) per day or €1 (Dh10.5) per hour, with a lounge, wi-fi and toilets. In Tangier, CTM Bus Station offers storage (Dh5 per bag).

BUS The most affordable way to travel long distances. CTM (booking.ctm.ma) and Supratours (supratours.ma) offer reliable services with air-conditioned coaches and online booking. Smaller operators serve remote areas but can be less comfortable. Buy tickets in advance for popular routes, especially during holidays.

PLANE Domestic air travel is growing in Morocco, with Ryanair operating 11 routes and Air Arabia providing key connections between major cities. It's the fastest way to cover long distances, though overland travel is often more scenic. Booking early secures the best fares.

DRIVING ESSENTIALS

Rent from a reputable firm like Avis, Hertz, Sixt or the well-regarded local company Locationauto.

Always opt for full insurance.

Drive on the right and stick to speed limits – 120km/h on highways, 80km/h on rural roads and 60km/h or less in cities – police are strict.

Use guarded car parks in cities; pay the attendant cash *(Dh3–5 for a few hours, Dh20–50 overnight).*

Road signs are in French and Arabic; a local SIM helps with navigation.

INSURANCE

Travel insurance for Morocco is essential, and should cover medical expenses, accidents and theft. Ensure your policy includes emergency medical evacuation, as private healthcare can be costly. If renting a car, opt for coverage that includes collision damage and liability. Adventure activities like trekking may require additional coverage. Always check exclusions and carry a copy of your policy while travelling.

TRAIN

Trains are comfortable and efficient, with the high-speed Al Boraq service connecting Tangier to Casablanca in just over two hours. Regular trains link major cities, though smaller towns rely on buses. First-class tickets offer assigned seating and air-conditioning.

BICYCLE

Cycling in Morocco suits experienced riders, with jaw-dropping routes through mountains, deserts and coastlines. Roads vary in quality, and city traffic can be nerve-jangling. Drivers are not always mindful of cyclists, so stick to quieter rural roads and carry spares. Repairs can be difficult outside major towns.

KNOW YOUR CARBON FOOTPRINT

Planes and cars have the highest carbon footprint for domestic travel in Morocco, while trains and buses are more eco-friendly. Shared *grands taxis* reduce emissions compared with private hires. To calculate your journey's impact and explore offsets, visit an online carbon calculator like carbonfootprint.com or myclimate.org.

ROAD DISTANCE CHART (KM)

	Fez	Marrakesh	Tangier	Agadir	Ouarzazate	Rabat	Casablanca	Chefchaouen	Merzouga	Zagora
Zagora	670	350	800	450	160	730	750	870	280	0
Merzouga	460	560	600	700	370	580	590	670	0	280
Chefchaouen	200	570	110	820	700	210	340	0	670	870
Casablanca	290	240	340	470	430	90	0	340	590	750
Rabat	200	320	250	550	510	0	90	210	580	730
Ouarzazate	580	200	720	350	0	510	430	700	370	160
Agadir	785	250	830	0	350	550	470	820	700	450
Tangier	300	575	0	830	720	250	340	110	600	800
Marrakesh	530	0	575	250	200	320	240	570	560	350
Fez	0	530	300	785	580	200	290	200	460	670

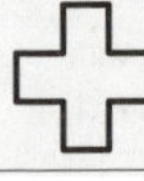

SAFE TRAVEL

Morocco is a welcoming destination, but smart planning ensures a smooth trip. From navigating bustling medinas to understanding local customs, knowing what to expect helps travellers stay safe and confident while exploring. Here's what to keep in mind before you go.

EARTHQUAKES Morocco experiences occasional earthquakes, most recently in the High Atlas. While tremors are rare, older buildings in mountain villages are vulnerable. If visiting, be aware of evacuation routes, follow local advice and carry essential supplies.

SANDSTORMS These mainly occur in the Sahara and arid regions, especially in spring. High winds reduce visibility and make driving hazardous. Protect your face with a scarf, wear sunglasses and stay indoors if a major storm hits. Flights and desert tours may be delayed, so check local forecasts.

FLASH FLOODS These are a serious risk in Morocco's mountains and desert wadis after heavy rain, particularly in autumn. Dry riverbeds can flood in minutes. Avoid camping in low-lying areas, check forecasts before hiking and never attempt to drive through flooded roads – water levels rise fast.

Scams Beware of unofficial guides, especially on trains, who may pressure you to cancel hotel bookings for their 'better' option. Stick to your plans, book accommodation in advance and only use licensed guides with official badges.

DRAGON IMAGES/SHUTTERSTOCK

TUPUNGATO/GETTY IMAGES

Drugs Drug laws in Morocco are strict, and penalties for possession can be severe, including prison time. Avoid any involvement with drugs, even in tourist areas, as enforcement is unpredictable and undercover police patrol popular spots.

SCORPIONS are found in arid and semi-arid regions, and parts of the Atlas Mountains, especially in summer. Shake out shoes before putting them on and avoid disturbing rocks. Seek medical help immediately if you get stung.

TAP WATER is safe in many Moroccan inland cities; coastal areas less so. To avoid stomach issues, it's best to stick to bottled water, especially in smaller towns and rural areas.

QUICK TIPS TO HELP YOU MANAGE YOUR MONEY

CASH & CREDIT CARDS

Cash is still king in Morocco, though hotels, restaurants, shops and transport hubs in main towns and cities accept credit cards. *Grands taxis* and *petits taxis* are always cash-only, as are market stalls. ATMs are widely available, but can run empty in smaller towns, so withdraw in advance when travelling to rural areas. Keep lots of change and small notes handy.

BANKS & ATMS

Attijariwafa, Société Générale and BMCE have branches across Morocco, with plentiful ATMs. Machines accept all major cards, with the exception of American Express.

TIPPING

This is much appreciated in Morocco. Give Dh10–20 to porters, and 10% in restaurants and to guides. Small cash tips for helpful service are always welcomed.

CURRENCY

Dirham (Dh)

HOW MUCH FOR A

Nus-Nus (coffee with milk) Dh12–25

Museum entry Dh20

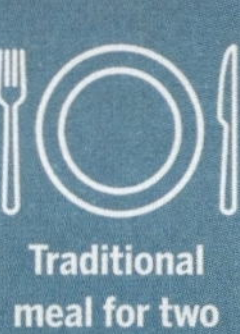

Traditional meal for two Dh500–750

INVESTING IN THE FUTURE

Morocco's economy is rapidly evolving, with major infrastructure projects shaping its future. The 2040 Moroccan Rail Plan aims to expand high-speed train networks, while the 2030 FIFA World Cup will drive investment in tourism and transport. Renewable energy projects, tech hubs and industrial growth further boost development.

CURRENCY

The dirham (Dh) is a closed currency, meaning it's not available outside the country. Upon arrival, exchange foreign currency at banks, official exchange bureaus, or withdraw dirhams from ATMs.

HAGGLING

All part of the fun in Moroccan souqs. Decide what something is worth to you, start there and negotiate with a smile. It's a friendly game – don't push too hard.

TAXES & REFUNDS

Morocco's standard Value Added Tax (TVA) rate is 20%. Tourists can claim VAT refunds on purchases over Dh2000 at the airport. Ensure you obtain tax-free forms from retailers and validate them upon departure.

STAY LONGER, SAVE MORE

For budget-friendly long-term travel, consider rentals with a kitchen to save on accommodation and meals. Public transport – buses, trains and shared *grands taxis* – is far cheaper than private hires. Eat at Moroccan canteens or street stalls for authentic, low-cost meals. Shopping in local markets is a great way to experience daily life and find fresher ingredients than in the supermarket. Travelling off-season, for example in the summer, means great deals on fancier hotels and fewer crowds.

UNIQUE AND LOCAL WAYS TO STAY

Morocco's accommodation is as characterful as its landscapes. Stay in a riad for romantic tiled courtyards and rooftop terraces, or a kasbah designed to withstand the desert heat. Sleep under Saharan stars in a luxury camp, or rent a dar (traditional house) for a longer stay with local charm.

HOW MUCH FOR A NIGHT IN A...

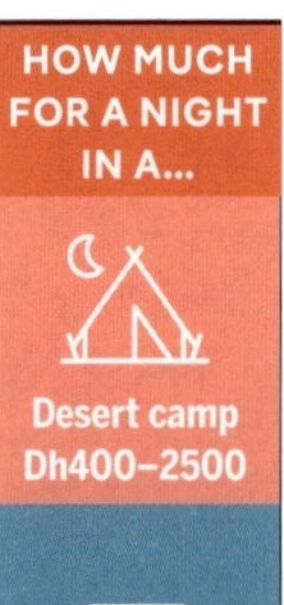

Desert camp Dh400–2500

Family-run *dar* Dh800–1500

Luxury *riad* Dh2500–4500

ARTUR DEBAT/GETTY IMAGES

KASBAHS

These traditional Moroccan fortresses, typically built from rammed earth and mud-brick, feature high walls and corner towers. Originally serving as defensive strongholds and residences for feudal leaders, many have been transformed into unique accommodation. Staying in a kasbah offers a glimpse into Morocco's architectural heritage and a chance to experience its storied past firsthand.

DESERT CAMPS

Desert camps range from simple rows of tents to secluded luxury stays with private bathrooms and gourmet dining. Reaching them often involves a camel trek or a 4x4 journey over dunes. Nights bring dazzling stars, Amazigh music and campfires.

If time is short, Agafay, just 45 minutes from Marrakesh, gives a taste of desert life without the long journey to the Sahara.

THOMAS BARWICK/GETTY IMAGES

RURAL TOURISM

Countryside guesthouses range from rustic auberges high in the mountains, to agrotourism stays on working farms, and breezy beach houses along the coast. Many are family-run, offering home-cooked meals, scenic settings and a slower pace of life – perfect for travellers seeking nature, authenticity and local hospitality.

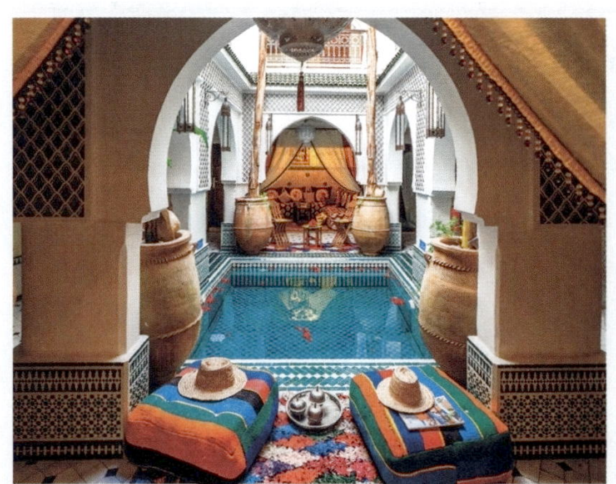

ZCPHOTOGRAPHY/SHUTTERSTOCK

HIDDEN HAVENS

Staying in a *riad* or *dar* is as much a part of the Morocco experience as wandering its souqs or sipping mint tea on a rooftop at sunset. Hidden deep within ancient medina walls, these traditional townhouses offer an escape from the frenetic bustle of the streets, their heavy wooden doors opening into a world of cool stone, intricate tilework, and birdsong echoing through a central courtyard.

The difference between a *riad* and a *dar* is subtle but distinct. A *riad* – meaning 'garden' in Arabic – typically has a larger courtyard, often planted with orange trees and jasmine, with a fountain at its centre. These houses were designed to provide shade and tranquility, an anti-dote to the jostling souqs. A *dar*, meaning 'house', is usually more compact, with a smaller, simpler courtyard, yet still embracing the inward-facing architecture that makes these homes feel like sanctuaries.

Both offer an intimate, immersive stay, with rooms overlooking the courtyard rather than the street. Mornings start with the scent of fresh bread and coffee, while evenings bring the glow of candlelight and the soft hum of conversation – a chance to slow down, enjoy the architecture and soak up the rhythm of traditional medina life.

BOOKING

When booking accommodation in Morocco, consider the diverse options available, from traditional *riads* and *dars*, to modern hotels and beach resorts, and decide accordingly. It's advisable to book in advance, especially during peak travel seasons, to secure your preferred lodging.

Always read recent reviews paying close attention to details like hot water, bed linen and noise, as well as checking the amenities promised to ensure the accommodation meets your expectations. Consider the location's proximity to attractions you plan to visit, and be aware of any local customs or regulations that may affect your stay.

Riads Morocco (riadsmorocco.com) Specialises in traditional Moroccan riads, providing curated selections in cities like Marrakesh, Fez and Rabat. Ideal for travellers seeking authentic experiences.

Secret Places (secretplaces.com) A hand-picked selection of countryside guesthouses and beach houses as well as luxury *riads* and hotels.

So Morocco (somorocco.com) Stretches beyond the usual accommodation picks to include cave dwellings, farmhouses and homestays.

ALESIAKAN/SHUTTERSTOCK

AIRBNB

Airbnb has taken Morocco by storm, ranging from sleek city apartments to sumptuous villas and designer *dars*, but standards vary widely. Villas often mean a garden and pool. A *dar* usually has a roof terrace.

RESPONSIBLE TRAVEL

Positive, sustainable and feel-good experiences around the country.

ON THE ROAD

Stay small and local Opt for Moroccan-owned guesthouses, *riads* and eco-lodges rather than international chains. These support local communities and often have a lighter environmental footprint.

Save water Morocco is a water-scarce country with many regions experiencing several years-long droughts. Take quick showers, turn off taps and avoid unnecessary laundry requests.

Shop smart Buy snacks and water from small *hanouts* (shops) and souqs instead of supermarkets.

Choose local crafts Many medina shops sell mass-produced imports. Seek out Moroccan-made textiles, pottery and woodwork to support artisans.

Travel sustainably Use buses, trains and shared *grands taxis* instead of private cars. Walk whenever possible.

Be aware of fuel consumption If hiring a car, choose a hybrid or electric model when you can. Charging stations are increasingly commonplace, especially in cities.

Right Carpet shop, Fez (p182)
Far right Market, Marrakesh (p42)

IURI S DESIGN/SHUTTERSTOCK

GIVE BACK

Protect nature Support conservation efforts by visiting eco-tourism projects like the High Atlas Foundation, which works on reforestation and sustainable agriculture.

Volunteer responsibly Opportunities exist in community organisations, like marine protection in Essaouira or permaculture initiatives in the Rif Mountains.

Support social enterprises Shop at organisations like Al Nour (employing disabled women in Marrakesh) or The Anou in Fez, which champions fair-trade craftsmanship.

Donate wisely Contribute to Moroccan-led NGOs focused on environmental and biodiversity issues, social enterprise and education, and women's rights organisations.

Choose ethical animal experiences Avoid attractions that exploit wildlife, including the monkeys and snakes on Marrakesh's Djemaa El Fna, and goats tied into trees in Essaouira.

SUPPORT LOCAL

Shopping locally in Morocco supports artisans and keeps traditional crafts alive. Seek out handwoven rugs, brass lanterns and hand-painted ceramics direct from makers. Spice markets brim with cumin, saffron and ras el hanout, perfect for home cooking. Opt for women's and artisans' cooperatives, and handcrafted goods over mass-produced souvenirs – your spending makes a difference.

LEAVE A SMALL FOOTPRINT

Stay in eco-conscious lodgings Choose *riads* and guesthouses with sustainable practices, such as solar power and water conservation.

Travel light Bring reusable bags, water bottles and cutlery to minimise plastic waste.

Eat local Support seasonal, Moroccan-grown produce and small, locally run eateries.

Respect nature Stick to marked trails when hiking and avoid disturbing wildlife.

Limit energy use Turn off lights, air conditioning and electronics when not needed.

KUDLA/SHUTTERSTOCK

DOS & DON'TS

Dress modestly Cover shoulders and knees, especially in rural areas and religious sites.

Greet respectfully A handshake is common; close friends may exchange cheek kisses.

Ask before photographing Many locals dislike being photographed.

Avoid public displays of affection Keep them minimal.

Use your right hand For eating, and giving and receiving items.

CLIMATE CHANGE & TRAVEL

Lonely Planet urges all travellers to engage with their travel carbon footprint, which will mainly come from air travel. While there often isn't an alternative, travellers can look to minimise the number of flights they take, opt for newer aircrafts and use cleaner ground transport, such as trains.

One proposed solution – purchasing carbon offsets – unfortunately does not cancel out the impact of individual flights. While most destinations will depend on air travel for the foreseeable future, for now, pursuing ground-based travel where possible is the best course of action.

The UN Carbon Offset Calculator shows how flying impacts a household's emissions:

The ICAO's carbon emissions calculator allows visitors to analyse the CO_2 generated by point-to-point journeys:

RESOURCES

mblaassociation.org

projectsoar.org

highatlastfoundation.org

efamorocco.org

amalnonprofit.org

ESSENTIAL NUTS & BOLTS

SMOKING

Smoking is common, especially in local cafes, bars and hotels. Many restaurants allow it indoors, so non-smokers may struggle in public spaces.

PUBLIC TOILETS

Public toilets in Morocco are scarce, often lacking seats and toilet paper – carry tissues and small change.

PUBLIC HOLIDAYS

Many businesses close or reduce hours for Ramadan, Eid Al Fitr and Eid Al Adha. Green March Day (6 November), Independence Day (18 November) and Islamic New Year also see widespread closures.

FAST FACTS

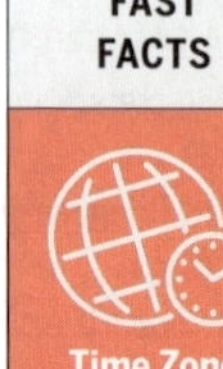

Time Zone
GMT+1 (except during Ramadan)

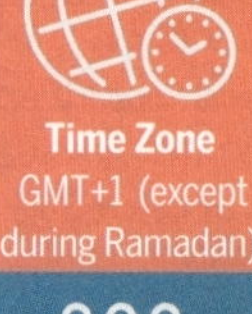

Country Code
212

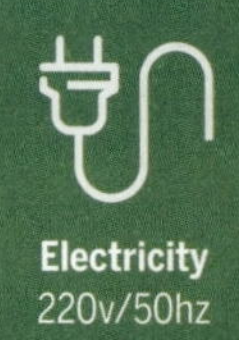

Electricity
220v/50hz

GOOD TO KNOW

The legal drinking age is 18, but enforcement varies, especially in tourist areas.

Many businesses and government offices close or have reduced hours on Friday afternoons for prayers.

Pharmacies are well stocked, and many medications are available without a prescription.

Moroccan dirhams cannot be taken in or out of the country, so exchange money on arrival and departure.

Morocco follows GMT+1 year-round, except during Ramadan, when clocks revert to standard GMT.

ACCESSIBLE TRAVEL

General accessibility Morocco is improving in accessibility, but streets in older medinas, like Fez, have uneven cobblestones, narrow alleys and lots of steps. Hotels in the Ville Nouvelle of cities like Casablanca, Rabat, Marrakesh and Fez are more wheelchair-friendly.

Mobility access While some hotels and new public spaces have ramps and lifts, many historic sites and *riads* don't. Larger train stations offer assistance, but buses and taxis are rarely adapted for wheelchairs. Supratours (supratours.ma) provides accessibility information for long-distance transport.

Vision-impaired travellers Braille signage and tactile paving are rare. Museums and cultural sites often lack audio guides. Bringing assistive technology is advised.

Hearing-impaired travellers Sign language is not widely understood, and public announcements are usually not displayed visually. Carrying a notepad or using a translation app can help with communication.

Resources Visit moroccoaccessibletravel.com for bespoke one-to-two week tours. For good-value package deals, see limitlesstravel.org/disabled-holidays/destinations/morocco. Tamaris Golden Tours (taxidumaroc.com/transport-for-people-with-reduced-mobility-in-morocco) has adapted vehicles for transfers for independent travellers.

SOLO FEMALE TRAVEL

Rewarding but requires awareness – dress modestly, stay in reputable places, ignore catcalls and trust your instincts.

DINING WITH A FAMILY

Wash your hands before eating, wait for the host to begin, and eat with your right hand.

WEDDING INVITATIONS

Dress elegantly but conservatively, bring a small gift, expect a late start and finish, plus lengthy, music-filled celebrations.

FAMILY TRAVEL

Kid-friendly stays Many *riads* welcome families, and larger hotels often have pools.

Transport tips Trains give kids space to move, bus journeys can be long and shared taxis cramped.

Street safety Keep a close eye on kids in crowded souqs. Getting lost is easy.

Food for kids Tajines, *msemen* pancakes and camel burgers are all kid-friendly.

Desert adventures Camel rides and camping in the Sahara are a hit, but nights get very cold.

MEDINAS

Medinas are the ultimate maze. Look for square signs marking through streets and hexagonal signs for dead ends. Use landmarks like hotels, restaurants and minarets to orient yourself as GPS can be unreliable. If lost, ask shopkeepers, not touts, for directions.

LEARN BASIC DARIJA

Beyond *'salaam,'* mastering a few words of Darija (Moroccan Arabic) unlocks richer interactions. Try *'bshal?'* (how much?) in markets, or *'shukran bzaf'* (thank you very much). Locals appreciate the effort, and it can lead to friendlier service, discounts or hidden recommendations.

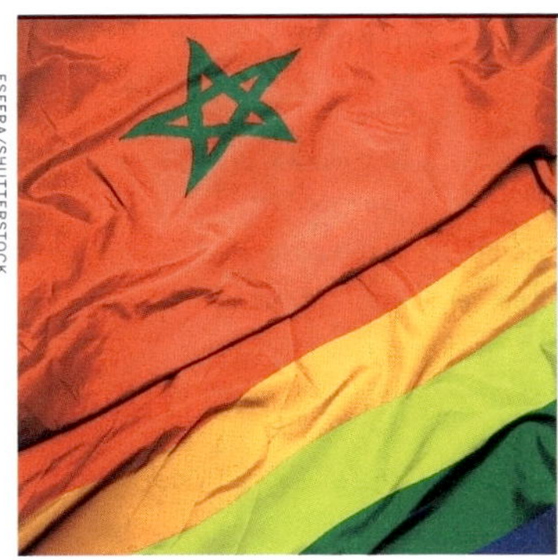

ESFERA/SHUTTERSTOCK

LGBTIQ+ TRAVELLERS

Morocco's laws criminalise same-sex relationships, but attitudes vary. In tourist areas, discretion is advised, though LGBTIQ+ travellers often experience few issues. Public displays of affection – regardless of gender – are generally frowned upon. Marrakesh and Casablanca have small, discreet LGBTIQ+ social scenes, often within private venues. Inclusive Morocco (inclusivemorocco.com), the country's first LGBTIQ-friendly travel agency, offers tailored experiences and guidance. Many foreign-run *riads* and international hotels welcome LGBTIQ+ guests, and respectful travellers can enjoy Morocco's rich culture without major concerns.

LANGUAGE

The official languages in Morocco are Arabic and Tamazight, the language of the Amazigh people. Tamazight is spoken by about a third of the population. Tashelhit and Tamazight are also major dialects. Most Amazigh also speak Moroccan Arabic, and French is still regularly used in the big cities.

Moroccan Arabic (Moroccan Darija) is a variety of Modern Standard Arabic (MSA) but is so different from it in many respects as to be virtually like another language. This is the everyday language you'll hear. Here, we've represented the Moroccan Darija phrases with the Roman alphabet using a simplified pronunciation system. In many former French colonies in the MENA region, it is customary to transliterate the 'sh' sound as 'ch'. Consider that as you read these.

BASICS

Hello.	*es salaam alaykum (polite).*
	Wa alaykum ssalaam (response).
Goodbye.	*bessalama/m'a ssalama.*
Yes.	*Eeyeh.*
No.	*La.*
Please.	*'Afak/'afaki/'afakum (said to m/f/pl).*
Thank you.	*Shukran.*
Excuse me.	*Smahleeya/smaheleeya/smahuleeya (said to m/f/pl).*
What's your name?	*Shno smeetek?*
My name is ...	*Smeetee...*
Do you speak English?	*Washkt'hdar bilengleezeeya?*
I didn't understand.	*Mafhemtsh.*
How much is it?	*Bishhaal?*
Please show me on the map.	*'Afak, werrini fi lkhrita.*

TIME & NUMBERS

What time is it?	*Shal fessa'a?*
morning	*assbah*
afternoon	*l'asheeya*
night	*lil/lila*
yesterday	*lbareh*
today	*lyoom*
tomorrow	*ghedda*

1	*wahed*	**6**	*setta*
2	*jooj*	**7**	*seb'a*
3	*tlata*	**8**	*tmenya*
4	*reb'a*	**9**	*tes'ood*
5	*khamsa*	**10**	*'ashra*

EMERGENCIES

Help!	*'Atqnee!*
Go away!	*Seer fhalek!*
I'm ill.	*Ana mreed/ana mreeda (m/f).*
Call a doctor!	*'Ayyet 'ala she tbeeb!*
Call the police!	*'Ayyet 'ala lbulees!*
I'm lost.	*(Ana) tlift*
I've been robbed	*Tsrqt*
I'm allergic to (penicillin).	*'Andee hasaseeya l (lbeenseleen)*

Index

000 Map pages

D

E

F

G

000 Map pages

000 Map pages

'With its ancient cities, boundless desert sands, majestic mountain ranges and delicious cuisine, Morocco is bewitching – and the country's friendly and hospitable people are what make it all sing.'

HELEN RANGER

'The cascading fifth waterfall at Setti Fatma is just beautiful. You'll likely have the rocky canyon all to yourself.'

NARINA EXELBY

'I've been lucky enough to see some ridiculously beautiful sunsets in the past… but nothing quite prepared me for the day's close at Merzouga (pictured right), among the shifting sands of Erg Chebbi.'

JADE BREMNER

'Arriving in Fez for the first time in 2005 was a falling through the looking glass moment into a swirling, medieval maze. Surreal, hypnotic, unforgettable. I was instantly hooked.'

TARA STEVENS

'The first time I visited Essaouira's flea market, I was delighted to stumble upon the fishermen's huts turned artists' studios.'

SARAH GILBERT

FROM LEFT: TATIANA BRALNINA/SHUTTERSTOCK, ELZBIETA SEKOWSKA/SHUTTERSTOCK

THIS BOOK

Destination editor
Zara Sekhavati

Production editor
Ailbhe MacMahon

Cartographer
Valentina Kremenchutskaya

Image editor
Virginia Moreno

Coordinating editor
Mani Ramaswamy

Cover researcher
Kat Marsh

Assisting Editors
Soo Hamilton, Fionnuala Twomey, James Appleton, Lucy Jones, Charlotte Orr

Thanks
Sofie Andersen, Alison Killilea, Saralinda Turner, Sanad Tabbaa, Charlotte McClelland, Ronan Abayawickrema